ācaðōhkīwina and *ācimōwina*

**Traditional Narratives
of the Rock Cree Indians**

ācaðōhkīwina and *ācimōwina*

Traditional Narratives
of the Rock Cree Indians

Robert A. Brightman

2007

Copyright © 2007 Canadian Plains Research Center
Copyright Notice
Reproduced with permission of the Canadian Museum of Civilization, © 1989

All rights reserved. No part of this work covered by the copyrights hereon may be reproduced or used in any form or by any means—graphic, electronic, or mechanical—without the prior written permission of the author. Any request for photocopying, recording, taping or placement in information storage and retrieval systems of any sort shall be directed in writing to the Canadian Reprography Collective.

Canadian Plains Research Center
University of Regina
Regina, Saskatchewan S4S 0A2
Canada
Tel: (306) 585-4758/Fax: (306) 585-4699
e-mail: canadian.plains@uregina.ca/http://www.cprc.uregina.ca

Library and Archives Canada Cataloguing in Publication
Brightman, Robert, 1950-
ācaðōhkīwina and ācimōwina : traditional narratives of the Rock Cree Indians / Robert A. Brightman.

(Canadian Plains reprint series : 1208-9680 ; 13)
Includes some text in Woods Cree.
Includes bibliographical references.
ISBN 978-0-88977-195-6

1. Cree Indians—Manitoba, Northern—Folklore. 2. Folk literature, Indian—Manitoba, Northern—Translations into English. 3. Folk literature, Indian—Manitoba, Northern—History and criticism. I. University of Regina. Canadian Plains Research Center II. Title. III. Title: Traditional narratives of the Rock Cree Indians. IV. Series.

E99.C88B748 2007   398.2089'97323071271
C2007-904994-X

Cover design: Donna Grant, Canadian Plains Research Center, Regina, Saskatchewan.
Cover image: Courtesy of Tim Jones

Printed by Imprimerie Gauvin
Gatineau, Québec

Publishers Note
We acknowledge the financial support of the Government of Canada through the Book Publishing Industry Development Program (BPDIP) for our publishing activities. We acknowledge the support of the Canada Council for the Arts for our publishing program.

Contents

Preface ix
Chapter 1: The Rock Cree and Their Literature 1
    The Rock Cree of Northern Manitoba 1
    Categories of Cree Oral Literature 6
Chapter 2: *ācaðōhkīwin*: The *wīsahkīcāhk* Cycle 9
    Cornelius Colomb Narrative 9
        Rolling Head 9
        Contest with *wīmisōsiw* 11
        The Women and the "Sickness" 14
        The Flood 14
        Marries Daughter 16
    Jeremiah Michel Narrative 18
        Contest with *wīmisōsiw* 18
        The Flood and the New Earth 21
        Goose Transformation 22
        Shut-Eye Dancers 23
        Squeezed by Trees 24
        wīhtikōw and Weasel 24
        Eye Juggler 25
        The Startlers 26
        The Farting Hunter 26
        Bear's Eye Medicine 27
        Muskrat Cools Grease 27
        Fly Transformation 28
        Fooled by Reflections 28
        Scab Eater 29
        Moose Transformation 29
        Marries Daughter 29
    Albert Umferville Narrative 31
        Tricks Moose and Squeezed by Birds 31
        The Startlers 31
        Fooled by Reflections 31
        Bear's Eye Medicine 32
    Other Versions and Narratives 33
        wīhtikōw and Weasel 33
        wīhtikōw and Weasel 35
        Marries Daughter 36
        Marries Daughter 37
        Contest with *wīmisōsiw* 38
        Eye Juggler 39

Goose Transformation	39
The Shut-Eye Dancers	41
The Shut-Eye Dancers	42
Fooled by Reflections	42
Muskrat Cools Grease	42
The Startlers	43
The Farting Hunter and Scab Eater	43
The Farting Hunter	44
The Flood and the New Earth	44
The Flood and the New Earth	44
wīsahkīcāhk and the Baby	45
wīsahkīcāhk Changes Frog, Muskrat, and Bear	45
Rolling Head	47
Chapter 3: Discussion of the Trickster-Transformer Cycle	**49**
wīsahkīcāhk and *nēnapoš*	49
Rock Cree Knowledge of *wīsahkīcāhk*	52
Syntagmatic Structure and Sequencing	54
The Stories	58
Rolling Head	58
Contest with *wīmisōsiw*	59
The Flood and the New Earth	60
Goose Transformation	65
The Shut-Eye Dancers	65
Squeezed by Trees	66
Tricks Moose and Squeezed by Birds	67
wīhtikōw and Weasel	67
Eye Juggler	68
The Startlers	68
The Farting Hunter	69
Bear's Eye Medicine	70
Muskrat Cools Fat	70
Fly Transformation	71
Fooled by Reflections	71
Scab Eater	71
Moose Transformation	72
Marries Daughter	72
Imitates Baby	72
wīsahkīcāhk Changes Frog, Bear, and Muskrat	73
Chapter 4: Other *ācaðōhkīwina*	**75**
Introduction: The *pawākan* and the *wīhtikōw*	75
Other *ācaðōhkīwina*	79
The Origin of Animals	79
God's Oven	80
Wolverine and Wolf	82
The Bear Abductor	84

mistāpēw.	85
The Thunder Women	86
ayās	88
maskōkōsan	95
mistacayawāsis.	99
The Hairy-Heart People	106
kayānwī Kills Hairy Hearts at the Beaver Lodge	108
kayānwī Kills Hairy Hearts with Trees	111
Wolverine, Wolf, and Fire Medicine	113
The *wīhcikōsisak*	115
cahkāpīs Kills Giants and Snares the Sun	117
The Dog Council	121
Wolverine Defeats Great Skunk	121
Wolf and Dog	124
Wolverine, Wolf, and Dog	125
Chapter 5: *kayās-ācimōwina*.	129
okimāw acāhpīy Kills a Caribou with Snow	129
mīmīkwīsiwak	129
manicōw	131
The Rival Suitors	132
Medicine Woman Defeats *wītikōw*	132
Repulsing a *wītikōw*	133
Flight from a *wītikōw*	134
wītikōw and the Big-Rock *pawākan*	136
Chapter 6: *kayās-ācimōwina*: *manitōkīwin* and Catholicism	137
Introduction.	137
The Arrival of the Priests	139
mīsīl Kills a *wītikōwak*	140
Simulated Crucifixion	141
Simulated Crucifixion II: Jesus at Highrock	142
Flying to Heaven.	143
Eskimo in Heaven.	144
Last Offering.	145
Chapter 7: *ācimōwina*: *wītikōw* Encounters and Medicine Stories	147
Barren Lands *wītikōw*.	147
Laurie River *wītikōw*.	148
P.B. and *wītikōw*	149
Moose Lake *wītikōw*.	150
Nelson House *wītikōw*	151
Introduction to the Medicine Narratives.	151
Sled Medicine.	152
Hair Medicine.	152
Soccer Medicine.	153
Insect Medicine.	153
Enlargement Medicine	153

    Dr. Young and the Saskatoon Medicine Man 153
    Dr. Young's Love Medicine 155
    Can't Refuse Medicine 155
    Goldsand Lake *wītikōw* 156
    Antoine Dumas's Prophecies 157
Chapter 8: *ācimōwina*: Humour 159
    Introduction 159
    Trapper Tricks *wītikōw* 160
    Drowning the Moose 161
    The Voluble Wolverine 162
    Edmund Sinclair in the Chimney 162
    The First Bush Pilot 163
    Jimmy Bighetty Rides a Moose 163
    The Dumb Partner: The Lost Ducks 164
    The Dumb Partner: The Cat Impersonator 164
    The Dumb Partner: Feasting in Heaven 165
    The Dumb Partner: Scabby Suitor 165
Chapter 9: Texts: Animal Marriages 167
    Introduction 167
    The Bear Husband 169
    The Beaver Wife 178
References Cited 181

Preface

The narratives included here were obtained in 1977–79 and 1985–86 in the course of research in the northwestern Manitoba Rock Cree communities of Pukatawagan, Granville Lake, and Brochet. As should be obvious, the book is a collaborative project between myself and the Cree narrators and translators, and the form the narratives assume on the written page necessarily reflects the variable circumstances under which they were recorded and translated. With very few exceptions, the stories were recorded on tape; those that were told in Cree were subsequently translated by the narrator, if bilingual in Cree and English, or by another individual.

Four approaches were employed in preparing the translations and committing them to writing. First, in certain cases, what appears is merely my written paraphrase of a translator's English retelling or summary. The stories obtained in this way are often attenuated and have little to recommend them as authentic renderings of Cree literature beyond our attempts to ensure accuracy in plot and details. A second and more successful method involved turning control of the taped Cree narratives over to the translators who listened initially to the entire story and then went back over it slowly, successively interpreting short passages. A third and related approach was employed with parts of the Jeremiah Michel transformer cycle, "The Hairy-Heart People," "*wīsahkīcāhk*" Changes Frog, Muskrat and Bear," "*mistacayawasis*," "*ayās*," and "Wolverine and Wolf." In these cases, I worked from transcriptions of the Cree text and prepared interlinear translations that then became the basis for the English versions. These narratives often retain stylistic, lexical, and syntactic features of Cree, often to the detriment of their lucidity or elegance in English. Two of these Cree texts are included as the final chapter: "Beaver Wife" and "Bear Husband." Finally, in the case of some stories related in English or of English translations, what appears is a word-for-word transcription with some normalization, editing out of so-called performance errors, and punctuation insertion.

In most cases, division into lines and paragraphs follows shifts in scene or dialogue exchange and bears no necessary relationship to the discourse properties of the oral telling or performance. In the cases of the two Cree texts,

Johnny Bighetty's "*wīhtikōw* and Weasel," and Cornelius Colomb's connected *wīsahkīcāhk* narrative, the organization of the narratives into lines is based on pauses in the oral presentation (cf. Tedlock 1983). With the exception of pause, there is no representation here of the prosodic and paralinguistic properties of the narrative instances.

The arrangement of the *wīsahkīcāhk* stories in Chapter 2 requires comment. Cornelius Colomb, Jeremiah Michel, and Albert Umferville provided connected narratives encompassing multiple stories that are represented here in their order of occurrence. *wīsahkīcāhk* stories are not named by Rock Crees, but I employed improvised titles to mark the transitions between distinct stories and used the same titles for alternate versions that were narrated separately.

The partitioning of narratives between chapters is relatively arbitrary. I grouped together no stories that Crees assign to different genres but distinguished subclasses within such genres. Thus stories of the *ācaðōhkīwin* category are divided between trickster stories (Chapter 2) and stories of other characters (Chapter 3). Similarly, stories of the *kayās-ācimōwin* genre are divided between those concerned with Catholicism and those describing spirit guardians and windigos.

Cree words are transcribed using Wolfart's (1973: 12) modifications of Bloomfield's (1930) orthography. When Cree expressions occur, they are retained from the speech of narrators or translators.

My acknowledgments extend beyond the narrators and translators themselves to encompass many individuals who shared hospitality and information. In Granville Lake, I am indebted to Johnny and Sarah Bighetty, and August Merasty. At Pukatwagan, I owe thanks to Julien and Nancy Bighetty, Pascal and Marie Bighetty, Cornelius Colomb, Solomon Colomb, Selazie Linklater, Luc and Caroline Dumas, Jeremy and Caroline Caribou, Angus Bear, Solomon Francois, Sidney Castel, Eli Castel, Sandy Dumas, Ken Dillon, Colin Ross, and Glen Monkman. At Brochet, I owe many thanks to Henry and Angelique Linklater, Albert and Philomene Umferville, Jeremiah Michel, Catharine Merasty, Lawrence Merasty, Jean-Marie Merasty, Jean-Baptiste Merasty, and Pierre Merasty. I gratefully acknowledge the support of the Canadian Ethnology Service and the National Museum of Civilization (then the National Museum of Man) for field research at Pukatawagan, Granville Lake, and Brochet in 1977–79. Finally, my thanks to Alice Ann Rocca for a heroic and formidable typing project.

CHAPTER 1
The Rock Cree and Their Literature

The Rock Cree of Northern Manitoba
The narratives collected here were obtained between September 1977 and April 1979 in the course of research in the Manitoba Cree communities of Pukatawagan, Granville Lake, and Brochet. The members of these communities identify themselves as *asinīskāwiðiniwak*, a term analyzed as "people of the country with abundant rock" (Rossignol 1939a, Smith 1975). When speaking English, Crees use the phrases "Rocky Cree," "Rock Cree," or "Rock People" as glosses; some persons also consider the name *kīwītināwiðiniwak* "northern people" as an exact synonym. Although the Oblate missionary Rossignol (1939a) described the "Assiniskawidiniwok" or "Cree of the Rocks" as a distinct and self-identified social division, contemporary awareness of the grouping among non-Indians derives from Smiths paper (1975) on the Cree of Brochet. As Smith points out, these people distinguish themselves from other divisions they identify as Cree including those they call *paskwāwiðiniwak* "Plains Cree," *maskīkōwak* "Swamp Cree," and *sakāwiðiniwak* "Woods Cree." In Manitoba, the Rock Cree/Swampy Cree distinction coincides precisely with the distribution of the *ð* and *n* dialects defined by different reflexes of Proto-Algonquian. These social and linguistic groupings are not, however, necessarily coordinate in Saskatchewan where both also occur. Some Saskatchewan users of the dialect define themselves as *sakāwiðiniwak* and apparently are not cognizant of the Rock Cree division (Pentland in Smith 1981: 270). Rock Crees also designate themselves as *nīhiðawak*, a noun which includes Crees of other divisions but excludes Saulteaux, Chipewyans, Assiniboines, and non-Indians.

It is clear that the name *asinīskāwiðiniwak* refers to a broad social division rather than any single regional or treaty band or local complex of the latter. Informants identify as Rock Cree the following communities in Manitoba: Pukatawagan, Granville Lake, Nelson House, Southern Indian Lake, High Rock, Brochet, and Churchill. In Saskatchewan, they identify Sandy Bay, Island Falls, Southend, Mirond Lake, Pelican Narrows, Sturgeon Landing, Sandy

Narrows, Lac Wollaston, and Lac La Ronge. This list coincides for the most part with that provided by Smith's (1975: 174) Brochet informants; the latter, however, included Split Lake and Cross Lake in Manitoba which Pukatawagan consultants identify as Swamp Cree.

It remains unclear upon what criteria aside from dialect and genealogy the Rock Cree distinguish themselves from the proximal Swamp Cree to the south. That the distinction has been a socially significant one is evident from genealogies: there has occurred some intermarriage between different Rock Cree regional bands, including links between communities as far apart as Pukatawagan and Lac La Ronge, but almost none with Swamp Cree groups. When speaking English, some persons reserve the term "Cree" for "Rock Crees" and refer to other Cree divisions as "Indians."

As is well known, the currency of the term "Cree" as an ethnic label for linguistically related groups from Quebec to British Columbia is the relatively arbitrary product of Euro-Canadian expansion in the boreal forest. The term was applied initially to groups resident north of the Great Lakes in Quebec and Ontario and extended gradually to culturally similar peoples encountered by the English and French on Hudson Bay and to the west. These groups were often initially designated with distinct names such as "Athapuskow," "Nahathaway," "Muskagoe," "Michinipee," and the like that presumably reflected to some degree the broader social divisions recognized by the Indians themselves. The Rock, Swampy, Plains, and Woods divisions now recognized by Crees and anthropologists conceal a complex history of amalgamations and migrations, and any attempt to provide an adequate historical account of the Rock Cree is beyond the scope of this introduction. Smith (1976a) has argued convincingly that Cree occupation of the boreal forest in Manitoba and Saskatchewan antedates European contact and the contemporary Rock Crees may be assumed to be the descendants of ð-speaking populations resident in the area before the period of Euro-Canadian colonization. It is clear from Pentland's historical dialect survey (1978: 107–10) that ð-speaking populations were formerly resident along Hudson Bay and inland in areas now occupied by n-speaking groups identified as Swamp Cree. No simple identification of the Rock Cree division with ð-dialect speakers in earlier periods is possible. All the persons consulted stated that they had heard the term *asinīskāwiðiniwak* in use for as long as they could remember, but its absence from eighteenth and nineteenth-century sources may suggest a relatively recent inception. The single earlier reference to it in the anthropological literature occurs as a label for what Skinner (1914) took to be a regional band of the Plains Cree.

The single link with a group attested in earlier Euro-Canadian documentary sources was provided by Mr. Julien Bighetty of Pukatawagan who identified a group he called *misinipīyiðiniwak* as an early component or progenitor of the

Rock Crees of the lower Churchill River. According to Mr. Bighetty, this group was accustomed to travel from the mouth of the Churchill to as far west as Alberta in the period preceding and immediately following White contact. The term is clearly cognate with the "Mishenipee," "Misshenippe," "Michinipi," and "Meshinnepee" who traded at York Factory and Churchill in the second decade of the eighteenth century (Knight 1932: 161–66). Uncertainty over the territory of this division arises from the multiple possible referents of the noun *misinipīy* "big water" or "great water." Pentland (1978: 107) identifies the noun as referring to Southern Indian Lake (presently known to Crees by that name), while Ray (1974: 53, 70) suggests that the name referred to Reindeer Lake and more broadly to the Churchill River upstream from its confluence with the Reindeer River at Southend. All three identifications are consistent with the mobility emphasized by Rock Cree oral tradition. Pentland (ibid.) suggests that the Misinipi were speakers of *r*-dialect Cree. The area was occupied, however, by *ð*-dialect speakers at least by the late 1700s. George Charles (HBC B/83/a) provided, for example, the form "*aw-pis-a-paw-athi-panna-coose*" as the name for Granville Lake in 1794. Thompson (1962: 73) occupied outposts at Sipiwesk Lake, Reed Lake, Reindeer Lake, Duck Portage and "Masquawegan" (Laurie River at Granville Lake) between 1792 and 1806. He identified the Crees of the region as using the *ð*-dialect and used the name "nahathaway" (Cree *nēhiðawawēs*/he is a Cree") to refer to them. Sipiwesk and Reed Lakes are now areas occupied by *n*-dialect-speaking Swamp Cree as is Cumberland House in Saskatchewan, although it was the territory of *ð*-dialect-speaking Crees self-identified as "*nathehwy-withinyouwuc*" in the early 1800s (Franklin 1823: 95–96).

Crees state that Pukatawagan and Granville Lake were summer fishing sites from time out of mind and both were the sites of Hudson's Bay Company and Northwest Company outposts during the late 1700s and early 1800s (Morton 1973: 441–42, HBC B/83/a). Although there were undoubtedly population shifts as posts were closed and re-opened in the wake of the 1821 coalition of the competing companies, the area was occupied by ancestors of the contemporary population since at least the early 1800s and probably much earlier. Following 1821 and the elimination of winter outposts, the Crees of the Nelson River District traded either at Nelson House or Southern Indian Lake. George Charles' Indian Lake (Southern Indian Lake) post journal of 1822–23 (HBC B.91/a/8) provides a census of the Nelson River District Indians together with a discussion of different hunting groups and their customary territories. Charles distinguished between "Swampy Ground" Crees on the lower Nelson River, Crees nearer to Nelson House on the upper reaches of the Nelson, and Churchill River Crees. The latter division comprised six bands whose populations and approximate territories are indicated on Table 1.

Table 1. Bands and Territories in 1822–23.		
Band	Size	Territory
1.	9	Loon Lake, Grenouille (Frog) Lake, Trout Lake
2.	34	Burntwood Lake and (upper?) Burntwood River west to Pelican Lake and south towards Cumberland House
3.	20	The Churchill River in the vicinity of Sisipuk (Duck) Lake and Pukatawagan Lake
4.	15	Reindeer River and Loon River
5.	12	"around the Burntwood River"
6.		Trade at Indian Lake; usually hunt at Paint Lake and Wapisu (Swan) Lake

Charles wrote of this division:

> To judge of the country from the furs we procure from it, this part of the District must be termed the worst, as the Natives have a great extent of Country to traverse and need not hunt two seasons on the same grounds, as to claiming any rights in the grounds in which they hunt they do not as one party are often on the land that may have been inhabited by others a season or two before. The furs that are procured are Very Good. Beavers, cats lynx, otters, and often martens, bear, and rats. The Natives are all Southern Indians or Crees and, like all the rest of their Tribe, very fond of Rum, they are a quiet, inoffensive people, and remarkably hospitable, as they seldom or ever fail to offer anything they possess and generally of the best. In their habits they are kind and generous to each other, seem very much attached to their children, though they pay very little attention to their morals or are anyway careful in keeping them properly clothed until real necessity obliges them.

Charles' conventionally ethnocentric views on Cree morals and prodigality aside, the passage provides some insight into the theoretically interesting question of Cree land tenure during the period. Although specific hunting groups appear to have been sufficiently localized at the time to make possible approximate delimitations of their territories, Charles makes clear that relationships between groups and territories were fluid and sometimes impermanent. That different groups serially occupied the same land may have exemplified hospitality or the use of land relinquished by others.

A second census of the Nelson River District taken in 1838 (HBC B239/2/10) does not indicate band divisions but demonstrates the continuity in the population. Such ancestors of contemporary Pukatawagan and Granville Lake families as *Ostikwān* ("Head"), *Okimāw Acāhpīy* ("Chief Bow"), *Apikosis* ("Mouse"), *Tāwipīsim* ("Half Sun"), and *Wāpask Okimāw* ("Polar Bear Chief") are listed. It is not clear where the Rock Crees of the area were trading during this period since Nelson House was closed in 1827 to allow beaver populations to recover (Fleming 1940:1x) and there are no records for Southern Indian Lake after 1823. Possibly the trade was carried on at the Split Lake post which apparently remained open through the period, although there may have developed a westerly trading orientation towards Pelican Lake and as far west along the Churchill as Lac La Ronge. In any event, Pukatawagan Lake continued to be a summer fishing site probably throughout the 1800s. The Oblate missionary Bonald visited Pukatawagan during the summer of 1878; his voyage was undertaken in the expectation of finding Crees assembled there, and he was evidently not disappointed since Oblate tradition states that mass conversions followed his arrival. By at least 1889, Nelson House was re-established on the northwest bay of Three Point Lake, within the boundaries of the present reservation, with outposts at Southern Indian Lake and Burntwood Lake (HBC D.25/6). By around 1900, permanant Hudson's Bay Company and Revillon Frères posts were located at Pukatawagan and maintaining outposts at Granville Lake and High Rock. By this time also, Pukatawagan, Granville, and such other sites as Burntwood Lake, Swan Lake, Trout Lake, Sisipuk Lake, Suwanee Lake, and locations on the Laurie and Prayer Rivers emerged as semi-permanent log cabin communities which were the winter focus of different hunting groups. Pukatawagan gradually emerged as the primary mission-trading post-summer fishery center for the area.

Administratively, the treaty Indians of Pukatawagan and Granville Lake are members of the Mathias Colomb Band, established in 1910 from a group formerly included in the Peter Ballentyne Band formed in 1901. Earlier members of the Ballentyne and Colomb Bands were included in the James Robert Band (now the Lac la Ronge Band) which signed adhesion to Treaty Number 6 at Montreal Lake, Saskatchewan in 1889. References to the Roberts and Ballentyne bands in government documents suggest that these were administrative labels for Crees occupying Lac la Ronge and points east along the Churchill who had not yet had reservations surveyed. Between 1904 and 1907, for example, the "Ballendine Band" was described as assembling at Pelican Narrows (on Pelican Lake, Saskatchewan) for its annuities, as lacking any settled abode, and as scattered across the country as far as Nelson House to the east (Canada 1899: 236, 1889: 132, 1900: 137, 1901: 139). The conventional Subarctic pattern for the period of relative sedentism and aggregation in summer and winter dispersal to the log cabin communities persisted until the 1950s when most members of the Mathias Colomb Band moved in to Pukatawagan and occupied houses there. Today, Pukatawagan is a conventional micro-urban reservation community with a school, band office and administration, nursing station, church, Hudson's Bay Company store, and RCMP detachment. Granville Lake, occupied both by treaty Indians and "Metis" or non-treaty Crees, is transitional between the old log cabin communities and the micro-urban reservation centers. Granville has a grade school and store but retains some of the isolation and autonomy of the earlier bush settlements. At the time of study, the population was approximately fifty persons in contrast to thirteen hundred at Pukatawagan. The Crees of Brochet trace their ancestry to families who moved north from Pelican Lake and Southend in the 1800s; the history of the community is discussed by Smith (1975).

Categories of Cree Oral Literature

Rock Crees class oral narratives either as *ācaðōhkīwin* or *ācimōwina*. Events in *ācaðōhkīwin* are understood as temporally antecedent to those in *ācimōwina* and comprise most of what is conventionally labeled "myth": the trickster-transformer stories, stories in which animals possess hominid characteristics, stories of powerful heroes, and accounts of marriages of human or proto-humans with animal or other nonhuman entities. Crees stress certain cosmological or experiential contrasts with the contemporary world in these stories, emphasizing that animals and other non-human agencies spoke and behaved like humans and that the landscape and fauna had not yet acquired their customary characteristics. Human beings were said to exist during this ancient period by Mr. Henry Linklater, but he emphasized that there were very few and that they were separated by vast expanses of territory. The stories are strongly identified with the trickster-transformer such that *ācaðōhkīwin* and "*wīsahkīcāhk* story" are almost interlingual synonyms; many stories, however, are classed as *ācaðōhkīwin* but lack *wīsahkīcāhk* as a character. A third and indexical characteristic of these stories is relevant: the characters are not persons of whom the narrators possess any direct knowledge or experience outside of esoteric contexts such as dreams or shaking lodge performances. Finally, stories in the *ācaðōhkīwin* class are generally said to be true accounts of events that transpired in an earlier condition of the world. The existence of different versions does not discredit their veracity since human knowledge of these events is understood to be imperfect. Originally, it is said, the stories were relations of then contemporary events that were handed down successively through the generations. Alternatively, some of the stories of the *ācaðōhkīwin* class were said to have been dreamed, a modality of learning that possesses, for traditional Cree, a validity sometimes exceeding the data of conventional waking perception.

Stories in the *ācimōwin* class focus upon human characters but this is not their defining feature since humans figure also in *ācaðōhkīwin*. They are temporally situated in a kind of "historical" time possessing continuity with the situation of narration. The narrator knows the characters or has direct or indirect knowledge of them through human intermediaries. Examples are stories relating the exploits of celebrated ancestors. *ācimōwin* is clearly the unmarked category, encompassing old and contemporary narratives, gossip, humorous stories and jokes, and serious tales of bush experiences and enigmatic encounters with non-Indians. Like the *ācaðōhkīwin*, the *ācimōwin* may contain events and characters which are supernatural or non-factual from a non-Indian perspective. Not all *ācimōwina* are regarded as true; many are appreciated as humorous fabrications. A sub-grouping called *kayās-ācimōwina* refers to stories which are temporally remote from the situation of narration, although people differ as to how remote the temporal setting must be. Prototypical *kayās-ācimōwina* describe the nineteenth-century exploits of famous ancestors, but some informants regard stories located prior to the sedentism of the 1950s as belonging to the category. In organizing stories into chapters, I grouped stories as their narrators identified them. There is sometimes lack of consensus (and often little interest) in whether a particular story belongs to one or the other category. Other discussions of Algonquian literary categories are provided by Preston for the Rupert's House Cree (1975: 288–93) and Hallowell for the Berens River Saulteaux (1955: 231–33, 1976: 364–65).

wīsahkīcāhk and the other dramatis personae of Rock Cree myth are alive and well in the 1980s, supplemented but not at this time displaced in many families by the incursions of television and non-Indian literature. The author did not observe formalized performances attended by large audiences such as that discussed by Darnell (1976), but the stories are related in households and in the bush for entertainment, instruction, and philosophical reflection. Some narrators perpetuate the widespread Algonquian convention of restricting narration to the winter months for fear that summer recitations would be attended by snakes or other undesirable consequences. An obvious imperative, one hopefully congenial to those Whites and Indians who design educational policy for northern schools, is the incorporation of this literature, with its Rabelaisian (or *wīsahkīcāhkian*) humour unbowdlerized and its cosmological surrealism unadulterated, into the curricula of schools with Indian clientele. Given the emerging interest in the poetic and stylistic characteristics of Indian literature and oral literary performance, Rock Cree narratives deserve recording in both Cree and English, ideally by bilingual individuals sensitive to the linguistic and cultural nuances involved. With plots and characters that reach back to archaic strata of Algonquian culture these narratives continue in the 1980s to express and engage the intelligence and emotions of the men and women who reproduce, transform, and perpetuate them.

CHAPTER 2

ācaðōhkīwin: The wīsahkīcāhk Cycle

Cornelius Colomb Narrative

Rolling Head

wīsahkīcāhk had a mother and a dad and a small brother. His dad used to—well, he was always hunting, eh? And whatever time the old man comes in, the old lady wouldn't be cooking. She'd be out in the bush all the time. Like she make believe she's out cutting wood. No time to dry meat or fix up the place, y'know. Always busy in the bush. Used to go where there's *misikinīpikwak*, big snakes, big snake. Used to go to the snake, that woman. Monkey around with the snake. By the time the old man comes in [to the lodge], the old lady would try and get there. Try and cook. But she caught hell from the old man.

So the guy got fed up with this woman. And he asked his boys, "What does your mother do every time I leave?" "Well, as soon as you're gone, she takes an axe and tells us she's gonna' cut wood. And she doesn't come back all day. We heard her making noise, pounding that big trunk of tree." That guy would come out, that big snake. That was her lover, that old bitch.

So—so the guy wanted to get rid of—kill that snake. So he went—He left two beavers one day's walk away [from the camp]. Like it would take the old lady all day to go and get those two beavers. So he told the old lady, "I left two beavers. You go and get 'em tomorrow." Oh, the old lady was anxious to leave, she wanted to leave the tent. "Sure, I'll get them back," she said.

So—He had one of those—what you used to call garters. He took one of them and he threw it in the—Well, people used to do things like that, you know—threw it in the fire. Said he's going to shorten up his trail. That's to shorten up his trail. So the old man took off. So he went and killed the snake. And he brought that snake head back to the tent. Then he sends his boys out. Then the old man left the tent, the old man left the wigwam.

When the old lady got back, the kids weren't there and the old man's not there. But she seen that snake head inside that wigwam. And this guy made a dummy to cut wood. So the old lady heard someone cutting wood over there towards where the snake was. So she right away took off. Went to see her lover, that snake. Well, the snake, his head wasn't there. Already she'd seen it. Sure enough, she seen just an axe and a dummy cuttin' wood. And the old man took off already besides.

And so the kids, when he got them out from that wigwam under the poles, he feed all the animals, that old man [to procure their silence]. And the crow—raven is always greedy. He didn't have enough feed.

So first she took off after the old man, that woman. Well, the old man chase her around and finally they took off in the sky.

I think that's where the old lady kill that guy, that man. That's where the Dipper is, that's part of the man. This side's gone [?] That thing came down except—That's the way she kills him up in the air, that's the Dipper now.

So after he [part of body] came down, the old lady came down. And then she wants to find out where the little boys were. She ask all the animals. Well, the raven didn't have enough to eat. So he told her, "That's where they took off from." Once she knows from where they took off, from there she knows the road.

And the old man gave them [previously] *oskācihk* ["awl"]. It's something you punch a hole with. We call it *oskācihk*. It's a nail. Like you punch a hole with it. It's sticking to a little piece of wood. You punch holes with it. We call it *oskācihk*. Another thing was that thing they use to strike fire. Strike sparks. That's one— And he give them that towel [?]. He gave them three things. "So if you notice that your mother's close by," he said, "you throw behind *oskācihk*. That thing, you throw it behind."

Yeah, the old lady come down with just the head, *ostikwān* ["her head"]. The old man cut the head off the old—the old bitch so there was just her head trailing after her kids. But the old man was killed up in the air. That's that Dipper. But the old lady wouldn't die, she ran after her kids with just a head. She wanted to kill her kids. So they threw those *oskācihk* behind. They made a fence of thorns. There was lots of them so she couldn't pass it. So the old lady—

I think she hires two slim things that crawl under the earth. Kind of snake-looking things. Worms that crawl under. So she asked them, "If you can make a hole for me underground, I'll marry you after I get back." So it said, "Okay, I'll make a hole through here, past these things." So away they went and then *Ha*! She was coming again. Those little kids, they heard her coming. "Oh, I want to kiss my kids for the last time," she keeps saying as she was rolling. They heard her coming, she was close back. So they threw that sparkler, they threw it behind. *Ha*! There was a fire across. *Ha*! The old lady couldn't pass the fire.

Somebody got her through again. Anyway, she said she was going to marry the guy again.

There was somebody anyway that got her underground again so she passes that. Oh, she was still coming. So the towel was the last one. "Oh, this is our last— From here on she's going to catch us," *wīsahkīcāhk* said. And he was going to throw it behind but it so happened he threw it ahead. And there was a river formed across and they couldn't cross it. Son of a gun and she was not far behind. So they seen this swan and he asked the swan if it could take them across. Oh, he said, "Sure." It was a big wide river. So it took them. "As long as you don't touch my neck," the swan said. "If you touch my neck, I'll throw you off." So they landed safely across. Ha! The old lady was just across and she hollered at the swan, "C'mon, you take me across. I'll marry you after I kiss my kids." Oh, the swan went back over and told her, "As long as you don't touch my neck I can take you across." *Ha*! The old lady, she was on top of the swan. Oh, just about when she figured she was going to make it to the shore she rolls into the swan's neck, bumps it. "What's wrong with your neck?" she said. And the swan swings his neck and he threw her off back in the middle of the river. So the old lady couldn't swim across with just the head. Keeps singing. So it came up—this was a sturgeon. She said, "I'm gonna' turn into a sturgeon. Too bad I couldn't kiss my kids but me, I'm gonna' turn into a sturgeon." So that was the last they saw their mother.

Contest with *wīmisōsiw*

And they were there all this time on the shoreline. Well, of course, the little kid was crying all the time, the little kid. He had this—Well, somebody came like a big bird, something like an eagle. So he give out these claws, he cut his claws off anyway, somehow. That's the story. Put them in a rope [to make a toy]. And he threw them claws in the air to make the kid keep quiet [amuse him]. *wīsahkīcāhk* did that for his little brother. So that was his dad's—Well, people used to dream about animals. Some were good, they were good to them. This was his dad's side [identifying eagle as father's dream spirit]. And his mother, that's that *wīmisōs*. That's *wīmisōs*, that's another story. He's rowing a boat. He lives in the sea. Well, the guy came rowing a boat. He seen those two kids. Ha! he had landed his boat alongside the little kid. Well, of course, he was their mother's side. Still the mother was after the kids to try and get rid of her kids.

It so happens that those things [claws] fall into the boat. And *wīsahkīcāhk* asked the guy to toss it back to him. The old guy said, "oh, come and get 'em yourself. You can step on my paddle," he said. Soon as *wīsahkīcāhk* got into the boat, the guy shoved the boat out and started rowing. *Ha*! The little kid was crying. *wīsahkīcāhk* was crying, he couldn't get off the boat. So finally they were far out already and he [*wīsahkīcāhk*] seen this wolf running around. He said, "I'll turn into a wolf." The little kid said, "I'll turn into a wolf." *wīsahkīcāhk* said, "That's good. But remember, never run—never chase a moose over the lake in the water." You know, water. A wolf wouldn't chase a—a moose to the lake. It's not true [that a wolf won't enter water at all], but as soon as a wolf—I mean this much water [indicates about two feet]. If a moose gets down in the lake about this much water, he'll—he'll turn around on the wolf. A wolf, he's got a hard time to move around in the water so he [moose] starts pounding him. That's why you never see a wolf do something to a moose in a lake 'cause they kill 'em right there, the moose'll kill him.

So anyway, *wīsahkīcāhk* told the wolf, that's his brother, "Never chase a moose to the lake."

So happens this guy *wīmisōs* took *wīsahkīcāhk* to his place. He had two daughters. *wīmisōs* was the guy's name. That's the guy that lives somewhere around the ocean. He's got his boat, rowing. So he dumped [overturned after landing] the boat with this *wīsahkīcāhk* at the bottom. He dump his boat and put *wīsahkīcāhk* under there. Went up [to his camp]. He had two daughters. So after awhile, he said to the older one, he said, "Go and check my boat. I brought a man in there," he said. "Go and wash him up. He might be looking red-eyed because he been crying all this time I was coming home." So the older daughter went down. Checked the boat. And there he was, *wīsahkīcāhk*, all red-eyed, eyes swelling up with crying all the way. Left him like that. Said, "Ah, hell, I don't want him. Much too ugly" [laughs]. Old man said to the youngest girl, "Oh, go on, go and get him. Wash him up good. He was a nice-looking chap when I first seen him. Only thing is, he's been crying all this time. He'll be alright after awhile." So the girl took the soap down and washed *wīsahkīcāhk* good. Took him up. He was alright looking after she comb him up and all that.

And the older girl said, "By Jesus, what if we sit on each side of him?" Ah, the young girl said, "No!" Said, "You didn't want him the first time. It's mine." The old man said, "No, don't do that. There'll be people. There'll be a lot of people, later years. They want—they're gonna' have—They'll be short of men a lot of times because—You sitting with your sister, that's what's gonna' happen later years anyway. If you don't do it [polygyny], nobody'll do it. If you sleep with him together, it'll be like that later on," he said. And so it happens. I used to hear the old people, they used to have five or six women. One old guy had six wives. That was before they were baptised. The older you grow, the more women you get.

So they stay with this *wīsahkīcāhk*. And that guy wanted to kill *wīsahkīcāhk*, that old man. He took him out after he was getting to be alright, forget about his brother.

He [*wīsahkīcāhk*] wanted to make a bow and arrow—arrows—and he had to have some kind of eagle feather on each side of the arrow so it goes straight, eh? He had nothing to do it with. So he told him [*wīmisōs*], "I seen" he said to the old guy, "young eagles somewhere here in the lake." "I'll take you over there." So those giant eagles, that's where he [*wīmisōs*] threw him off on the shore. He told the eagles to eat him.

Oh, I guess the guy [*wīsahkīcāhk*] kill those eagles. Took the feathers. The old man was out on his way home rowing. And *wīsahkīcāhk* turned into a seagull to get home. And he seen his father-in-law rowing and he duck down and he shit on him. *Ha*! The old man, the eagle shit on him. He says, "Ah, you son of a bitch, I bet you wouldn't help the guys eating my son-in-law" [laughs]. Got home and he seen his son-in-law in there fixing his arrows and he says, "How in hell you get home?" So he was trying to kill him all the time.

Another time, he took him in the reef again. He said, "Any kind of feather you find, you gotta' fly in to the reef with it [transform into bird]." "Ah, okay," he said. "I'll match you," he said to the guy. So *wīsahkīcāhk* found this *cīscīskisis*. It's a little bird that sticks around the shoreline. You've seen him fly. He flies low, right above the water just as if he was going to cave [fall] in. What do you call it in English? Not a kildeer, I know. Kildeer is bigger, eh? And this old man, he found this whiskeyjack (Canada jay) feather. *wīsahkīcāhk* took off first [transformed into a *cīscīskisis*]. Well, he took off from the shoreline. *Ha*! away he goes to the reef, just about touching the water. The old man keeps hollering, making lots of noise, hitting his boat so the guy would fall in 'cause if he'd just fall in, he'd drown. Oh, he made it and the old man was next [to transform into a whiskeyjack]. You see, a whiskeyjack, every time you watch a whiskeyjack and he wants to go across [a water body], he keeps climbing the tree [higher altitude]. Right from the top, that's when he start. And he *wīsahkīcāhk* keeps doing this, hollering. If you holler at a whiskeyjack going across, he'll fall down. You try sometimes. Or if you get a shotgun you holler same time as you shoot. Damn thing fall down right away. They have no strength on 'em, eh? That's what happened to that old man. *wīsahkīcāhk* hollered as he was coming. He keep flying up and down and finally he got in—into the water. That's how he drown this old man. From there on he was a free man. Took off.

The Women and the "Sickness"

So anyway after that he left his family, he left his women. Oh, he was travelling lots.

And finally he's coming to two women. Oh, he's coming to these women. There was two. Oh, he wanted them pretty bad. He said [to them], "There's sickness behind. I'm running away from it," he said. "How far back?" the woman said. "Oh," he said, "maybe a day behind. Two days at the most," he said. "I'm just now about two days ahead of it, I'm running away from it.

Well, anyway, I'm on my way. But there, I'll tell you," he said. "If you hear it coming, pull your dresses up and on the door side [lodge entrance] stick your butts out like that, you know?" So away he went. He made a circle and he went and cut birch. Went and cut the birch and put it in the sunshine where they dry up. Where the leaves would dry up right away, eh? Ha! Two days afterwards, the leaves were drying up. He went back again and went and got those and he drag them. Those ladies heard it coming. The leaves made a lot of noise. "Oh," she said, "here comes the sickness. We'd better do what that *wīsahkīcāhk* said," she said. Ha! they took their dresses off. They were pointing their butts to the door. They heard it coming right to the door. Ha! *wīsahkīcāhk* took his clothes off, peeped in at these two women. He did it with each one of them. After he was through, he took his leaves and moved on. I guess he threw them off on the way.

And the lady shortly after he was gone say "*Nicākwīy*—" That's how they say it in Cree, Something like in English "partner." "How'd you like—how'd you feel about the sickness?" one said.

And the other woman said, "By Jesus! I wish the damn thing would come back again!" [prolonged laughter].

The Flood

Yeah, that's what they say about *wīsahkīcāhk*. There's no ending story, they say. Old people, they all used to make lots of stories over that. They say that a guy who die old would tell stories and he would never end the story. I don't know, I used to hear the old people stories. Used to give them tobacco so they'll tell stories. They'd be laying around the wigwam listening to a guy telling stories about *wīsahkīcāhk*.

So finally, anyway, that was his brother, the wolf. So then he start wondering about what happened. So he seen this kingfisher. He was looking—well, of course, he's looking for a fish, the kingfisher. This was in the rapids. Big falls, y'know. The guy was looking to the falls. So he said—Well, *wīsahkīcāhk*, everybody was his—he was the brother of all the animals. Supposed to be, *wīsahkīcāhk*, he called everybody *nisīmis* ["my younger sibling"]. So he said "*nisīm*! What are you looking at?" "Oh," he said, "I'm watching those *misipisiwak* ["water lions"]. They're playing with wolf hides." "Ah, ča-ča-ča-ča-ča-ča, what'd you say?" "Playing with wolf hides," he said. "Oh, Jesus!" he said, "What'd they do?" He tried to find out right away. "Well, after they start playing, when they're tired of playing, they come up on that reef. And they spread those wolf hides and on them they sleep. They start playing and sleeping." "Oh, so that's what they do." "Yeah, that's what they do." So, *wīsahkīcāhk*—what the kingfisher told him was that they come up on the shore, sleeping. Come and rest after playing. So he make himself like a dead tree. That's the ones that are cut off. You see them, dead trees, eh? Part of it gone? So he make himself one like that, look like one. Standing there. So these *misipisiwak* come up in the evening. Oh, he notice right away the guys were—they were kind of—there was something. They keep looking at the tree. They kind of notice something strange. They never see that tree standing in there. They spread the hides. They went and lay—lay down. After they got to sleeping, he [*wīsahkīcāhk*] had this spear. He made himself spears. After—once they fall asleep, he took the spears and stab those *misipisiwak* in the ribs. Took the hides and I think he made a raft. The water came up right away. And he was floating on top of the raft with the hides. So after the thing got—the water went down again, coming to shore. He put life—he brought them back to life. The wolves. And he starts shaking him [brother]. Well, wolf came up again [returns to life] and he said, "Don't do that again, I had a hard time to catch you."

So as he was wandering around he ran into a frog. He was a medicine man, the frog. He happened to hear him [frog] coming. So he—The frog was hopping. He keep saying he was going to cure those *misipisiwak*. Ah, he stopped him and he said, "What the hell you saying?" "Oh," he said, "I'm a medicine man. I've just about got them, got everything off. *wīsahkīcāhk* stuck those spears on them." "Oh the dirty guy. I don't know who's *wīsahkīcāhk*," he [*wīsahkīcāhk*] said. After the frog told him everything, he killed the frog and skinned it and put the hide on him. That way he went hopping. Soon he got into the place where those guys were laying. They were staying underwater, I guess.

Well, after he got there, they were laying there with spears on them. They were just about—the frog had just about got everything out [removed spears from wounds]. Well, everybody had to leave the place. Just him, the medicine man in the place. So he shoved that spear right into him [*misipisiw*], right clean through him. Ah, he keep saying, "*Ha*! Just about cured now. It won't hurt anymore." After he kill him, he got to the other one. Did the same thing. So after he was through killing them, he came out. And the guy noticed. One of those guys [other *misipisiwak*] said, "It don't seem to be—it's not that medicine man. He acts different. He usually stick around after, tell a few stories. Then go home. But him, he just—" After he kill them, he just come out and go. So the guy was kind of feared of something wrong. So he went and chased the frog to find out what the frog was doing, the big frog. That's when he seen the [discarded frog] hide hanging. He track the guy from there. "Oh," he said, "the son of a bitch. That's *wīsahkīcāhk*." So he went and check those two *misipisiwak*. They were dead. That's how he got rid of those *misipisiwak*. That's why there's none now. They're just a story now [Mr. Colomb later qualifies these remarks].

That's all. He kill the *misipisiw*. Yeah, that was his brother [wolf]. He chased a moose into the water. That where the *misipisiw* got him. Skin him and they play with the skins. So you don't see a wolf chasing a moose.

Marries Daughter

wīsahkīcāhk did it with his daughter. Well, he married now and then, you know. Of course he was—they say he was trying to cover the whole world. That's what he was trying. Well, he ran into a woman. Oh, he stayed with the woman. They had a girl. Oh this girl is coming to be a beautiful woman. So he really wanted to do it with his daughter. But, "How in the hell am I going to do *that*?"

So this was in wintertime. Oh, he turned sick. He said, "I'm sick." Anyway, he had enough meat, I guess. He haul a lot of meat first. Lots of dry meat. Plenty meat. So he turned sick. *Ha*! He didn't eat. Make believe he was sick. *Ha*! He was getting weaker. He keeps saying he's gonna die. Now he says to his wife, "If I die, you leave. Just keep on trapping. If you run into people—or you might run into a man, sometime you might run into a man. You give him to our daughter so the guy, he'll hunt for you. As long as you guys don't starve." She says, "Okay, we'll do that. Just as soon as you die." "You make a *tīsipicōwin* [platform stage]. Make one. You hang me over there after I'm dead. So nobody [animals] will eat me." She said, "We'll do that." So he died that night. I don't know how in the hell. Anyway, he didn't breathe, I guess. Stiffened up.

"Well, too bad you're dead. You're dad is dead." The old lady say that to the girl. So they hang him up. They left.

So of course there was a lot of meat there. He said [before "dying"], "Don't try to take all that meat. There'll be too much to pull. Leave some." When he said that, he figured he was going to stay there for awhile. Cool off things. He have this—

Wigwams, they used to make them out of wood, you know? He didn't have no canvas. Nothing, just wood. Wood, make a wigwam, cover it with moss. Then spruce boughs. Then snow. Then it's just like a house, you make a fire inside. I had one like that in the bush, but I put a stove in. Just like a house.

So the old lady took off. Then he got up. After they were gone, he jump off the platform and went inside and made fire. *Ha*! He stayed there for maybe a week and a half. Maybe two weeks. There was a lot of meat there. And then he start trailing his wife. They were about—He made a big circle and he came up where they were. Well, of course, he never changed. He didn't grow old, same looking all the time. Only thing is, he had a birthmark on the ass here. Just above here he had a birthmark.

So they told the story to this guy that comes in, a man. "Oh, my husband died a month ago. We left. He told us to keep looking for people. If you're not married, you can stay with my daughter," she said. This old lady said that. "Oh," he said, "no, I'm not married." Boy, he really wanted to sleep with his daughter. So the old lady said, "Oh sure, go ahead, sleep with her. You marry my daughter, she's your wife now." *Ha*! They kind of notice him. His accents, you know, trying to change. But he—The girl says, "Sometimes he acts like my dad," she said to her mother. "Ah," the old lady says. "sometimes—yeah, the way he used to make fun." I guess *wīsahkīcāhk* couldn't help it sometimes, making jokes like that. He can't change all of a sudden. But anyway, the old lady, she was pretty sure it was *wīsahkīcāhk*. Same age. Only thing, I guess he dressed different. He didn't want to use the same clothes. Maybe everything a little bit different. So this was in the summer. I guess he had all kinds of fun at night. No covers on that morning. The old lady got up. Well, she used to see *wīsahkīcāhk* naked like that. Seen the birthmark. So she took that big piece of burned wood, eh? So she shoved that up his ass! Said, "You son of a bitch, *wīsahkīcāhk*! That's what you were after, your daughter!" Well, the guy, he was always ready. *wīsahkīcāhk* had everything outside in case of some trouble if the old lady find out. He was always prepared. Ha! He run out like that. No clothes on. Ha! Away he went, laughing.

Robert A. Brightman

Jeremiah Michel Narrative
Translator: Caroline Dumas

Contest with *wīmisōsiw*
The stories about *wīsahkīcāhk* were not originally told by Indian people. [Interpreter interjects, "That's not true!"]. *wīsahkīcāhk* and his younger brother were staying by the shore and playing with their fingernails. There was an old man *wīmisōsiw* who was travelling around. *wīmisōsiw* possessed a canoe which he could direct through the water simply by striking the prow. The old man knew where *wīsahkīcāhk* was and approached his camp in the canoe. He came toward the shore where *wīsahkīcāhk* and his brother were playing. *wīsahkīcāhk* and his brother had been throwing their fingernails into the air. *wīsahkīcāhk* lost his fingernails and he thought that they had fallen into *wīmisōsiw*'s canoe. *wīmisōsiw* told *wīsahkīcāhk* to come into the canoe so that he could retrieve his fingernails. *wīsahkīcāhk* got into the canoe to get his nails and the canoe moved away from the shore and began moving down the river. Behind them on the shore, *wīsahkīcāhk*'s *osīma* ('his younger sibling') was crying because he was left behind. Then they heard the howling of a wolf. That was *wīsahkīcāhk*'s *osīma*; he had become a wolf after being left on the shore. To his younger brother *wīsahkīcāhk* called back, "If you are hunting caribou, don't follow them into the water or you will be drowned!"

wīmisōsiw was taking *wīsahkīcāhk* to his camp. There he had three daughters who desired husbands. *wīsahkīcāhk* was crying all the way they travelled because he didn't want to go there. They arrived at *wīmisōsiw*'s camp and went ashore. To his daughters, *wīmisōsiw* said, "I've brought a young man here with me for you." Before, *wīsahkīcāhk* had been a handsome man but now he looked ugly from having cried all the way there. So then the oldest of *wīmisōsiw*'s three daughters walked down from the lodge to the edge of the shore. She looked *wīsahkīcāhk* over. So then she walked back up to the lodge and to her sisters she said, "Our father is telling us a lie. No one would marry that man, the way he looks." The second oldest daughter went down and she too looked at *wīsahkīcāhk* who was still crying. Just like her older sister she said, "No one would marry this one, the way he looks." Finally the youngest of the three sisters went down to the shore. She looked at *wīsahkīcāhk* and thought, "I like him." "Don't cry," she said. "I'll stay with you and I'll fix your appearance. It doesn't matter if you're ugly. I'll stay with you so don't cry." So that youngest sister began to clean *wīsahkīcāhk* up and comb his hair and she fixed him up good. So she took his hand and they went up together to the lodge. So then the oldest sister, the one who had gone down first, said to her younger sister, "All right *nisīmī* ("my younger sibling"), let him sleep between us when we lay down for the night." But that youngest sister said, "You were the first to go down and see him and you didn't want him, so he won't sleep between us tonight." So *wīsahkīcāhk* became that youngest sister's husband and they stayed together for a long time and had two children.

wīmisōsiw hated his son-in-law and planned to use his *pawākanak* ("spirit guardians") to harm him. *wīsahkīcāhk* knew that his father-in-law intended to harm him. And then he said to him, "I wish that I had wings. If I had wings, then I'd be able to fly. I would be able to provide myself with a fine bow and arrows. Perhaps also then I would be able to know what others are thinking about me." Then *wīmisōsiw* said to *wīsahkīcāhk*, "I know where small eagles can be found. From them you can get the wings." So then together they traveled away down the river in *wīmisōsiw*'s canoe. Far ahead of them, *wīsahkīcāhk* saw what looked like small eagles hovering around a nest and said to his father-in-law, "Those small eagles are doing a good job building their nest." They passed around a bend in the river and approached closer and *wīsahkīcāhk* saw on the shore huge rocks that resembled giant eagles. These rocks that looked like huge eagles, these were the *pawākanak* of *wīmisōsiw*. And when they approached closely, *wīmisōsiw* said, "My *pawākanak*, I come to feed you." And then he threw *wīsahkīcāhk* from the canoe far into the air and he landed up amidst the stone eagles.

To these eagles, *wīsahkīcāhk* said, "Don't harm me because truly I'm your *kistīs* ("your elder brother")." [Mrs. Dumas remarks that *wīsahkīcāhk* always addresses others as *nisīmiy* "my younger sibling"]. So thus *wīsahkīcāhk* tricked those stone eagles and they didn't eat him because they believed that he was their elder brother. And then *wīsahkīcāhk* began picking up molted eagle wings and truly he became a seagull and flew down over the river away from the stone eagles. And below him as he flew he saw his father-in-law reclining on his back inside the canoe which was floating back toward his camp. And then *wīsahkīcāhk* flew down low over his father-in-law and defecated directly in his face. And *wīmisōsiw* said this about that seagull, "He has smelly excreta—truly he stinks. I guess he was helping those eagles devour my son-in-law." *wīsahkīcāhk* flew back to the camp where they stayed, and once again he became a man. And then he walked back up to the lodge and went inside and he began to manufacture a bow and arrows. Presently, he heard *wīmisōsiw* coming up from the shore. And then *wīsahkīcāhk*'s son ran down to the shore and said to his grandfather, "My grandfather, you're very late. Our father returned a long time ago." To this, *wīmisōsiw* said, "My poor grandchild, a long time ago I fed your father to my *pawākanak*." And then *wīmisōsiw* walked into the lodge and saw *wīsahkīcāhk* sitting there manufacturing arrows.

To *wīmisōsiw*, *wīsahkīcāhk* said, "I need some good willow stalks for my arrows." And his father-in-law said, "I know where there are some fine willows, and I'll take you there." So they traveled in *wīmisōsiw*'s canoe to a place where there were many willows, and *wīsahkīcāhk* saw many fine stalks. But when he approached more closely, he saw *misikinīpikwak* ("giant snakes") crawling over the bushes. And then his father-in-law, desiring once again to kill him, threw him up into those willows and then abandoned him. But again, *wīsahkīcāhk* addressed those snakes as "younger brother," and they left him unharmed. Quickly, *wīsahkīcāhk* cut the willows he needed and travelled back to their lodge. He arrived there before his father-in-law returned, and when *wīmisōsiw* came in, again he saw *wīsahkīcāhk* sitting there making arrows.

As he finished making his arrows, *wīsahkīcāhk* said to *wīmisōsiw*, "I wish we had a little swing. I desire to swing myself." And then *wīmisōsiw* said that he knew of a place where there was a swing, and once again they traveled away in *wīmisōsiw*'s canoe. They came finally to the place where there was a swing, and *wīsahkīcāhk* saw bones scattered all across the ground. And to himself, *wīmisōsiw* thought, "Soon my son-in-law's bones will be lying here on the ground." It was *wīsahkīcāhk*'s turn first to get onto the swing, and *wīmisōsiw* began to push him until he was swinging very high in the air and he feared that he was going to fall. So he stopped the swing, and it was *wīmisōsiw*'s turn to get on. *wīsahkīcāhk* pushed the swing higher and higher until finally *wīmisōsiw* fell off. *wīsahkīcāhk* sat there for a long time after *wīmisōsiw* fell off; he believed that his father-in-law was dead. Finally, he travelled alone back to the camp in *wīmisōsiw*'s canoe, and tied it carefully to the shore when he landed. *wīmisōsiw* did not return that night. Then, the next night, far in the distance, *wīsahkīcāhk* heard *wīmisōsiw* calling for his canoe, and truly that canoe left the shore and moved through the water to where *wīmisōsiw* was calling for it. And then *wīmisōsiw* got inside his canoe and came back again to that camp.

"Well, I have just about overslept," he said to *wīsahkīcāhk*. Again those two stayed there together and they were thinking of ways to outsmart one another. So then *wīsahkīcāhk* said to his father-in-law, "Let us go out traveling," and they set out walking. That night, they put up a camp and built a large fire to dry their clothes. And as they dried their clothes, *wīmisōsiw* kept on building the fire larger and larger, until *wīsahkīcāhk* thought to himself, "Maybe he will try to burn up my clothes tonight." Thus later he folded his own clothes for a pillow, and moved his father-in-law's clothes to where his own had hung. And as he had thought, *wīmisōsiw* arose in the night and took those clothes and burnt them in the fire. And *wīsahkīcāhk* said, "What are you doing to your clothes, my father-in-law? My clothes are over here where I'm using them as a pillow." And then *wīmisōsiw* looked into the fire and saw that he had burned his own clothes. They sat awake until morning and they didn't know how they were going to travel the next day because *wīmisōsiw* was naked. And finally, *wīmisōsiw* found a round flat rock and he placed it in the fire until it was red-hot, and then he rolled that rock in front of him as they traveled homeward. And many times, *wīmisōsiw* by accident rolled the stone into the muskeg where it was cooled, and he had to stop many times to make a fire to heat it up again. And when finally they arrived home, *wīmisōsiw* said: "That's all! There will be no more fighting! I can't beat *wīsahkīcāhk* and he always gets the better of me." *wīsahkīcāhk* had won that contest. And there where *wīmisōsiw* had stood was standing *wākinākan* (tamarack), so all the tamaracks come from *wīmisōsiw*.

The Flood and the New Earth

After this, *wīsahkīcāhk* did not return to his family, but went in search of his younger brother the wolf. He searched and searched and finally he came upon his younger brother's tracks. They were the tracks of a wolf following a small herd of wood caribou. For a long time he followed those tracks until they disappeared into the water near a small waterfall. He went across but couldn't see his younger brother's tracks coming out of the water. He didn't know what to do, but he kept looking for those tracks. It was a nice evening now at that place and as he was looking around he saw *okiskimanisiw* ("kingfisher") sitting in a tree and looking down at something by the falls.

"*nisīmī*("my younger sibling"), what are you doing there? What are you looking down upon?"

"*nistīsī*" ("my elder brother"), said one kingfisher, "I'm looking at *cimiskiwanihīsiwak*. They're playing with a wolf hide in the water."

"What do they do when they finish playing?"

"They swim ashore and then they go to sleep." *wīsahkīcāhk* knew then that these animals had killed his brother and he was angry.

"Let's see then, *nisīmī*("my younger sibling")," he said to the kingfisher. "Let's see what happens if someone kills them."

And then it started to flood and water began coming up onto the land. *wīsahkīcāhk* made six spears and he tried them out to see how they worked. "Soon someone will feel spears," he said. And then because he was worried about the rising water he built a big *mitot* (raft) of great size. But then he forgot about the moss that he was going to need later. Then, carrying his spears, he went walking quickly to where those *cimiskiwanihīsiwak* were staying. As he was walking, he remembered the moss and he collected a pile and hung it from a tree branch before continuing on his way. When he came to where those *cimiskiwanihīsiwak* stayed near the falls, *wīsahkīcāhk* turned himself into a dead tree. When they came ashore, one said, "That's the first time I ever saw a dead tree standing there." The other said, "No, it's been standing there for a long time." They tried to pull the tree down but *wīsahkīcāhk* wouldn't let them do it. The wolf hide that they had played with, they threw up into the tree branches. That was all that was left of *wīsahkīcāhk*'s brother. It was as though his *osīma* ("his younger sibling") was asleep. He then took one of his spears and stabbed that *mahēhkanēwayān* (wolf hide) through the eye. When he did this, the spear broke in half. And then *wīsahkīcāhk* went after those *cimiskiwanihīsiwak* and he killed all of them there in the water.

Suddenly the water began to rise very high. *wīsahkīcāhk* grabbed the wolf hide and ran to where he had built his raft. He forgot to pick up the moss he had hung up in the tree. He jumped aboard his raft as the waters rose higher and higher and finally all of the land was covered with water. *wīsahkīcāhk* began to think about how he could get some moss. He called to a beaver and an otter and told them to dive under the water and bring moss to the surface. But the water was so deep from the flood that the beaver and the otter drowned. Then *wīsahkīcāhk* saw a muskrat swimming toward him.

"*āstam, nisīmī*," ("come here, younger sibling"), he called at that muskrat. "I want you to try to dive and find some moss under the water. If you find some moss down there, put it into your mouth and hold onto it as long as you stay alive." The muskrat dived and far below the surface of the water he found moss. *wīsahkīcāhk* pulled him up and as he pulled him onto the raft he saw that he had moss in his mouth. The muskrat was nearly drowned, but *wīsahkīcāhk* restored him to life. *wīsahkīcāhk* took the moss and squeezed the water from it before blowing on it. He intended in this way to create land. Then it started to turn back into the earth just like it was before the flood.

And that's how *wīsahkīcāhk* made the earth. And then he started traveling. He kept on going all the time. He couldn't do anything for his brother but he carried that wolf hide with him. And when he traveled around, he did anything that he could do. To anybody he sees, he says "*nisīmī*."

Goose Transformation

As he traveled along, *wīsahkīcāhk* saw a flock of geese preparing to fly south for the autumn. "My younger siblings," he said to them, "I really admire what you are able to do [ability to fly]."

"Well, we'll give it to you, older brother," those geese said. "You'll also be able to fly." They transformed *wīsahkīcāhk* into a goose. Before they began to fly, one goose told *wīsahkīcāhk*, "If someone shoots at us while we're flying, don't look down because if you look down, you'll fall." So they were flying south, and *wīsahkīcāhk* was the biggest of all those geese. He flew in front of all the others. Then they passed over a place where there were people and the people began to shoot at them. Well, *wīsahkīcāhk* looked down at them and he fell. Those hunters were happy. "We killed the big goose," they said and they ran towards where it had fallen. Then they saw someone poking his head out. "That must be *wīsahkīcāhk*. We'll take him and fix him good," they said. They grabbed him and brought him to their camp. And when they got there, they asked, "What shall we do with him?"

"We'll go tie him up in the bush, and when anyone wants to defecate, they can go there." So they tied *wīsahkīcāhk* on the ground out in the bush, and whenever anyone had to defecate they went there and defecated on *wīsahkīcāhk*. Then later, one old women went out there to where he was and said, "What are they doing to *wīsahkīcāhk*, shitting on him like that?"

"My grandmother, untie me," *wīsahkīcāhk* said. So the old lady went and untied him and after she untied him she wanted to defecate on him also. *wīsahkīcāhk* struck that old woman and killed her and then threw her up in a tree. He took her dress to use as a blanket for himself and then he ran away. Later, those people missed the old lady who had gone out to defecate and they went there and saw her hanging in the tree where *wīsahkīcāhk* had thrown her.

The Shut-Eye Dancers

As *wīsahkīcāhk* was traveling along, he saw many *nīpinayisak* ('water birds') floating on the water and flying overhead; there were geese, ducks, and loons. He thought to himself: "What can I do so that I can get these to eat?" Then he thought: "I'll fool them. I'll pack some moss in my pack-bag." He filled his pack-bag with moss, and they began walking along the shore where the birds were swimming. Those birds saw him and they were interested. "Our older brother is carrying something. I wonder what it is?" They called to him, "Older brother, what are you carrying?"

"I'm carrying *ninikamona* ("my songs")," he said.

"Truly, our older brother is going to give us a dance," those birds said. So *wīsahkīcāhk* began preparing a dancing lodge for those birds and he fixed it up good so that it would be hard for anyone to get out. The birds came inside, and *wīsahkīcāhk* began to sing. He told them that it was a special dance which they should dance with their eyes shut.

There were many birds and they made a lot of noise dancing. *wīsahkīcāhk* was singing special songs for the fat birds to make them dance well. As he sang, he would grab the fat birds one after another and twist their necks. "Keep dancing all together," he sang. Loon was dancing near the door. He began to think: "It's getting quieter and quieter in here." He opened his eyes for a minute, and saw *wīsahkīcāhk* twisting the birds' necks. "My brothers, my brothers!" he shouted, "*wīsahkīcāhk* is killing us!" Loon ran for the door, and *wīsahkīcāhk* kicked him in the legs as he escaped; that's why the loons today have flat feet, because *wīsahkīcāhk* did that. All the other birds tried to escape from the lodge. *wīsahkīcāhk* grabbed all those that he could catch and twisted their necks.

"Stupid *nīpinayisak*, now I'll eat good," he said. He roasted many ducks and ate a big meal. Those he didn't eat, he planted in the ground with their feet sticking up so that they would be easy to find.

Squeezed by Trees

After he finished his meal, *wīsahkīcāhk* went out traveling. He had eaten so many water birds that he needed to be squeezed in order to defecate so that he could eat more. He came to where there were two large birch trees growing close together. He got between them and said, "Squeeze me, *nisīmīyak* ("my younger siblings")." Those trees did as he asked and squeezed him hard. Finally he said, "Stop now, that's enough." But the birch trees said, "We won't let you go. You told us to do this to you." *wīsahkīcāhk* struggled but he couldn't release himself. To those trees he said, "I'm angry at you for doing this. I intend to call my brothers and they will destroy you when they get here." *wīsahkīcāhk* called to the lightning and it came and struck the trees, splitting them down the middle and freeing him. So he went back again to where he had left his birds. He saw the feet sticking out and thought to himself, "They're still there." But when he pulled them up, he found that someone had eaten them and left only the feet. *wīsahkīcāhk* was angry at the trees for holding him while his ducks were stolen. So as he traveled he picked up a willow branch and began striking the birch trees, causing them to become cracked and knotted. "If there will be people living in the future time," he said, "they will call this *otasak* ("knots") and when they find cracks and knots in the birch trees it will be my doing."

wītikōw and Weasel

As *wīsahkīcāhk* was traveling, he found large tracks. Lying in the tracks were bits of excreta that looked like they contained human bones. He thought, "I wonder whose excreta this can be?" And as he was looking around, he saw *mistāpēw* ("Great-Man," "Giant") approaching. *mistāpēw* came towards him and said, "Why are you talking about me, *wīsahkīcāhk*? I'm going to roast and eat you so you'd better go out and cut roasting sticks. Hurry up because I'm hungry." *wīsahkīcāhk* went out to cut the sticks and he was crying in fear because he knew he would be eaten. [Mrs. Dumas wonders at this point why *mistāpēw* doesn't simply swallow his victim whole.] Then he saw *sīhkos* ("weasel") going by.

"Come here, little brother, come here! *mistāpēw* intends to kill me and eat me. You see that door [*mistāpēw*'s anus] that's open there? Run in there and go up inside to the heart. When you're inside, bite his heart and he'll die. Chew it up and you'll kill him. Don't worry about dying because I'll save you anyway," he said.

So that Weasel crawled into the hole. And just as *wīsahkīcāhk* had told him he began to chew on *mistāpēw*'s heart. And *mistāpēw* said, "Hurry up! Hurry up! I'm sick from not eating in a long time. I'm almost fainting." And then *mistāpēw* fell over dead because that Weasel had killed him. And then *wīsahkīcāhk* cut apart *mistāpēw* and found that Weasel in there who had drowned from all the blood. *wīsahkīcāhk* took him to the lake and washed him clean. Then he wrang all the water from his tail and began to blow on it and that Weasel came alive once again. And *wīsahkīcāhk* said: "Younger brother, in the future when there will be people, they will call you *sīhkos*." So that was *wīsahkīcāhk*'s doing that the Weasel has that name.

Eye Juggler

wīsahkīcāhk started walking along again. All at once he heard singing and he went in that direction. He came to a place where he saw birds singing. While they sang, the birds threw their eyeballs up into the air and then caught them again in their empty sockets.

"My younger siblings, I greatly admire what you are able to do," he said. "Sometimes I myself also have sore eyes."

"Our elder brother, we'll give it to you so that you'll be able to do it also. But we'll tell you this. You'll only be able to do it twice. Don't try to do it more than two times." So they taught *wīsahkīcāhk* the song for throwing his eyes. And then *wīsahkīcāhk* went walking through thick brush and the twigs began to hurt his eyes. So he removed his eyes from his face for awhile and then tossed them in the air and caught them in his sockets. Soon his eyes again began to hurt from the brush and again he removed his eyes and tossed them in the air and caught them in his sockets. And then a third time his eyes hurt him and so he tossed them in the air and instead of landing in his eyesockets they fell somewhere where he couldn't find them. *wīsahkīcāhk* crawled all over the ground looking for his eyes. Not anywhere were his eyes to be found. All at once someone began poking him in his eye sockets.

"Don't poke me in my hollow eyes!" he yelled. That person that was doing it kept poking his eye sockets. *wīsahkīcāhk* suddenly reached out and grabbed that person and it was Fox. "I'm going to fix you, Fox," *wīsahkīcāhk* said. "It was you who stole my waterbirds and now you poked my eye sockets. I'll twist your arms and legs so that you can't walk."

"No, no, my elder brother, don't do that to me. I'll look for some spruce gum to use for your eyes."

"Alright, younger sibling, you find the best spruce gum that you can and bring it to me." So that Fox went to look for that *oskisīkōkanatikwa* ("spruce gum") and when he found some he rolled it into balls and made two eyes. And he gave them to *wīsahkīcāhk* and *wīsahkīcāhk* could see again.

The Startlers

wīsahkīcāhk began traveling again until he came to a small house. When he looked inside, he saw several small *piðīyak* ("spruce partridge") and he wondered who they were.

"What's your mother's name?" he asked these birds.

"*okoskohōwiðawīsīw* is our mother's name and she likes to frighten people." To this *wīsahkīcāhk* said, "Why should she scare me? I doubt it that she'll scare me." So he grabbed those small birds and he defecated on them. Then he left them and started going again until he came to a rocky place where he lay down to sleep.

When the mother came home later, she looked at her children and asked, "Why do you look like this?"

"*wīsahkīcāhk* did this to us. He asked us what your name was and we told him that your name was 'Startler' because you like to frighten people. He said that he doubted you could scare him and then he defecated on our heads and our faces."

"I'm angry at that *wīsahkīcāhk*," she said, "and I'm going to follow him." So she came to where *wīsahkīcāhk* was staying at that rocky place and she came up to him while he was sleeping and poured cold water suddenly into his ear. *wīsahkīcāhk* jumped up and then he fell into the water of a nearby lake and made a great splash.

"My younger sibling," he said, "you woke me up and frightened me greatly while I was sleeping."

"Before, you said that I couldn't frighten you," said that Startler.

The Farting Hunter

wīsahkīcāhk started traveling again and as he walked he heard voices talking so he went in the direction of the voices. But when he came to where he had heard the voices, all he could see were *okinīyak* ("rose berries"). There was only that big red bunch of rose berries.

"What are you talking about, my younger siblings? What happens to a person if he eats rose berries?"

"Oh, older brother, if anyone eats us they will become itchy." So *wīsahkīcāhk* grabbed a handful of those berries and ate them.

"I'm itchy! I'm itchy!" cried *wīsahkīcāhk*. He began to travel again and then again he heard the voices of many people talking and he went toward the hill where the voices were coming from. But again when he got there he couldn't see any people. All he could see was *asinīyowākona* ("rock tripe").

"Why are you talking, younger siblings? What happens to a person if he eats rock tripe?"

"Oh, older brother, if someone eats us, he will fart continuously." *wīsahkīcāhk* ate lots of lichen and began to travel again. As he walked, he began to fart loudly.

"*nipawīkiton!*" (I'm farting!) he cried as he walked along. He kept farting as he walked. When he tried to catch spruce chickens to eat, they were always scared away by his farts. Finally, *wīsahkīcāhk* got angry with his rear end. He built a large fire and put a large flat rock in the middle of it to heat it up. Finally, when the rock was very hot, he sat down on it and burned his rear end. While his rear end was burning, it continued to fart. Finally he got up off the rock and began walking and his farting had stopped.

Bear's Eye Medicine

wīsahkīcāhk kept traveling and looking for food and finally he found a bear eating berries. "I'll go with you, younger sibling, as you go around looking for berries," said *wīsahkīcāhk*.

"All right, elder brother, we'll go together and eat berries." They stayed together during the summer and when it came to be autumn *wīsahkīcāhk* complained that his eyes were sore. He picked up some cranberries, squeezed them, and pretended to put the juice in his eyes. Then he told the bear to do this also. The bear put juice in its eyes and they began to burn.

"Older brother, my eyes are sore," that Bear said.

"Well, you didn't put enough in, younger sibling. You should use more. Then certainly your eyes will not burn." That Bear put more juice in his eyes and they became worse.

"Older brother, I can't open my eyes."

"Wait a minute, younger sibling, I'll take care of you," *wīsahkīcāhk* said. He told that Bear to lay down on the ground and to turn over. As soon as the Bear had turned over, *wīsahkīcāhk* struck him on the head with a big stick and killed him. And then he cooked that Bear up and ate it all and had a good meal.

Muskrat Cools Grease

wīsahkīcāhk kept the grease from the bear and put it in a birch bark box and took it down to the shore of the lake to cool it. There he saw a Muskrat swimming towards him.

"Come here, younger sibling. My bear grease is too hot. Carry it around with you on your back as you swim so it will cool off." The Muskrat swam closer.

"I will do what you ask me, older brother, but be sure not to do anything to scare me. Don't scare me or your grease will be spilled." Then the Muskrat took the container of grease and swam back and forth with it in the water. And then *wīsahkīcāhk* did something to scare that Muskrat, and he dived underwater and disappeared with the grease. Right away, *wīsahkīcāhk* ran to the bank and started drinking the lake water, saying, "I still intend to taste my grease!"

Fly Transformation

wīsahkīcāhk again began traveling. As he wandered about, he saw flies feeding on the inside of an old caribou skull which still had the antlers attached.

"My younger siblings, I really admire what you're doing there. I wish that I too was inside there eating."

"Well, older brother, if you admire it so much, we'll give it to you." So then *wīsahkīcāhk* became a fly and went inside and started eating with the others. Later, when he was full, he desired to become himself again and he changed his body back. That old caribou skull was stuck to his head. He wasn't able to get the skull off from around his head. He wandered around like that until he came to a lake near where there were people camped and then he began to swim across the lake with that skull still stuck onto his head. Those people saw him crossing. They said, "Really, there's a big caribou swimming across!" They ran for their canoes and came after him. *wīsahkīcāhk* came to the shore and ran into the bush, and all the hunters followed, thinking that they would kill a caribou. Finally, the skull got turned around so he couldn't see where he was going. He ran headfirst into a tree and the skull broke and fell off of his head. So he ran away from those people laughing.

Fooled by Reflections

wīsahkīcāhk began traveling again, and he came upon a Beaver laying motionless on the ground.

"Get up, younger brother, get up!" he shouted. But the Beaver didn't move.

Again he shouted, "Get up, my younger brother." Still the Beaver didn't move.

"Now I'm going to be able to eat a beaver," he said. So he put that Beaver into his game bag and slung it over his shoulder and carried it down to the shore of a lake where he intended to cook it. Then he went back into the bush to find roasting sticks. And while he was in the bush he heard a Beaver splashing in the water. And he though to himself, "I wonder if that's the Beaver that I just brought down to the shore?" He went down to the shore, and he saw that Beaver swimming in the water. When he went to get cooking sticks, he had left the Beaver in his game pouch. Now the Beaver had that pouch in the water.

"Throw my game bag ashore or it will get wet." he said to that Beaver. The Beaver threw the game bag toward the shore, but it landed in the water. *wīsahkīcāhk* saw where it lay under the water. He kept reaching for it but couldn't grab it. Finally he got the water muddy, so he could no longer see his pouch.

"I'll take a rest and wait for the water to clear," he thought. Again he tried to grab the pouch, and again he muddied the water so that he couldn't see it. Then he lay down on his back to wait for the water to clear again and he saw that the bag had landed on a tree limb and that he had been trying to pick up the reflection that it cast in the water. He picked up his pouch and began traveling again.

Scab-Eater

As *wīsahkīcāhk* wandered around, he found little pieces of dry meat on the ground. He began picking them up and eating them. Many birds saw him eating the pieces and began singing, "*wīsahkīcāhk* is eating his scab! *wīsahkīcāhk* is eating his scab! *wīsahkīcāhk omīkī mīcisōw*!"

wīsahkīcāhk said to those birds, "Why do you say this? This is my mother's dry meat that she dropped on the ground. That's what I'm eating." Those birds kept singing that *wīsahkīcāhk* was eating his own scab. He reached around to where he had burned his rear end and found that it was raw there as though a scab had dropped off. "Maybe those birds are right," he thought. He picked up all the pieces of the scab and rolled them together and then he looked until he saw a *waskway* ("birch tree"). He threw his scab at the birch tree.

"If there are people in the world in the future, they will call this *posākan* ("birch fungus"). They will use it to tinder fires," he said. So when you see *posākan* on the trees, that's *wīsahkīcāhk*'s scab.

Moose Transformation

wīsahkīcāhk did many things. Everyone he met, he addressed as "younger sibling." He met a Moose and transformed himself into a moose and they traveled together. And when they traveled, if *wīsahkīcāhk* heard a branch or a twig cracking, he would run away in fear but there would never be anyone there. The Moose always knew immediately if hunters were near, but *wīsahkīcāhk* never knew. If the Moose heard real hunters, he would run away and *wīsahkīcāhk* would follow him. It was so cold during that winter that *wīsahkīcāhk*'s moose hooves almost froze. Finally, *wīsahkīcāhk* tranformed himself back to his own shape and he left that Moose.

Marries Daughter

wīsahkīcāhk started traveling around again. Everyone he met, he called "little brother" in order to deceive them. He did all kinds of things to trick and deceive them. He was married also, that *wīsahkīcāhk*. He wanted to get his own daughter. He told his wife that he was going to die. To his wife, he said, "Any man that comes to your lodge, don't object to him. If he's a good hunter, let him stay with our daughter. Because soon I am going to die."

So his wife did just as he instructed. After *wīsahkīcāhk* died, a man came to that lodge and he began staying with their daughter. That was *wīsahkīcāhk* in a disguise [transformed appearance]. They all thought that he had died. No one said anything about that man because they didn't know who it was. But one of his young sons recognized *wīsahkīcāhk* while he was staying there. He said to his mother, "Mother, my father is sleeping with my sister."

"Don't say that," his mother said. "Your father is dead. That's another man that stays with your sister." So that little boy didn't bother them anymore that night and went to sleep. But the next night he watched them again and he told his mother that it was his father staying there.

"I wonder if it could be true," that woman thought. So she looked close and she saw a big white scar on that man's buttocks just where *wīsahkīcāhk* had burned himself. Then she knew it was *wīsahkīcāhk*. She grabbed a piece of firewood and began beating *wīsahkīcāhk* with it. *wīsahkīcāhk* ran out of there and he was ashamed to come back to the camp again. [End of Jeremiah Michel narration.]

Albert Umferville Narrative

Tricks Moose and Squeezed by Birds
wīsahkīcāhk came to the shore of a lake and out in the water several yards from shore he saw a moose swimming.

"Hey, brother," he yelled at the moose, "where are you going?" The moose told him that he was going to swim across to the other side of the lake. *wīsahkīcāhk* asked the moose if he would carry him across and the moose agreed to it. *wīsahkīcāhk* jumped on the moose's back and the moose began swimming. As they were crossing the lake, *wīsahkīcāhk* took out his knife and began trying to cut pieces out of the moose's back.

"You're hurting me!" said the moose. "What are you doing?"

"I'm not doing anything!" *wīsahkīcāhk* kept trying to cut meat off that moose's back. Finally, just as they got to the shore on the other side, *wīsahkīcāhk* cut through the moose's neck and killed him. He dragged that moose up on shore, butchered it, and began roasting the meat. *wīsahkīcāhk* ate and ate until he was so full that he could hardly move. He ate so much that he couldn't relieve himself and he asked two birds who were there to get on either side of him and squeeze him. The birds squeezed and *wīsahkīcāhk* began evacuating copiously. But the birds refused to let him go and kept him caught between them while other birds came and stole all that was left of the moose meat. After they had taken it all, the two birds let *wīsahkīcāhk* go. He was mad at the birds for stealing his meat. He took a willow branch and began whipping those birds. Today you can see the marks on those birds [species unidentified] where *wīsahkīcāhk* whipped them.

The Startlers
wīsahkīcāhk traveled along until he came to a river. The river was pretty big and he figured that he would have to jump it. He got ready to jump over it, thought about it, and then went further back to give himself more of a running start for the jump. Twice more he stopped and backed up further. Finally, he ran toward the river and jumped. A bunch of spruce partridges flew up out of the brush by the banks and frightened *wīsahkīcāhk* so that he fell into the river. He got mad at those partridges and shortened their wings so that they would never be able to do that again. Even today, when you see partridges, they have short wings and can't fly along very well. That's from *wīsahkīcāhk*.

Fooled by Reflections
wīsahkīcāhk walked along and decided that he'd like to have a smoke. He reached around for his tobacco pouch and pipe but he couldn't find them. "Well," he

thought, "I must have dropped them somewhere along the way." He began going back the way he came. Finally he came back to that river and walked up and down the shore. There by the shore he could see his pipe and tobacco pouch underwater. He kept reaching down under the water to grab them but couldn't do it. Finally he looked up and saw that his pipe and bag were up in a tree and he had been trying to grab their reflection.

Bear's Eye Medicine
After he retrieved his pipe and tobacco bag from the tree, *wīsahkīcāhk* continued walking until he saw a Bear stretched out on the trail ahead of him. The Bear was moaning.

"What's wrong with you, brother?" said *wīsahkīcāhk*. "My eyes are sore. I can hardly see anything."

"Well, brother, you should let me help you. I have a medicine for it." *wīsahkīcāhk* went and gathered cranberries. He squeezed the berries until he collected a quantity of the juice. Then he put some into the bear's eyes. That Bear yelled in pain [narrator explains that the juice is very strong].

"Well, brother," said *wīsahkīcāhk*, "how are your eyes now?"

"My eyes still hurt," said the Bear. "I still can't see well."

"Well, brother, we'll use more medicine." He got more juice and poured it into the Bear's eyes. The Bear yelled.

"Are your eyes better now?" asked *wīsahkīcāhk*. "No! Now I can hardly see anything!"

"Well, my brother, we'll use still more of this medicine." For the third time, *wīsahkīcāhk* put berry juice into the Bear's eyes.

"How are your eyes now?" asked *wīsahkīcāhk*.

"Now I can't see anything at all!" said the Bear. So *wīsahkīcāhk* grabbed a big stick and smashed it over the Bear's head, killing him. Then he cooked and ate that Bear.

Other Versions and Narratives

wīhtikōw and Weasel
Narrator: Johnny Bighetty (English)

Well the story came this way. Ah, once upon a time there was a *wīsahkīcāhk*. You know, ah—he seen the fire, the smoke out on the point. So *wīsahkīcāhk* was wondering, "I bet you I'll get a meal if I go to that smoke. Maybe some hunter kill something that's cooking on the fireplace." So he walked to that fireplace. When he came to that fireplace, he found out that *wīhtikōw* was making fire there. So this *wīsahkīcāhk* was very surprised, he was very scared. He know what *wīhtikōw* is going to do with him once he get ahold of him, he's going to roast him in the fire. So *wīsahkīcāhk* asked that—"Who are you?" Oh the *wīhtikōw* didn't say nothing. So this *wīhtikōw* look up. "Oh it's you *wīsahkīcāhk*," he said. "Well I'll tell you what, *wīsahkīcāhk*," he said. "You make—gather all the wood," he said. "Don't go no place," he said. "You make fire for me and after you make big fire get all kinds of sticks. Get the willow sticks, straight ones," he said. "Cause I'm going to roast you," he said. "After you finish that you tell me. You count your—how many pieces of your body," he said. "Don't forget you got two legs, two arms, that's four sticks, and your head, that's five and your two ribs, two ribs, that's seven sticks. Cut about dozen sticks," he said. "You'll have enough for the whole body to roast you on every stick," he said. So *wīsahkīcāhk* got scared when he heard that from *wīhtikōw*. So—so finally—*wīsahkīcāhk* didn't like to do that. So he started to cut sticks, roasting sticks. While he was doing that he was crying. He was crying but he had to do it for *wīhtikōw*, it's *wīhtikōw*'s orders. So while he was doing it he seen a weasel. So he whisper at the weasel, "Hey brother! Brother! Come here!" he said. "Come here!" So weasel came running, came running. "What do you want, brother?" he said. "Sht," he said to weasel not to talk loud because *wīhtikōw* was going to hear him. He's asking that weasel for help. So, "What do you want, brother?" he said, weasel said to *wīsahkīcāhk*. "Hey brother," he [*wīsahkīcāhk*] said. "You see that *wīhtikōw* there. He's going to kill me," he said. "That's why I'm cutting all the sticks. He's going to roast me in the fireplace," he said. So they thought for awhile and ahh—And ahhh—

This weasel said: "Okay brother, I'll do whatever you want me to do," he said—So this *wīsahkīcāhk* was still whispering. He said— *wīhtikōw* was sitting on the—right beside the fire. So he told, ahh—this weasel: "You see that little hole?" he said. "See that hole in the *wīhtikōw*'s—behind that *wīhtikōw*?" he said. "There's a hole in there, that's—you go in that," he said. "You go inside that hole," he said. So this—When you go inside that hole, it'll be dark," he said. "You'll see—it'll be dark inside," he said. "But keep on going," he said. "Wait until you reach something beating. That's the *wīhtikōw*'s heart, eh? You'll start—

use your teeth on that thing that's breathing, eh? "You'll chew up that thing, chew it up till it stops," he said. "Once it stops, this *wīhtikōw* will die because you cut up its heart." And so, "Okay brother," he said. "I'll do it, I'll do it for your sake," he said. "Because I love you brother. If you die, I'll have no brother," he said. "I gotta save you." So he give this weasel a lesson too. "You'll die. Maybe you'll drown in the blood. Because when you start eating that heart," he said, "lots of blood will come inside—it'll be full inside of the body—you might drown in the blood," he said, "but I'll save you," he said. So—"Okay, don't worry," he said, "You go in that hole." So—

After he instruct the weasel—So the weasel went running. He went inside that hole. So crawling, he find whatever he sees inside. Follow that hole there 'till he reach that heart. It was still beating, eh? So that's where that weasel remember, remember what *wīsahkīcāhk* told him. "You got to eat that—start biting that heart."

So there was lots of blood coming out. And that's what *wīsahkīcāhk* told 'em. So this weasel start to worry, eh? Start to worry he's gonna drown. He didn't know where to go—got lost comin' back [rising pitch, amused]. So he drowned on the way.

So this *wīsahkīcāhk* start to jump with joy when he seen that *wīhtikōw* keel over. Dead. He didn't breathe because that weasel kill him. Kill that *wīhtikōw*. That weasel kill that *wīhtikōw*.

wīsahkīcāhk was happy. He seen that *wīhtikōw* dead. So he grab his knife, little knife, eh? Had a little knife so he—so he throw that *wīhtikōw* on the side this way and start to cut him open, cut him open. He look for his little brother inside. So he found him halfways in here halfways in the chest someplace. He was drowned but his little heart was still beating. The weasel's heart was still beating. So—he was dead though. It was snowy—there was a little bit snow on the ground. Soooo, he said: "Little brother." So he started to sing a song that *wīsahkīcāhk*. He was going around, he was wiping—He was full of blood that weasel, eh? Black. All black.

And ah—he drag him around the snow, drag him around. And finally this weasel start to breath. Breath. So he rub him and rub him and rub him and rub him. And finally the weasel came alive, came alive, came alive. So he start to talk to him, "Hey brother," he said. "Thank you brother, you saved my life. I also save your life," he said. "From now on we'll be real brothers," he said. "Now in the future," he said to the weasel. *wīsahkīcāhk* told this to the little weasel. He said: "In the future time there'll be memories of this story about you and me," he said. "Your—I'll turn you white as the snow," he said. "But this—I'll leave a little black at the tip of your tail," he said. To the weasel he said: "I'll leave this mark so the people in the future generation," he said. "They'll remember this story for a long time," he said. "So I'll leave this little black tip at your tail," he said. *Wās*, the weasel was happy. Now "What do we call you, brother?" he said. "Oh, they call me 'Small Mink'," he said. "No that doesn't—That's no good," he said. "I'll call you—I'll give you a better name," he said. "You go in there, in that big rock," he said. "You crawl in that big rock and you come out all of a sudden and I'll give you a name," he said. So the weasel did what *wīsahkīcāhk* told him. He went inside that rock. So he all of a sudden jump out of that rock. "Hey *sēhkos!*" he said. That's—now you call that *sēhkos*. No more *apiscisākwīsis* you call 'em, eh? "Small mink" you used to call that before. And now *wīsahkīcāhk* reward this weasel. He give 'em a name and he give him that color. White and he leave that back tip at his so he call him "*sēhkos*." "Hey *sēhkos!*" he said. Yeah, that's—Now today they still call him that name "*sēhkos*." Yeah, that's the—That's the only—There's some more added to it but I don't remember.

wīhtikōw and Weasel
Narrator: Jean-Baptiste Merasty
Translator: Albert Umferville

One day *wīsahkīcāhk* decided he was going to go for a walk. He was going visiting; I guess that's what he was figuring on doing. So he had a good meal first and cooked some meat for himself. After he had his lunch, well then he started off. So he was walking along and he blazed a trail for himself by breaking branches off on trees. So anyway while he was walking along he started thinking, "If I were to meet this *wīhtikōw*," he says, or a werewolf as you'd say, a flesh eater, he says, "I'd do the same thing with him [that he'd do with any other being], I'd snap his neck just like that." But apparently this *wīhtikōw* was coming towards him too, but he never seen him. But the *wīhtikōw* heard him.

So he says, "What did you say, *wīsahkīcāhk*? Say that again." *wīsahkīcāhk* got pretty scared and he couldn't speak. He knew that he was in trouble then for sure. So the *wīhtikōw* says, "You start picking up all these dead trees and branches and pile them in one place. And after that," he says, "when you're through," he says, "I'm going to make a big fire and I'm going to throw you in there." Of course, he had no alternative but to do what he was told. So he started gathering dead trees and branches. He had quite a pile already when he saw a Weasel come running up. So right away he had an idea of what he was going to do. So he told...he says, "Come here, my brother," to the Weasel. He said, "I want you to help me out."

He [Weasel] says, "What can I do to help you out?"

Well, he says, "I'm in very serious trouble," he says. "That *wīhtikōw* wants to burn me up on that pile of wood that I'm gathering there," he says. "I've got quite a bit already. But I want you to do something for me."

"Well," he says, "I'll do what I can to help you."

"Well," he says, "you see him there, sitting over there?" he says.

He says, "Yeah."

He says, "I want you to climb up his asshole," he says. And he says, "And go to his heart and bite off the veins to his heart. That way," he says, "you'll kill him. When you do that," he says, "I'll reward you very nicely."

Well, the Weasel says okay and he sneaks over and, of course, the *wīhtikōw* was sitting there. And he never even knew when the Weasel climbed up his asshole. Climbed up to his heart and he bit him and he bit the arteries and pretty soon the Weasel climbed out again and he was, of course, pretty dirty when he came out.

Anyway, *wīsahkīcāhk* waited for a little while and pretty soon he seen the *wīhtikōw* cough and then all of a sudden he threw up. Pretty soon he fell over dead. So he says, "Oh, I'm so happy," he says to the Weasel, "that you've killed him," he says. "You saved my life." He says, "I'm gonna' reward you now." So he picks up the Weasel and he takes it down to the lakeshore and he gives him a good washing. Washed him so long that he turned white. And then he says, "I'm going to decorate you," he says. "I'll turn the tip of your tail black." So that's the reason why today the weasel in the winter time turns white and his tail stays black, the tip of his tail. That's the end of that one.

Marries Daughter
Narrator: Selazie Linklater
Translator: Caroline Caribou

wīsahkīcāhk had seven sons and one daughter. When she began to grow up she was very good looking, that daughter of his. *wīsahkīcāhk* wanted to go after his own daughter. So he told his sons that he was going to die. "Really, I won't be alive on this earth much longer," he said. He gave instructions to his sons. "Make sure my face is pointed to the west when you put me on the burial scaffold," he said. Then he pretended to die. His sons put him on the burial platform but forgot his instructions about facing him west. Later on they remembered what their father had said. "Really, we should do what he told us," they said. They went back to move the body in the right direction. When they got there, the body was gone.

In that camp where *wīsahkīcāhk* had lived, word got around that a stranger had come. One of *wīsahkīcāhk*'s sons went out and told his mother about the stranger. *wīsahkīcāhk* was that stranger. He had changed his shape so that he looked handsome. He recognized one of his own sons and asked him if his mother had a daughter. The boy replied that he had a sister alright. *wīsahkīcāhk* told his sons that he wanted to marry that girl. He told his son to go and ask the old lady if he could have her. The son went back and asked the old lady. He told her that the stranger looked alright. The old lady gave her permission.

So *wīsahkīcāhk* married his own daughter. They were all living in the same lodge. One night *wīsahkīcāhk*'s sons saw him in bed with their sister. They saw burn marks on that stranger's buttocks. (Translator adds that *wīsahkīcāhk* still had the scar from when he had burned himself with hot rocks.) They thought that he looked like their father. So they told their mother. She went and looked and recognized that it was *wīsahkīcāhk*. She went out and made a fire, put a stick in the fire until it was charred and hot, and then ran in and gave *wīsahkīcāhk* a wallop with it. *wīsahkīcāhk* jumped up and ran out of the village.

Later he came back to that camp after changing his appearance again so that no one would be able to recognize him. He asked everyone what had been happening in the village. Everyone told him, "It was that *wīsahkīcāhk* again. He was sleeping with his own daughter."

Marries Daughter
Narrator: Jean-Baptiste Merasty
Translator: Albert Umferville

wīsahkīcāhk was always into different predicaments like wanting to marry his own daughter-in-law. Now the story goes that he married twice. Well, the first wife that he had, she had a daughter. And the second wife he had, she had a little boy. So anyway it goes on that this young woman, this young lady, got to be quite beautiful. So he kind of falls in love with his own daughter and he decided he was going to marry her without the old lady knowing. So he took sick all of a sudden. Very, very sick. He had cramps in the stomach and every ailment that he could think of. And so he calls his wife and he said, "I'm dying." He says, "After I die, I want you to make a scaffold," he says, "and cover me up with whatever you can find, canvas or some hide, deer hide, and hang me up on the scaffold," he says, "and after you're finished move away from here." And he told them where to go to a certain place. And he says, "After a certain time, there'll be a young fella' there to come and look after you. And when he comes there," he says, "I want you to give our daughter to him in marriage." So the wife said, "Yes, I'll do that."

So anyway he eventually dies. And they buried him in...they hung him up in the scaffold just as he wanted it to be done. And they all got ready and took their horse and got two poles and tied some hide in between and placed all they had on it. And away they went and left him on the scaffold. So anyway, as soon as they're gone, he comes back to life. Or at least he made out that he had died. So he gets up and climbs down and off he goes.

So he eventually gets there to where they're camping. So he comes into camp and sure enough he started cutting wood and hauling water, making it comfortable for the widow, and the daughter and the boy. And finally the woman said, "You can have my daughter in marriage." Well, she didn't recognize him, her husband, for some reason. But the little boy seemed to recognize his dad. And he was always playing with him. So the old lady says, "You leave him alone. You leave your brother-in-law alone. He's tired and he's come a long ways to get married."

This little boy knew that it was his dad all the time because, I guess, apparently he loved his dad and when he died he felt very sorry. And so he was always hanging around. So anyway he lived with his daughter and that's where the story ends.

Contest with *wīmisōsiw*
Narrator: Catherine Merasty
Translators: Albert Umferville, Denise Umferville

This is the story of *wīsahkīcāhk* and *misōsiw*. *misōsiw* was paddling along one day and he came to where *wīsahkīcāhk* and his brother were sitting along the shore, on the rocky shore. Before *misōsiw* came there, *wīsahkīcāhk* and his brother were playing with their fingernails. *misōsiw* had three daughters. So he told *wīsahkīcāhk* that he wanted him for his son-in-law. So he said, "Jump in" [to the canoe]. But his brother was with him. His brother was going to jump in, but Misosiw said, "Not you! *wīsahkīcāhk* is the one I want!" So *wīsahkīcāhk* jumped in and they paddled away. They say that his younger brother turned into a wolf then.

They camped somewhere for a couple of days. And *misōsiw* had a contest with *wīsahkīcāhk*. Running, wrestling, and every other kind of thing he could think of to beat him. But *wīsahkīcāhk* beat him in all these games. So that *misōsiw* had a boat. A canoe. He didn't have to paddle that boat. All he had to do was hit his canoe with a stick and away it goes. Just as though it had an outboard. So *wīsahkīcāhk* admired this boat very much and he wanted it for his own. So he asked *misōsiw* if he would have a contest swinging with him. But *wīsahkīcāhk* knew what he was going to do already. When he got hold of *misōsiw* in that swing, he pushed it so hard that *misōsiw* fell out and hit the ground so hard that he passed out. So while the old man was knocked out, he swiped this boat. In the meantime, the old man was still passed out and unconscious. And when he woke up, his boat was gone. But that boat of his was very obedient to him. All he had to do was call for it and it would come to him. So he started calling. *wīsahkīcāhk* had that boat tied up along the shore. And that boat began to tug away from shore out onto the open water. So *wīsahkīcāhk* ran down to the shore and got ahold of it. But the boat was too strong. It broke the rope and pulled *wīsahkīcāhk* into it. The boat floated back to *misōsiw* so the old man got his boat back.

They paddled someplace and camped. The old man's daughters were there. The oldest daughter looked at *wīsahkīcāhk* and said, "No, I don't want to marry him." The younger daughter looked at him and said, "No, he's too ugly. I won't marry him." The third daughter, the youngest of the three, had pity on him so she said, "I'll marry him." And *wīsahkīcāhk*, in the meantime he was crying for three days because the oldest girl wouldn't marry him. He was so disappointed.

Eye Juggler
Narrator: Catherine Merasty
Translators: Albert Umferville, Lorna Cook

As he was walking along, wīsahkīcāhk saw a bunch of birds sitting in a tree. The birds were taking their eyes out, throwing them up in the air, and then popping them back into their sockets. wīsahkīcāhk was very curious. He asked the birds if he would be able to do that trick.

"Sure," they said, "it's easy." So wīsahkīcāhk popped one of his eyes out of his head and tossed it up in the air. Instead of landing back in his eye socket, it fell on the ground and rolled off. "Try the other one, olderbrother," said those birds. "You'll be sure to succeed." wīsahkīcāhk took out his other eye and threw it up in the air. He waited for it to fall back into the socket. That one got lost too. wīsahkīcāhk started feeling around on the around for his eyes. All the birds were laughing at wīsahkīcāhk.

That Fox who had stolen the ducks passed by and saw wīsahkīcāhk feeling around for his lost eyes. The Fox picked up a dry stick and began poking it in wīsahkīcāhk's eye sockets.

"Well, older brother, what have you been up to?" said the Fox.

"I was trying to find my eyes," said wīsahkīcāhk. The Fox knew that he was blind and kept teasing him with the stick. Suddenly wīsahkīcāhk reached out and grabbed that Fox.

"I'm going to wring your neck," said wīsahkīcāhk. "Don't!" yelled the Fox.

"Yes I will! You swiped my ducks too! You owe me lots! I'm going to teach you a lesson!"

"Don't!" said the Fox. "If you let me go, I'll help you get your eyes back again."

"Okay, but you'd better." That Fox went to a spruce tree that had a nick in it. He got two little pieces of dry resin and he rolled them until they looked like eyes. He brought them to wīsahkīcāhk. wīsahkīcāhk put them in his eyes and he could see again.

Goose Transformation
Narrator: Albert Umferville

One time wīsahkīcāhk was way down south. I guess he went down south. I guess he went down there for a visit. So he was there all winter and then he wanted to come home. It was getting towards Spring. He saw the geese flying. Flying towards the north. "Brothers, come here!" he yelled. Well, they landed.

"What do you want?"

"I'd like to go home, back up north. I'm getting lonesome. And it's such a long way for me to walk. Can I travel with you?"

"Sure you can," said the geese. "But you can't travel this way (in his present form). We're too small to carry you. We'll have to do something." So one of the old ganders there said, "Well, I'll tell you. You stand here and we'll dance around you and sing." So they started dancing and *wīsahkīcāhk* was standing there in the center. They danced around him and they were singing away. And pretty soon *wīsahkīcāhk* turned into a big goose. So after he turned into a big goose, they all started honking and they were going to fly up. They were going along and *wīsahkīcāhk* said, "Let me go ahead. I know the road good!" So they said, "Okay, you lead." But that old gander said, "Don't look down! If anyone says anything to you while you're flying, don't listen to them. Because if you do you're going to fall down."

So anyway, *wīsahkīcāhk* was flying along. The people below were looking up. "Oh, there's *wīsahkīcāhk* going along," they said. "You can tell him right away." He never paid any attention. They came to another village where a bunch of people were living. They looked up and they saw *wīsahkīcāhk* flying across the sky. And they said, "Oh, there goes *wīsahkīcāhk*! We know it's you! You big liar!" *wīsahkīcāhk*, he still didn't pay any attention. And they came to another village. It was quite a ways north there, pretty near home. And the people looked up.

"Oh, there comes *wīsahkīcāhk*. I wonder how he managed to learn to fly with those geese! The big liar! The big bastard!" They called him all kinds of names. Of course, *wīsahkīcāhk* got mad then.

"Shut up!" he yelled. Down he fell.

So the people got hold of him and they tied him up. And they staked him down behind the teepees there. Once in a while, someone would go over to the toilet. And they'd shit on him. So anyway this kept on and on and on. And all of a sudden, one old lady said, "What are you people doing?"

"Oh," they said, "we're having a heck of a time with *wīsahkīcāhk*. He's tied over there."

"Can I go and see him?" said the old woman.

"No you'd better not go, grandmother. That *wīsahkīcāhk*, he's one big liar. You don't want to go there." But the old lady said, "I want to see him too."

"No, don't go." Well, when no one was looking, the old lady sneaked over there. And she goes and sits down. And *wīsahkīcāhk* was all covered with shit. And so the old lady, she was going to sit down.

"Don't do that, grandmother," said *wīsahkīcāhk*. "Why not? Everybody else is doing it."

"But it's not nice for you to sit down here like that because you're a woman."

"Oh, that's okay."

"But it's not nice for me to look at you," said *wīsahkīcāhk*.

"Well, what do you want me to do?"

"If you'll untie me," said *wīsahkīcāhk*, "I'll give you lots of money." The old lady thought that she was going to be rich so she untied *wīsahkīcāhk*. As soon as he got untied, he grabbed hold of that old lady and tied her there instead. And, of course, he ran off.

So towards nightfall the old lady was missing. So the people said, "Where's our grandmother?"

One little boy said, "Well, I saw her running off into the bush." So they all went over there and that's where they found the old lady among the shit. That *wīsahkīcāhk* was gone.

The Shut-Eye Dancers
Narrator: Catherine Merasty
Translators: Albert Umferville, Lorna Cook

wīsahkīcāhk was walking around and he saw water birds by the river. He began to think how he could kill a lot of them. He went into the muskeg carrying a bag and filled the bag with moss. Then carrying the bag, he walked right by the river where many ducks, geese, and loons were swimming. Those birds were curious.

"Hey, older brother, what are you carrying in that bag?"

"I'm carrying my songs," said *wīsahkīcāhk*.

"Songs?" those birds asked. *wīsahkīcāhk* built a *mīkīwāp* (three-pole lodge) for the dance. All kinds of birds came there that night. Ducks, loons, and geese were there. *wīsahkīcāhk* told the birds that there was a special dance that they should dance with their eyes shut. *wīsahkīcāhk* began to sing. All the birds closed their eyes and began to dance. *wīsahkīcāhk* kept singing. While the birds danced, he would grab them, one after the other, twist their necks, and throw them outside the lodge. He killed lots of ducks.

Finally, one loon got tired of dancing with his eyes closed and opened his eyes.

"Oh, our older brother is killing us! Our older brother is killing us!" he yelled. It was almost too late. *wīsahkīcāhk* had killed almost all of those birds. That loon made a dive for the lake. *wīsahkīcāhk* went after that loon and kicked it in the legs. That's why loons have short legs today.

wīsahkīcāhk cooked and ate the birds that he killed. He ate and ate and ate. Finally, he couldn't eat any more, but he still had some ducks left. He decided to save them for later. He buried them in the ground but left their legs sticking up so they would be easy to find again. He went away for about three days. While he was gone, Fox traveled by that place and saw the duck legs sticking up out of the ground. He dug around and found those ducks all cooked and ready to eat. He ate all those ducks. Then when he was finished he planted their legs back in the ground as though no one had disturbed them. Then he left. *wīsahkīcāhk* came back. He was very hungry and looking for his ducks. He pulled up the legs and found that someone had eaten the ducks that he had left there. He was still hungry so he went on to look for something to eat.

The Shut-Eye Dancers
Narrator: Henry Linklater (English)
wīsahkīcāhk wanted to eat a lot of birds. He began blowing into a flute ("something that looked like a flute") which called lots of birds to the area. He invited them to a large dance which he was having in his lodge. All the birds came and danced. For a certain dance, wīsahkīcāhk insisted that all the birds had to dance around the fire with their eyes shut. They all did this. At one point, Loon opened his eyes and saw wīsahkīcāhk sneaking up behind the birds and twisting their necks. Loon began to shout, "Open your eyes! wīsahkīcāhk is killing us!" All the birds who were still alive ran out of that lodge. wīsahkīcāhk ran after the Loon and kicked it in the rump. That's why the loons have ruffled feathers there today.

Fooled by Reflections
Narrator: Henry Linklater (English)
wīsahkīcāhk was traveling around in the bush and came to a river which he had to cross. He jumped across it but just as he was leaving the ground, spruce partridges flew up from the brush and startled him so that he fell into the river. He waded ashore to the other side but found that his pipe and tobacco pouch had fallen into the river. So he began walking along the bank, looking in the water in order to try and find them. He walked along and finally he thought that he saw his pipe and tobacco bag in the water a few feet from shore. He waded out and leaned over, groping around in the water in order to grab his stuff. He kept doing this for a long time but he couldn't grab onto them. Finally, he happened to look up and saw his pipe and tobacco pouch hanging in a tree where they'd landed when he fell in the river. He had been trying to pick up their reflections in the water.

Muskrat Cools Grease
Narrator: Joe Michel
wīsahkīcāhk was alone by himself. No one was with him. All of a sudden ī-cikā-ciwīðikot, he knew somebody was around.

"Hey, nisīm ("my younger sibling"), come here!" he said. "Come with me, nisīmī ("my younger sibling"). Don't let anything bother you. Just follow me, nisīmī. So you'll become fat." wīsahkīcāhk is trying to fool him. So he started making akaskwa ("arrow"). "So come here, nisīmī," he said after he made that arrow. "Let's go toward the north."

So that guy says, "Okay, let's go."

"If there's going to be people in the future, maybe they'll see us." Let's see how fast you are." He's trying to fool him. *wīsahkīcāhk* sure likes to fool people. *wīsahkīcāhk* said this, "Keep going with me, *nisīmī*. You'll become fat if you keep going with me." He's looking ahead for himself [looking out for his interests]. "See how good of a meal I can get out of my *nisīmī*. I'm like that, *nisīmī*, I like to fool people. We'll go someplace else after." He seen an *atik* ("caribou") and he killed him, but it was eaten up 'cause he was busy. That's why he lost his meal because he was busy with his *osīmisa* ("younger sibling"). There was no people at that time. Maybe just the animals. "Let's see," he says. He was going around alone, *ipapīyakōw papāðakot*.

So he said he was going to go down to the lake. It was a nice day. So he seen a muskrat in the water. He was standing there. And he knows already what he's going to say to that rat. So he said this to him, "*nisīmī*, how come you're swimming slow?"

And the Rat says, "My tail is too heavy."

"Come here, *nisīmī*, come here." So the Rat went to him. "How come your tail is making you mad? So you can't swim fast? Wait, *nisīmī*, I'll help you to swim fast." So he fixed the tail for the Rat. "You try it now and see *mātikwa* how fast you'll go." So he let her go and the Rat started jumping fast in the water and that's what *wīsahkīcāhk* wanted. *īkwānī*.

The Startlers
Narrator: Julien Bighetty
Translator: Sidney Castel

wīsahkīcāhk came to the side of a lake where he found a nest of small *piðīyak* ("spruce partridge"). As a joke, he grabbed these birds, told them not to be frightened, and then farted on them. Then he went along on his way. The parents of those small birds were now angry at *wīsahkīcāhk*. They knew he was traveling towards a river and would soon have to jump across it. They got together and flew ahead and then concealed themselves by the bank. Just as *wīsahkīcāhk* was jumping across, the birds flew up from the bank and scared him, making him fall into the water.

The Farting Hunter and Scab Eater
Narrator: Henry Linklater (English)

wīsahkīcāhk ate too many *okinīyak* ("rose berries") and began to fart continuously. All his hunting is ruined by his farts. Whenever he was about to catch an animal, he'd fart and the animals would run away. *wīsahkīcāhk* got angry with his rear end and he decided to burn it in order to stop the farting. So he heated rocks in a fire and then he sat on them. He burned his rear end until it was crusted over with scabs. Then he reached around, picked off some of the scab, and began to eat it. All the birds up in the trees saw him doing this and they began singing together, "*wīsahkīcāhk* is eating his own meat! *wīsahkīcāhk* is eating his own meat!" *wīsahkīcāhk* got madder and madder at those birds and finally he yelled at them, "No, I'm not! I'm eating the pemmican!"

The Farting Hunter
Narrator: Julien Bighetty
Translator: Sidney Castel
One time *wīsahkīcāhk* was walking around. While he was walking, he heard someone talking and went to see who it was. He reached the place where he had heard the voices, but couldn't see anyone there. Finally he saw a bunch of plants, "a kind that grows in the rocks" ("rock tripe"). He stood and listened. The plants called him "brother" and told him that they were doing the talking. *wīsahkīcāhk* asked the plants what would happen if he ate them. The plants told him that if he ate them it would cause him to fart for a long time and to fart very hard and loudly. Disregarding them, *wīsahkīcāhk* picked some of the plants and ate them. Later on, he became hungry again and began tracking a caribou herd. Every time he came close to the herd, he would fart loudly and scare the caribou away. Those caribou would think, "That must be *wīsahkīcāhk*."

The Flood and the New Earth
Narrator: Selazie Linklater
Translator: Caroline Caribou
This story explains why wolves are so frightened of people and so wild. *wīsahkīcāhk* had lost his brother the wolf and was traveling around looking for him. *wīsahkīcāhk* was the brother to all the animals. As he was walking, *wīsahkīcāhk* saw a kingfisher sitting on top of a tree and crying. "Why are you crying, little brother," he said. That kingfisher said he was crying because the fish in the water were playing with a wolf hide. *wīsahkīcāhk* hung the hide up in a tree. Then he climbed up into the tree and slept there and made his dreams. When he woke up, he said to the wolf hide, "Look out! I intend to chop down this tree and it will fall on you and kill you." So that wolf hide came to life. His brother came back to life. *wīsahkīcāhk* told his brother never to go into the water since he was killed by fish when he did this. That's why wolves never follow moose into the water today.

The Flood and the New Earth
Narrator: Catherine Merasty
Translators: Albert Umfreville, Denise Umfreville
[The first section of the narrative, dealing with the conflict between *wīsahkīcāhk*

and the water beings, was confusing or incomprehensible to the translators. They noted that the water beings were called *misipisiwak*, that the lupine brother was involved, and that *wīsahkīcāhk* killed the murderers of his brother.]

A great flood came. All the land was flooded. The water got higher and higher and *wīsahkīcāhk* climbed to the top of a tall tree and sat there. *wīsahkīcāhk* saw muskrats swimming around.

"My little brothers, come here," he called. They swam to where *wīsahkīcāhk* was sitting. *wīsahkīcāhk* told one muskrat to dive down to the bottom of the water and bring up some earth. The muskrat agreed to this and *wīsahkīcāhk* tied a long cordage line to its tail. That muskrat dove into the water from the top of the tree. He swam further and further down under the water and the rope that *wīsahkīcāhk* had tied to him unwound further and further. Finally, that muskrat came back to the surface. He had a little mud in his paw. *wīsahkīcāhk* told him that it wasn't enough. "Just one more, little brother," he said. Again the muskrat dived below the water. Finally he came back up with a little more mud in his paw. *wīsahkīcāhk* took that mud and began to blow on it. It got bigger and bigger and finally the land was formed. That is how the earth we live on today was made: from *wīsahkīcāhk* blowing on the mud brought up by the muskrat.

wīsahkīcāhk and the Baby
Narrator: Henry Linklater (English)

wīsahkīcāhk was going around and he came by a camp of human people. Those people had a new little baby in the camp. *wīsahkīcāhk* waited until they weren't looking and he grabbed that baby and ran away and took it to his camp. He used to spend a lot of time watching it. You know, babies can bend themselves...they can put their foot in their mouth like that. "I really think that I should be able to do this," *wīsahkīcāhk* thought. So he keeps trying to do this. Trying to put his foot into his mouth like that baby. But he can't do it. He tries and tries. So you know what then? He has admiration for this baby. So he starts calling the baby "older brother" because the baby can do this and he can't.

wīsahkīcāhk Changes Frog, Muskrat, and Bear
Narrator: Marie Wescope
Translator: Charles Hart

Now then, at one time *wīsahkīcāhk* is traveling from place to place and those animals who are there begin following him; they go walking after him. But *wīsahkīcāhk* continues on his way.

"Let's follow him and watch him to see what it is that he'll do," they say about him as they follow him. Now then, they weary *wīsahkīcāhk* with their following. In this fashion he thinks about it, "Let's see. I will get the better of those animals.

Whatever it may be, I will do something to them. Let's see if it doesn't happen. They continuously follow me. I hate them. I lack the time to eat with them following me."

Now then, he crosses over a hill to the side of a lake. Now then, that frog [one of the environing animals] is there and *wīsahkīcāhk* grabs him as he jumps about. Now then, he grabs a log. Pushing and pulling, he pins the frog down right there with that log. Now then, that frog [with legs entrapped] jumps strenuously until he progressively lengthens his legs. So much did he leap in trying to escape that he now has long legs.

wīsahkīcāhk continues walking. Now then that bear approaches and *wīsahkīcāhk* seizes him. Now he intends to entrap the bear's tail in the crack of a split log held open by a wedge. At that time the bear had a long tail.

Now he says to him, "Don't bother me, bear! I intend to do something! Come here and I'll show you something. Go in there, underneath that log." So then this bear goes in underneath. Now then *wīsahkīcāhk* traps the bear's tail in the split log. Now then he leaves him there, paying no attention to his bellowing: "Come release me, *wīsahkīcāhk*!" Now then, *wīsahkīcāhk* pays no attention; really he only continues walking.

Now then, that muskrat is following him and *wīsahkīcāhk* is angered by it. So then, he seizes that muskrat and he ties his tail to a stone and he throws him into the water. Now then, that muskrat struggles very hard to escape; he is nearly drowning. Then really *wīsahkīcāhk* was very happy to have dealt with all of them because they had angered him by following him about.

Now then, that frog frees himself and his legs are now very long as he hops around. "Really that *wīsahkīcāhk* has angered me by trapping me and stretching my legs," he says. Then he goes trailing after *wīsahkīcāhk*. As he hops along, he sees that bear, trapped by his tail in the split log.

Now then, he says to him, "What happened to you?"

"That *wīsahkīcāhk* trapped me by the tail," the bear says to him.

Now that frog says to him, "I can't free you in any other way than by cutting off your tail." So then he cuts this bear's tail off. Now then, the frog and bear together trail *wīsahkīcāhk*. Now then, they arrive at a little lake and they see that muskrat trying to free himself.

"Why are you caught like this in the water?" they say to him.

Now then he says, "That *wīsahkīcāhk* threw me into the water after tying a rock to my tail."

"We can't help you," they say to him. "The only thing we can do to release you is to skin your tail." So then they skin the muskrat's tail, narrowing it. At that time, the muskrat had a tail like a beaver. It is because of their skinning his tail that the muskrat has a small tail today.

Then he says to them, "Let's trail that *wīsahkīcāhk*." Now then *wīsahkīcāhk* knows that they are close behind him and he leaps into the water [to escape them]. They come up to where he is.

"Better for you that we don't see you again," they say to him. "Why did you do these things to us?"

Now then, *wīsahkīcāhk* says to them, "Just such things are my responsibility and I therefore make use of anything. You, frog, are not intended to walk but are intended to hop. It is for that reason that your legs are now lengthened." "And you then," he says to the bear, "you are not intended to have a long tail and for that reason your tail is now cut off. And you muskrat, you are not intended to have a tail like a beaver. You are not to be formed that way. So for these reasons this has happened."

Now then those animals say, "It appears that this *wīsahkīcāhk* knows everything."

Addendum
Narrator: Charles Hart

The animals, still angered, continued to trail *wīsahkīcāhk*. *wīsahkīcāhk* knew they were following closely behind him and, fearing their vengeance, decided to do something about it. So he stopped and, pulling down his pants, leaned over so that his butt pointed behind him down the trail.

So frog was in the lead. When the frog saw *wīsahkīcāhk*'s butt, he said "That's the log with which *wīsahkīcāhk* trapped me." When the muskrat came up, he saw *wīsahkīcāhk*'s testicles and said, "That's the stone he was using to drown me." Finally the bear came up and saw the crack in *wīsahkīcāhk*'s rear end and said, "That's the crack in the log where he caught my tail." So they all got frightened and they stopped trailing *wīsahkīcāhk*.

Rolling Head
Narrator: Jeremiah Michel
Translator: Pierre Merasty

That woman married a snake. That woman was staying with her husband and she married a snake. *ī-pawāmit kinīpikwa*, she was dreaming of the snake. Her husband *nitanipakahōw*; he's a good hunter and he kills lots of animals. That man went out and he killed a moose. That man went where his wife was in a bunch of trees. So he started hitting the *mistik* ("tree"). And (as) he was hitting the tree, a *misikinīpik* ("giant snake") came out of the log (trunk). When it was coming toward him, *ī-pawāmit kinīpikwa* ("he kills the snake"). And when he kills it, he takes the snake's blood, that *kinīpikomihko* ("snake blood") home. And that moose he killed, that lady make a stew out of it. And him, he made a stew out of that snake's blood. He told his kids to run away.

"Just leave," he said to his kids. "I'll look after her myself." And then I'll run away too." *īkwānītāhpwī*("so truly"), so when his wife got there he fed her the snake stew. The woman started eating it. While he was eating it, the man said to his wife, "Do you taste that blood?"

"It's not moose blood. I went and cut off the head of that big snake, your husband. That's where I got that blood from and that's what you're drinking." The woman got mad. She went and checked right away in those trees and she saw it laying there. And she got mad and she ran back home. So when she ran back, that man, her husband, cut her head off. So the man run away. His kids had left already. But her head comes alive and starts following him. He ran everywhere but he couldn't escape from her. So he ran to the water and he started running on top of the water. But that *tihtipistikwān* ("rolling head") kept following him. They got into the middle of the lake and then the head sunk down into the water. So she died there and drowned. That's all I know about the woman. *opawāmīwin* ("her dreams/visions") did that to her.

CHAPTER 3
Discussion of the Trickster-Transformer Cycle

wīsahkīcāhk and nēnapoš

wīsahkīcāhk (Plains Cree and Swampy Cree wīsahkēcāhk) is the combined transformer-trickster-culture hero character of Cree oral literature from the Quebec-Ontario border west to British Columbia. In common with some comparable characters in North American Indian literature, wīsahkīcāhk combines attributes of sacredness, spiritual power, altruism, maliciousness, cleverness, and stupidity. Early Euro-Canadian observers confused wīsahkīcāhk with the benign creator deity kicimanitōw (Isham 1949:5, Graham 1969:160), an identification that was clearly erroneous. Of greater complexity are the historical relationships between wīsahkīcāhk and comparable characters in the literatures of other Algonquian-speaking peoples in the Subarctic and Eastern Woodlands areas.

Broadly speaking, wīsahkīcāhk appears as the transformer character among all Crees west of Quebec; among the Cree, Montagnais, and Naskapi of Quebec, mēsū (variants mēšū, mēš, mēs) is the equivalent character (LeJeune 1898: 154–55, 1899: 156–59; Speck 1935: 98–99; Savard 1979: 26–32; Bauer 1971: 28–35). The most widely known such character to non-Indian audiences is nēnapoš of the southeastern and southwestern Ojibwa. The name is given here in the Walpole Island dialect described by Bloomfield (1958); such cognates as wēnapošō, nēnapošō, and mēnapošō are attested from different dialects in the present century.

Although the Cree and southwestern/southeastern Ojibwa transformer cycles are distinct in many respects, the attributes of the characters are similar and many stories are common to both (Dixon 1909, Fisher 1946). Consequently, Europeans and some Algonquians have understood wīsahkīcāhk, mēsū, and nēnapoš with its cognates as names for the identical character. The earliest seventeenth and eighteenth-century references to the Ojibwa transformer do not use nēnapoš or its cognates but rather variants of Ojibwa missāpōs "big/large rabbit" that were glossed as "Great Hare" (Perrot in Blair 1911 1: 31, Allouez 1899: 201 [*"michabous"*], Raudot in Kinietz

1965: 371–72 [*"michapoux"*], Rasles 1900: 155 [*"michabou"*]. Although *nēnapoš* and its cognates are not readily analyzable as reflexes of *missāpōs*, it is probable that the two were concurrent or successive names for the same character. *nēnapoš* has certain leporine characteristics and at least some contemporary Ojibwa define him as the "Great Rabbit" or "Great Hare" (Coleman, Frogner and Eich 1962: 56, Landes 1968: 22). The earliest form of *nēnapoš* I have discovered occurs in a passage by Henry the Younger identifying it with the cognate "Minabojou," *missāpōs*, and the Quebec Algonquian *mēsū*; the passage pertains to the 1770s:

> Nanibojou is otherwise called by the names of Minabojou, Michabou, Messou, Shactac, and a variety of others, but of all of which the interpretation appears to be, The Great Hare. (Henry 1969: 204)

Henry's "Shactac" is unknown to the author, unless it is a garbled and contracted form of *wīsahkīcāhk*. Regarding the identification of *nēnapoš* with the Quebec Algonquian *mēsū*, it is worth noting that the Montagnais in the seventeenth century recognized also a mythological character called "*michtabouchiou*" whose name is analyzable as "he is a great hare" (LeJeune 1898: 31–32). It is possible that *mēsū* and "*michtabouchiou*" were synonymous names for the same transformer character. The "Misabos" character in contemporary Montagnais mythology (Basile and McNulty 1971) is perhaps cognate with these beings.

The first reference to *wīsahkīcāhk* I have encountered pertains not to the Cree but the Ojibwas and Ottawas of the Mackinac region in 1669:

> They say it is the native Country of one of their Gods, named Michabous [*missāpōs*] īthat is to say, "the great Hare," Ouisaketchak, who is the one that created the Earth. (Allouez 1899: 201)

Allouez treats the *missāpōs/nēnapoš* and *wīsahkīcāhk* characters as identical, but the Ottawas described by Rasles (1900:155-59) in 1723 distinguished *missāpōs* the transformer from "ouassakita," possibly a variant of *wīsahkīcāhk*, who controlled terrestrial animals and birds. Like Allouez, Alexander Henry the Elder identified *wīsahkīcāhk* with *nēnapoš*, but his remarks do not clarify whether Algonquians conventionally made the same equation. In 1792, Henry wrote:

> Their [Fort Vermilion Cree] ideas of creation are nearly the same as [Ojibwa] and they have the same wonderful stories concerning Nainauboushaw, who they call Wee-suc-ha-jouck. Their tales, however, are not related so clearly and distinctly; many things appear obscure to them and to such they can give no proper signification. (Henry in Coues 1896 2: 512)

It is clear that some Algonquian groups or individuals identified *wīsahkīcāhk* and *nēnapoš* as the same personage. In, for example, a Plains Cree version of the

"Winged Startlers," the transformer states:
> Everything that breathes has two names...I myself have three: Wesaykaychak, Nanaposo, and Mutchekewis. (Ahenakew 1929: 333)

Howard (1977: 11) provides a similar equation among Plains Ojibwa.

The distribution of cognates of *wīsahkīcāhk* as names for the primary transformer character among northern Ojibwa, Lake Winnipeg Saulteaux, Algonquin, and the more northerly southwestern Ojibwa groups suggests either a long history of reciprocal literary influence or Cree influences on Ojibwa literature. Around 1804, Grant (Masson 1890 2: 353–54) stated that the mixed Cree-Ojibwa bands from Lake Nipigon west to Lake Winnipeg recognized "*wiskendjac*" as the creator of Indians and their country. Among the Lake Winnipeg Saulteaux, *wīsahkīcāhk* appears to have displaced *nēnapoš* as the primary transformer character, although the literature preserves the *missāpōs* character and a story of his conflict with Flint that parallels southeastern/southwestern Ojibwa versions (Hallowell 1976: 365, 367–69, cf. Simms 1906: 338–39). The Sandy Lake Band of Ontario, self-identified as Cree but speaking a language of the Severn dialect group of Ojibwa, uses a cognate of *wīsahkīcāhk* but retains also identifiable Ojibwa plot elements (Ray and Stevens 1971). The northern Ojibwa of Marten's Falls Post also use a cognate of *wīsahkīcāhk* (Skinner 1911: 173–75), while the Timagami band uses *nēnapoš* (Speck 1915). Most southwestern Ojibwa use *nēnapoš* and its variants, but *wīsahkīcāhk* figures as the primary transformer in stories from Dinorwic, Ontario (Radin and Reagan 1928: 63–67) and Lake of the Woods, Ontario (Cooper 1936: 12). The Tete de Boule use a cognate of *wīsahkīcāhk* (Davidson 1928a). Most Algonquian groups use cognates of *wīsahkīcāhk* (Speck 1915 [Timiskaming], Aubin 1982 [Golden Lake]), while the Grand Lake Victoria Band uses *mēsū* (Davidson 1928b).

In a number of cases, groups have used names cognate to those of the primary transformer in the literature of proximal peoples to refer to secondary characters in their own literature. The Montagnais, for example, use a cognate of *wīsahkīcāhk* to name a character in one of the *cahkāpēs* hero tales (Speck 1935: 49). The most interesting cases of such borrowing are versions of the *wīsahkīcāhk* myth in which *nēnapoš* figures as the younger brother or cousin whose death motivates the transformer's battle with water beings and the ensuing deluge. (Brown and Brightman [Lac La Ronge Cree], Radin and Reagan 1928: 63–67 [Dinorwic, Ontario Ojibwa]). Norman's (1982) enigmatic "*wichikäpäche*," the hero of a series of "poems" from Swampy Cree sources, parallels *wīsahkīcāhk* in many of his exploits and may represent the latter's identification with the hero *cahkāpēs* (Plains Cree transcription) who appears in the literature of the Montagnais-Naskapi and eastern Cree (Speck 1935), Lake Winnipeg Saulteaux (Hallowell 1976: 368), the

Swamp Cree of James Bay (Honigmann 1956: 68), the Severn dialect Sandy Lake Band (Ray and Stevens 1971), the Rock Cree and apparently some Plains Cree (Ahenakew in Faries 1938: 255). Among these latter groups, the two characters are always distinguished.

Despite derivation from a shared Algonquian literary stratum and evident reciprocal borrowing of plot and motif, the *wīsahkīcāhk* and *nēnapoš* cycles are distinguished by many features including details of the transformer's parentage and the incorporation of Midewiwin origin stories in the Ojibwa cycle. The transformer character of such Eastern Woodlands Algonquian groups as the Potawatomi, Sauk, Fox, and Kickapoo resembles *nēnapoš* in these respects, although the names appear to be cognates of *wīsahkīcāhk*.

Reconstruction of the earlier distributions and histories of the Cree and Ojibwa transformer characters will depend upon and perhaps contribute to continuing research on the location and movements of proto-historic and early contact period Ojibwa-speaking groups. If Ojibwa or mixed Ojibwa-Cree populations were resident in the northern boreal forest before European contact (cf. Greenberg and Morrison 1982), it would appear that *wīsahkīcāhk* is not a distinctively Cree character but was shared with some Ojibwa-speaking groups. Alternatively, if Ojibwa-speaking groups first entered the northern boreal forest to become permanent residents in the 1730s (Bishop 1981), the presence of *wīsahkīcāhk* as the principle transformer character among Saulteaux, Northern Ojibwa, and some Southwestern Ojibwa may represent Cree influence. In either case, a clear-cut distinction between the Cree *wīsahkīcāhk* cycle and the *missāpōs/nēnapoš* cycle of the Southeastern and southwestern Ojibwa and the Ottawa appears to have existed around the time of contact.

Rock Cree Knowledge of *wīsahkīcāhk*

As the character of his exploits might suggest, Rock Crees view *wīsahkīcāhk* with mingled contempt, respect, and affection. Although concrete exemplifications in the stories are infrequent, it is said that *wīsahkīcāhk* both modified the boreal forest environment to make it suitable for human occupation and introduced technological knowledge to human beings. As one narrator from Granville Lake put it: "*wīsahkīcāhk* was the first one up here in the North. He fixed things up for the old Indians and taught them to live in the Churchill River country." For example, rivers during the *acaðōhkīwin* period ran in straight beds and were unnavigable; *wīsahkīcāhk* is said to have introduced the curves which slowed the flow of water and made them navigable by canoe. In his capacity as culture hero, *wīsahkīcāhk* is said to have originally introduced the knowledge underlying the Euro-Canadian technology brought in by the traders. Angelique Linklater related this tradition which was translated by her husband Henry Linklater:

That *wīsahkīcāhk*, this is a good teacher, eh? For *wīmistikōsiw*, for the White Man. He learned the *wīmistikōsiw* how to make things. How to make any-thing: plane or carpenter work or any-thing. This is the guy that...they got it from *wīsahkīcāhk*.

Rock Crees are aware that *wīsahkīcāhk*'s behavior juxtaposes great cleverness and spiritual power with unutterable stupidity but see none of the supposed inconsistency between these attributes that Western scholars (cf. Boas 1914, Radin 1914) have remarked upon. The trickster episodes are the occasion of great hilarity and both narrators and audience were, on many occasions, nearly incomprehensible with laughter. Some narrators observed that certain individuals, especially those strongly associated with the Catholic Church, were offended by the stories, and emphasized that they were innocent jokes and good fun. I was requested not to repeat the stories either to the priests or to disapproving persons in the Cree community, but people were pleased when I stated that I would tell the stories in other Cree communities and that they would eventually be published in a book.

One person stated that *wīsahkīcāhk* obtained his name from the propensity for playing dirty tricks on people. This etymology concurs well with the identification of the element *wīsak* as a component of the name; *wīsak* occurs in several words with the sense of "bitter" or "suffer" but the phonological shape is clearly different and the connection is problematic. Neither is the name to be derived from *wiskacānis* "grey jay" as Speck (1915) erroneously suggests.

There is no consistent identification of *wīsahkīcāhk* with any biblical character and the tenor of scriptural dissemination in the area would have tended to discourage such equivalences. The only one noted was predictably inauspicious: *wīsahkīcāhk* was identified with the Biblical Cain.

Certain characteristics are repeatedly emphasized when Rock Crees discuss *wīsahkīcāhk*. Of these, the most important appears to be his ability to transform into other organic and inorganic forms. His ability to converse with animate and inanimate objects, his trickiness, his foolishness, his use of the ubiquitous *nisīmīy* "younger sibling" in address, his sexual voracity, his continual hunger, and his modifications of the environment are all emphasized. Most of these abilities are related to his possession of *mamāhtawisīwin* or extraordinary power; he "used his mind," as Caroline Caribou put it, to do things.

Opinion as to the taxonomic and ethnic status of *wīsahkīcāhk* differ. One person regarded him as an extraordinarily powerful Cree Indian. Others identified him as an Indian human being, but were uncertain as to what kind of Indian. Angelique Linklater expressed the opinion that *wīsahkīcāhk*, in common with most other *ácðōkiwin* characters was not a human being. She then paused and added *pakākam* "maybe."

Syntagmatic Structure and Sequencing

The comparative discussion of the Rock Cree *wīsahkīcāhk* stories below makes reference to other collections of Cree narratives. These sources are noted in Table 2 together with information on the Cree divisions and communities from which the stories were obtained. Page references are given infra for specific narratives.

Although *wīsahkīcāhk* stories are often narrated singly, some narrators possess explicit assumptions about the order in which they occur and this is sometimes evidenced in the temporal order of narration when more than one story is told at the same time. As Table 3 indicates, there is no invariant sequence either between or within Cree communities where such connected narratives have been obtained. For example, the Rock Cree *wīsahkīcāhk* stories presented here were collected primarily in Brochet, but Jeremiah Michel's sequence contrasts with those of Henry Linklater and Albert Umferville. Presumably individual narrators tend to reproduce approximately the same sequence from one occasion of connected

Table 2. Sources on Cree Narrative
Rock Cree and ð-dialect Thickwoods Cree
Franklin 1823. Cumberland House, Saskatchewan.
Brown and Brightman [George Nelson] 1988. Lac la Ronge, Saskatchewan.
Thompson 1962. Churchill and Nelson River drainages, northern Manitoba.
Swampy Cree
Clay 1938. Fisher River, Manitoba.
Cresswell 1923, Norway House, Manitoba.
Godsell 1938. Northern Manitoba.
Russell 1896. Grand Rapids, Manitoba.
Skinner 1911. Fort Albany, Ontario.
Swindlehurst 1905. "James Bay" (possibly Eastmain Cree or Montagnais).
Plains Cree
Ahenakew 1929. Thunderchild, Saskatchewan.
Ahenakew and Hardlotte 1977. Saskatchewan.
Bloomfield 1930, 1934. Sweet Grass, Saskatchewan.
Curtis 1928.
Dusenberry 1962. Rocky Boy, Montana.
Hamilton 1894. St. Peter's Reserve, Manitoba.
Maclean 1896. "Saskatchewan River."
Paget 1909. Qu'appelle, Saskatchewan.
Skinner 1916. Crooked Lake, Cowessess and Sakimay, Saskatchewan.
Thickwoods Cree
Petitot 1886. Fish Hook Lake and Cold Lake, Alberta.
Vandersteene 1969. Wabasca, Alberta.
Severn "Cree" (Severn Ojibwa Dialect)
Ray and Stevens 1971. Sandy Lake, Ontario.

Table 3. Sequencing of Episodes in the *wīsahkīcāhk* Cycle		
1) Michel Contest with *wīmisōsiw* The Flood and the New Earth Goose Transformation The Shut-Eye Dancers Squeezed by Trees *wītikōw* and Weasel Eye Juggler The Startlers The Farting Hunter Bear's Eye Medicine Muskrat Cools Fat Fly Transformation Fooled by Reflections Scab-Eater Moose Transformation Marries Daughter	2) Umferville Scab-Eater Tricks Moose Squeezed by Birds The Startlers Fooled by Reflections Bear's Eye Medicine	3) Linklater The Farting Hunter Scab-Eater The Startlers Fooled by Reflections
4) Ahenakew 1929 Rolling Head Contest with *wīmisōsiw* Destroys Short-Noses Wolf and Wolverine The Flood and the New Earth The Shut-Eye Dancer Squeezed by Trees The Startlers	5) Ahenakew and Hardlotte 1977 Rolling Head Contest with *wīmisōsiw* The Flood and the New Earth	6) Bloomfield 1930 Rolling Head Contest With *wīmisōsiw* The Flood and the the New Earth The Startlers Fooled by Reflections Pursued by Stone
7) Bloomfield 1934 Rolling Head Contest with *wīmisōsiw* Muskrat Cools Fat The Startlers Fooled by Reflections The Shut-Eye Dancers Eye-Juggler Fly Transformation Tricks Buffalo Squeezed by Trees The Farting Hunter Fight with Bear *wītikōw* and Weasel Becomes Woman	8) Clay 1938 The Shut-Eye Dancers Scab-Eater The Startlers Fooled by Reflections Bear's Eye Medicine Muskrat Cools Fat Squeezed by Trees	9) Dusenberry 1962 Lives with Wolves The Flood and the the New Earth The Farting Hunter Scab-Eater The Startlers Contest with Coyote Tricks Buffalo Squeezed by Trees Muskrat Cools Fat Fly Transformation Marries Chief's Daughter
10) Maclean 1898 Rolling Head Contest with *wīmisōsiw* The Flood and the New Earth	11) Ray and Stevens 1971 The Shut-Eye Dancers Scab-Eater	12) Russell 1896 Rolling Head Contest with *wīmisōsiw* The Flood and the New Earth The Shut-Eye Dancers Scab-Eater Tricked by Beaver Fooled by Reflections
13) Skinner 1911 The Flood and the New Earth The Shut-Eye Dancers The Farting Hunter Muskrat Cools Fat Squeezed by Trees	14) Skinner 1916 Lives with Wolves The Flood and the New Earth Bear's Eye Medicine Squeezed by Trees The Farting Hunter Scab Eater	15) Vandersteene 1969 Rolling Head Contest with *wīmisōsiw* The Flood and the New Earth

narration to the next. To this degree, individual narrators severally possess sequence designs which they reproduce in individual instances of narration; the coexistence of different designs in the same community reflects generally the rather loose integration of stories in the cycle and perhaps also individually evolved arrangements and/or different lines of transmission between families.

To the degree that narrators string stories together randomly and improvisationally, the sequence of stories in individual narrations can be regarded as an emergent property of the particular occasion of telling. This would be of considerable interest to examine further since the narrator would be, in such a case, creating novel kinds of cross-reference and discourse cohesion between different stories in the sequence. To the degree that there are individual, kindred-based, community-wide, or even more general constraints over improvisation and randomness in sequencing, they regulate the contiguity or sequencing of two or more particular stories and not, of course, the entire corpus. Insofar as general constraints or tendencies can be shown to underlie and influence sequencing in individual narration instances, one can speak of a syntagmatic structure of the cycle that encompasses certain of the constituent stories.

Whether a story is told singly or as one element in a longer connected narrative, events in certain stories presuppose or cross-reference events in others which were either related earlier or are conventionally known to be antecedent. For example, *wīsahkīcāhk*'s unmasking in "Marries Daughter" comes about through the burn scars he incurred in "The Farting Hunter." Other means of identification are both imaginable and possible, but Jeremiah Michel in "Farting Hunter" specified the location and cause of the scars as did Caroline Caribou in translating Selazie Linklater's singly narrated version. In the first case, "The Farting Hunter" precedes "Marries Daughter" in a temporal narrative sequence; in both, there appears to be a conventional assumption that the events in the one story antedate those in the other. The stories need not be contiguous, but the tendency would be to narrate them in the order indicated.

Table 3, in which the spaces separate bundles of consecutive stories occurring in the same source, suggests certain other tendencies. Of these, the most interesting for the comparative study of Algonquian literature is the greater than random occurrence of the sequence "Rolling Head", "Contest with *wīmisōsiw*," and "The Flood and the New Earth." Although Jeremiah Michel regarded "Rolling Head" as detached from the transformer cycle, all other Cree stories that account for *wīsahkīcāhk*'s parentage identify him as the oldest of the two children of the tragic couple in that narrative. Seven versions (Bloomfield 1930, Bloomfield 1934, Russell 1898, Maclean 1896, Ahenakew 1929, Ahenakew and Hardlotte 1977, Vandersteene 1969) locate "Contest with *wīmisōsiw*" immediately after "Rolling Head." In all cases where they both occur as elements in a connected narrative, "Contest with *wīmisōsiw*" precedes "The Flood and the New Earth," although in one case (Ahenakew 1929) they are separated by two intervening stories. Taking Bloomfield (1930) as a point of reference, the cycle relates sequentially *wīsahkīcāhk's* flight (with his younger brother) from their mother's animated and murderous rolling head, the destruction of the head, the abduction of *wīsahkīcāhk* by *wīmisōsiw* and the abandoned brother's simultaneous transformation into a wolf, *wīsahkīcāhk*'s marriage and his duels with *wīmisōsiw*, the latter's death or transformation, the killing of the lupine brother by water beings, *wīsahkīcāhk*'s attack on these beings, the ensuing deluge, the earth-diver motif, and then the recreation of the world and the testing of its size.

That there is no canonical "necessity" for this sequence is made abundantly clear by the table. In Jeremiah Michel's version, the "Rolling Skull" is detached. Skinner's (1911) Fort Albany version begins with the flood. In two Plains Cree versions (Dusenberry 1962, Skinner 1916) *wīsahkīcāhk* lives with wolves prior to the flood; Skinner's version is unique in identifying *wīsahkīcāhk* as having originally been a wolverine. Nelson's (Brown and Brightman 1987) version from Lac la Ronge borrows the "Virgin Birth" story that usually explains the origin of *nēnapoš* in the Ojibwa transformer cycle. Neither are there evident cross-references between the three stories when they occur together. *wīsahkīcāhk* could presumably have encountered his Draconian father-in-law at any point in his career rather than before the flood and after his escape from the skull. The identification of *wīsahkīcāhk* and his brother as children in "Rolling Skull" necessarily locates that story at or near the beginning of the cycle but does not specify what should follow it. The most evident link is between "Contest with *wīmisōsiw*" and "The Flood and the New Earth"; in the first, the younger brother becomes a wolf upon being abandoned and is warned to avoid water, while in the second the killing of the brother by the water beings motivates *wīsahkīcāhk*'s vengeance and thus the flood. The presence of the ordering in Plains, Woods, and Swamp Cree versions suggests at least some antiquity and perhaps the organization of sequencing in terms of such structural characteristics of the myth as the association of abandonment with loss of humanity and the antagonism between terrestrial and aquatic beings. That there are other possible arrangements is again attested by other versions. In what probably represents borrowing from Euro-Canadian sources, the flood is sometimes unmotivated by the lupine brother's death and represented instead as the creator deity's punishment for human wickedness (Thompson 1962, Vandersteene 1969, Dusenberry 1962).

Other tendencies in sequencing are favored by events in stories that can motivate or explain events in later ones. Comparison suggests that narrators often create, within limits, these motivating relationships by choosing certain sequences from among several possible ones that will provide cohesion between consecutive stories. In order for *wīsahkīcāhk* to eat his own scabs all versions have him previously burn himself either to silence his rear-end in the "Farting Hunter" (Linklater, Michel, Ray and Stevens 1971, Skinner 1916) or to punish some part of his anatomy for being a poor sentry (Clay 1938, Russell 1898, Ray and Stevens 1971, Skinner 1911) in "The Shut Eye Dancers." In all instances, the autocannibalism is preceded by self-inflicted burning. Similarly, *wīsahkīcāhk*'s motivation for being squeezed by birches is always surfeit and the desire to make room for food; his gluttony is variously preceded by tricking a buffalo or moose (Umferville's "Tricks Moose and Squeezed by Birds," "Tricks Buffalo" in Dusenberry 1962 and Bloomfield 1934), by tricking a bear and asking a muskrat to cool the fat ("Bear's Eye Medicine" and "Muskrat Cools Fat" in Clay 1938 and Skinner 1911), or by feasting on deluded birds ("The Shut Eye Dancers" in Michel and Ahenakew 1929). In all these instances narrators choose or conform to a sequence which motivates *wīsahkīcāhk*'s overeating. In five versions, "The Startlers" precede "Tricked by Reflections" as the agencies that cause *wīsahkīcāhk* to lose his pipe or bag (Michel; Linklater; Bloomfield 1930, 1934; Clay 1938). Although the combinatorial possibilities are unlimited, there are recurrent specifiable sequences linking such groups of stories within the cycle suggesting either the dissemination and/or the inheritance of particular syntagmatic orderings or their repeated invention by narrators familiar with similar literary repertoires.

The Stories

Rolling Head

As discussed earlier, "Rolling Head" appears to be recognized as the beginning of the *wīsahkīcāhk* cycle in most western Woods Cree and Plains Cree communities, and Mr. Colomb's narrative coincides with other Cree versions in identifying the protagonists as the transformer's parents (Ahenakew 1929: 309–13, Ahenakew and Hardlotte 1977, Bloomfield 1930: 14–16, Maclean 1896: 71–72, Russell 1896: 202–03, Vandersteene 1969: 44–47). Most of these accounts include the wife's adultery with giant snakes, the transformation of the father into a star, the use of magical objects to create obstacles for the murderous head, and the climactic transformation of the head into a sturgeon.

Mr. Michel's connected narrative is probably unusual in omitting "Rolling Head" and beginning with "Contest with *wīmisōsiw*"; his version of "Rolling Head" was related separately and lacks any reference to *wīsahkīcāhk*. Rather than viewing the omission as random, it may represent an ideological change in progress. Mr. Michel regarded "Rolling Head" as a "powerful and wicked" story, sentiments which are shared by some other persons who explicitly disassociate it from the *wīsahkīcāhk* cycle. Conjecturally, those who find the story's content objectionable are motivated to reject or deny the connection, a tendency which could, under the appropriate circumstances, encompass other of the hero's exploits as well.

"Rolling Head" also appears detached from the transformer cycle among the Severn Ojibwa of Sandy Lake where the being cognate to *wīsahkīcāhk* is represented as the third child of a female earth spirit called "*o-ma-ma-ma*" (Ray and Stevens 1971: 20–21). In a Woods Cree version from Lac la Ronge, *wīsahkīcāhk*'s birth results from the magical impregnation of the North Wind's daughter by the Sun, a motif clearly borrowed from Ojibwa accounts of the birth of *nēnapoš* (Brown and Brightman 1987). An unusual Plains Cree version (Skinner 1916: 344) has *wīsahkīcāhk* assume hominid form after a prior existence as a wolverine.

Contest with *wīmisōsiw*

Other Cree versions of *wīsahkīcāhk*'s contests with his murderous father-in-law were recorded by Ahenakew (1929: 313–19), Ahenakew and Hardlotte (1977), Bloomfield (1930: 16–18, 1934: 277–79), Maclean (1896: 72–73), Russell (1898: 203–05), and Vandersteene (1969: 47). The character of *wīmisōsiw* as a malignant father-in-law is of wide distribution in the Algonquian Subarctic. Two Cree versions (Skinner 1911: 168–73, 1916: 352–53) are detached from the transformer cycle, as is the case with two Ojibwa versions (Chamberlain 1890: 149–54, Speck 1915: 39–47). Among the Severn-dialect "Cree" of Sandy Lake (Ray and Stevens 1971: 52–55, 68–71, 112–20), the same story, detached from the *wīsahkīcāhk* cycle, is told of a character called "Ginosays" and the character "Way-mishoos" occurs in two other tales, as a jealous brother-in-law and as the evil stepfather in *ayās* (infra).

All versions that begin with the "Rolling Head" proceed immediately to the "Contest with *wīmisōsiw*," although the latter story is sometimes attenuated (Bloomfield 1934, Maclean, Ahenakew and Hardlotte) and describes only *wīsahkīcāhk*'s abduction and the consequent transformation of his abandoned younger brother into a wolf. Most versions describe *wīmisōsiw*'s duplicity in enticing *wīsahkīcāhk* into his magical canoe by inviting him to retrieve some possession that has fallen there. In Michel's version, various persons noted that *wīsahkīcāhk* would be anxious to retrieve his fingernails from the canoe in order to prevent their utilization in sorcery. The details of the ordeals and also the transformation of *wīmisōsiw* are variable between different versions, although most describe *wīsahkīcāhk*'s marriage to the youngest of his adversary's daughters. In the Michel version, *wīmisōsiw* becomes the first tamarack tree. Naomi Sinclair of Pukatawagan recalled an alternative ending in which *wīmisōsiw* became the first northern pike; small bones found in the pike's head today are said to resemble the bow, arrows, and canoe paddles used by *wīmisōsiw*. In a Swamp Cree version (Russell), the villain becomes a Canadian jay or whiskey jack.

The character of *wīmisōsiw* is sometimes evoked metaphorically by Crees as the prototype of malicious or demanding senior affines. Today, as in the past, post-marital residence arrangements are extremely flexible in Rock Cree communities. Young married couples may reside in their own home or live with or contiguous to the families of either spouse, and arrangements for residence in the bush may differ from those in the reserve community. In cases of uxorilocal residence some formality is said initially to exist between man and his father-in-law, although observation indicates that this formality varies according to individual circumstance. To the degree that such husbands find themselves under the control of their fathers-in-law, it becomes possible to interpret such remarks as "Well, I have to go cut wood for *wīmisōsiw*" or "Anything bad I think about my wife's dad, that's *wīmisōsiw*." It is probably unnecessary to observe that simplistic extrapolations from residential arrangements to wicked fathers-in-law in narratives are unwarranted; most such relationships appear to be characterized by reciprocal respect and often affection. In keeping with the persistence of "cross-cousin marriage" in some instances, the father-in-law may be a first, or second "uncle" in the *-sis* or "mother's brother"/"father-in-law" category.

The Flood and the New Earth
The flood and earth diver stories, widely distributed in North America, are included in most collections of Cree literature. In addition to the three Rock Cree versions discussed here, other variants occur in Ahenakew (1929: 324–27), Ahenakew and Hardlotte (1977), Bloomfield (1930: 18–19), Brown and Brightman (1988), Clay (1938: 16–23), Dusenberry (1962: 68–71), Franklin (1823 1: 133–14), Godsell (1938: 92–93), Maclean (1896: 71–76), Paget (1909: 170–77, 177–84 [two versions]), Petitot (1886: 472–74, 474–76 [two versions]), Ray and Stevens (1971: 21–26), Russell (1896: 205–07), Skinner (1911: 83–84; 1916: 344–46), Swindlehurst (1905: 139), and Vandersteene (1969: 47).

As defined here, "The Flood and the New Earth" comprises the consecutive events beginning with the death of *wīsahkīcāhk*'s lupine brother and culminating in the transformer's recreation of the earth after the deluge. As in Michel's version, *wīsahkīcāhk* may simply search for his brother and learn of his death (Bloomfield 1930); alternatively the story may begin with a reunion and co-residence (Ahenakew, Ahenakew and Hardlotte, Clay, Nelson, Maclean, Russell) or with *wīsahkīcāhk* acquiring a wolf as a classificatory nephew (Skinner 1916) as in many cognate Ojibwa myths. In some versions, *wīsahkīcāhk* dreams of or otherwise anticipates his brother's death and warns him to avoid water (Clay, Ahenakew, Russell, Skinner 1916). Michel's version exemplifies narrative cohesion in this respect in that *wīsahkīcāhk* warns his brother to avoid water much earlier, immediately before their separation at the beginning of "Contest with *wīmisōsiw*." In all versions in which the wolf figures, it pursues game into the water and is slain by aquatic beings. Nelson's (Brown and Brightman 1988) Ojibwa-influenced version identifies the younger brother as *mišwāpos* ("Great Hare") and has him pursue a deer into the water in the company of a wolf. This otherwise inexplicable juxtaposition results from the blending of Cree and Ojibwa transformer cycles.

Of the Rock Cree versions of the "Flood" story, only Colomb and Merasty identify the aquatic beings as *misipisiwak* (literally "Great Lynxes"), paralleling Nelson, Ray and Stevens Skinner (1916), and Russell. The "sea lions" of Clay and Ahenakew and the "lions" of Maclean are almost definitely inexact English glosses of *misipisiw*. Bloomfield (1930) mentions both *misipisiw* and *misikinīpikwak* or "giant snakes" together with a "chief fish" as the wolf's killers, and Paget (Second Version) mentions two giant snakes in this role. In the Michel version, the killers are called *cimiskiwanihīsiwak* (plural) which Caroline Dumas translated as "sea lions." The conventional word for "seal" is *ahkik* and it is probable that *cimiskiwanihīsiw* is a synonym or circumlocution for *misipisiw* or refers to similar beings. *cimiskiwanihīsiw* is obviously related formally to "*chemiskwana*" (animate obviative form) cited in a Plains Cree version (Ahenakew and Hardlotte 1977) whose accompanying illustrations show feline *misipisiw*-like beings with long tails. The verb *cimiskiwan*—"have a short nose" (Faries 1938: 253) suggests that *cimiskiwanihīsiw* and its cognates are the Cree names for the animal beings called "Short Noses" who prey upon humans in a *wīsahkīcāhk* myth recorded by Ahenakew (1929: 319–20). If this is the case, the interchangeability of *misipisiwak* and "Short Noses" in the flood myth would be suggestive since both are associated with the predator-prey relationship between humans and animals. The "Short Noses" are animals who prey on humans and the *misipisiwak* or other aquatic beings in some Cree (Clay 1938: 16) and Ojibwa (Ellis in Chamberlain 1891: 196–98, Jenness 1935: 69–70, Barnouw 1977: 34) versions of the myth resent the lupine brother's excessive predation on animals.

The image of the *misipisiw* is widespread among Subarctic and Woodlands Algonquians with obvious parallels in the mythology of other Eastern American Indian groups. The earliest references pertain to Ojibwas and Ottawas in the 1600s among whom cognates of *misipisiw* appear to have been proper names for an aquatic feline being which exerted influences over navigation and fishing (Perrot in Blair 1911 1: 59–62, Rasles 1900: 159–61, Allouez 1899: 289, Pachot in Kinietz 1965: 286). Rock Crees identify *misipisiw* both as a class of malignant water beings and as the proper name of their leader; they are described as resembling lynxes but with horns and long tails that they employ to create waves and currents. Today, some Rock Crees associate the *misipisiwak* with unexplained misfortunes and deaths both in the bush and on lakes and rivers, and many persons are uncomfortable discussing the beings or uttering their names. The motivation for the killing of the wolf is left interestingly opaque in most versions of the myth.

Vandersteene's account, which does not connect the wolf's death with the flood, states that the wolf is killed by the giant sturgeon into which the rolling head transformed. Most Cree versions (Michel, Stevens and Ray, Linklater, Nelson, Clay, Ahenakew and Hardlotte, Russell, Ahenakew, Maclean) concur with the cognate myth in the Ojibwa cycle in having *wīsahkīcāhk* search for his missing brother and follow his trail to a lake or river where he encounters a kingfisher gazing at events transpiring underwater. In Mrs. Linklater's version, the kingfisher is weeping; the translator suggested that this was either because it was hungry for the "fish" playing in the water or because it pitied the remains of the lupine brother. In order to secure the bird's cooperation or to reward it for its information, *wīsahkīcāhk* provides it with a sharp beak (Russell, Clay) or more attractive plumage (Ahenakew, Maclean). In one version (Ahenakew and Hardlotte), an eagle functions as *wīsahkīcāhk*'s informant. The kingfisher tells *wīsahkīcāhk* that the water beings are playing with a wolf's hide or tail underwater and that they sometimes come up on the shore to sleep. Some versions (Maclean, Paget) note that the wolf skin is suspended as a trophy over the entrance to the water being's underground lodge. *wīsahkīcāhk* determines to revenge himself on the water beings and, as in Michel's version, anticipates the flood to come by building a raft or canoe (Nelson, Clay, Ahenakew, Ahenakew and Hardlotte). In other versions (Paget, Russell, Maclean, Stevens and Ray, Bloomfield) the raft is built only after the waters begin to rise. Michel's version is paralleled by two others (Nelson, Maclean) which relate that the transformer lays aside moss for the re-creation of the world and then forgets about it.

The details of *wīsahkīcāhk*'s assault on the water beings are variable between different narratives. In several versions, the transformer disguises himself as a stump at the site where the water beings come out to sleep and then attacks them with spears and kills them (Michel, Nelson, Clay, Russell). In other versions, which parallel the cognate Ojibwa myth in the *nēnapoš* cycle, *wīsahkīcāhk* only wounds the leader of the water beings who then retreats to its underwater lodge. The transformer then kills and impersonates a female frog shamaness and after travelling to the underwater or terrestrial domain of the leader, delivers the *coup de grace* by killing him (Ahenakew, Maclean, Ahenakew and Hardlotte, Ray and Stevens, Skinner). In Bloomfield's version, both assaults occur underwater and in Russell's the episode of the frog impersonation occurs, perhaps erroneously, as a separate story in the cycle. In Paget's second version, *wīsahkīcāhk* simply encounters the terrestrial lodge of giant serpents and, angered by their wolfskin door covering, kills them.

Some interesting variations relate to the wolf hide which becomes the trophy or door covering of the water beings. The Michel and Linklater Rock Cree versions parallel others in having *wīsahkīcāhk* retrieve the wolf hide (Russell, Ahenakew, Maclean, Skinner, Paget [second version]), and the restoration of the brother upon which Mrs. Linklater's Rock Cree segment focuses, occurs also in the Russell, Ahenakew, Ahenakew and Hardlotte and Skinner (1916) versions. The Rock Cree narratives are apparently unique in associating the wolf hide with trees. In Michel's version, the wolf hide, which remains unanimated, is tossed disparagingly up into the branches of the tree into which *wīsahkīcāhk* has transformed. His act of spearing the hide through the eye may simply be a gesture of retrieval, although the breaking of the spear remains enigmatic, or it may represent an attempt at the reanimation successfully accomplished in the Linklater version. There, *wīsahkīcāhk* hangs the retrieved hide on a branch overnight and then seemingly "frightens" it back to life by threatening to chop down the tree. This passage, like one in the *ayās* narrative (infra), is consistent with Rock Cree premises regarding the rebirth or regeneration of slain animals, processes that are influenced or prefigured by respectfully hanging animal bones or skinned-out carcasses in trees.

Most versions represent the flood as proceeding reflexively after the wounding or killing of the water beings, although Michel's version is of interest in having the waters begin to rise after *wīsahkīcāhk*'s portentious utterance: "Let's see what happens if someone kills them." The occurrence of a preliminary flood which begins and then recedes when the transformer wounds the chief of the water beings occurs in Colomb's Rock Cree narrative and also in several of the cognate Ojibwa myths (Jones 1917: 235–78, Radin and Reagan 1928: 70–76, Jenness 1935: 69–70). In more attenuated versions of the flood story, different explanations are given for the deluge. The Swamp Cree version from Fort Albany (Skinner) relates the flood to the destruction of the dam built by *wīsahkīcāhk*'s enemies, the giant beavers. Petitot's Woods Cree versions relate the flood to a giant fish which tries to swamp the transformer's canoe by beating its tail in the water to create waves, and Franklin (1823 1: 113–14) also identifies a fish as the transformer's antagonist. Although these accounts lack or omit the death of the lupine brother, they reproduce the theme of antagonism between *wīsahkīcāhk* and beings associated with water. Several Cree versions also disassociate the flood from the death of *wīsahkīcāhk*'s brother and explain it as resulting from the decision of the creator being to destroy the inhabitants of the earth because of their wickedness. This variant is almost certainly influenced by the scriptural account of the flood but it occurs as early as the late eighteenth century (Thompson, cf. Vandersteene, Dusenberry), well before missionary entrepreneurs were established in the northern areas of Cree territory.

As the flood waters rise, the transformer retreats hastily to his canoe or raft and takes refuge upon it. Mrs. Merasty's Rock Cree narrative is the only known Cree version to parallel several cognate Ojibwa myths in having the transformer seek refuge in a tall tree rather than a raft. A number of versions specify that *wīsahkīcāhk* took animals with him onto the raft in order to preserve them (Nelson, Franklin, Russell, Ahenakew, Ahenakew and Hardlotte, Maclean, Skinner 1916, Ray and Stevens, Paget); certain of these (Petitot, Skinner 1911, Bloomfield, Dusenberry, Godsell) may reflect scriptural influence in specifying that a male and female pair of each species was taken aboard.

The Rock Cree versions omit mention of water monsters attacking the canoe while it is adrift in the flood (Bloomfield, Russell, Nelson), but the details of the "earth diver" episode are remarkably uniform across different versions. Having neglected to bring moss onto the raft, *wīsahkīcāhk* either calls aquatic animals to the raft or deputizes some already present and dispatches them beneath the water with instructions to swim to the bottom and return with a small quantity of earth. In the vast majority of versions, a beaver, an otter, and a muskrat successively make the dive and it is the muskrat that finally succeeds. Skinner's (1911) version is unique in having the muskrat drown without succeeding and *wīsahkīcāhk* uses instead a bit of earth found on the raft. Michel's version neglects mention of the rawhide line that is often secured to the muskrat in order to retrieve it; in another Rock Cree version, the muskrat's tail magically lengthens while *wīsahkīcāhk* holds onto it. The appropriateness of the muskrat as the successful diver is evidenced in Petitot's Woods Cree version:

> *Wissaketchak* prit cette terre, en forma un petit disque, la pt'trit, l'affermit, et placa le disque sur l'eau, ou it surnagea. Il ressemblait a ces petits nids ronds que construisent les rats musqut's sur les eaux congelt'es. (Petitot 1886: 474)

Among other successful divers are the beaver (Swindlehurst) and the otter (Clay). Other unsuccessful divers include the muskrat in the last two cases, a diving duck (Petitot), a fish (Skinner 1911), a mink (Paget [first version]), and unspecified waterfowl (Franklin). Michel's version parallels most others in having the transformer create the new earth by blowing on the mud brought up by the "diver." Absent from Michel's version is the incident in which *wīsahkīcāhk* sends animals or birds out to test the size of the earth (Nelson, Clay, Russell, Ray and Stevens, Ahenakew, Maclean, Ahenakew and Hardlotte, Dusenberry, Paget, Skinner 1911, 1916), and also the creation or re-creation of human beings which occurs as a post-fluvial event in some versions; the latter are discussed under "The Creation of Human Beings," infra. In a few versions, *wīsahkīcāhk* ordains the diets and other characteristics of his animal companions immediately after the flood (Skinner 1911, Paget [first version], Stevens and Ray) and in one (Nelson), he orders the animals to make themselves available as prey to the human beings he has created.

Goose Transformation

A number of other versions have been published (Ahenakew 1929: 351–52, Bloomfield 1934: 289, Clay 1938: 13–14, Curtis 1928: 132, Paget 1909: 194–96, Ray and Stevens 1971: 40–41, Skinner 1911: 87, Skinner 1916: 348) although often in expurgated forms that omit the climactic killing of or defecation upon the old woman. The circular dancing accompanied by song, with which the geese transform *wīsahkīcāhk* in Mr. Umferville's version, is here associated with the exertion of *mamāhtawīsiwin* or strong spiritual power, as also in the reanimation of the weasel in "*wītikōw* and Weasel." In another Rock Cree version, the transformer proposes sexual intercourse rather than money as the old woman's reward. Almost all versions exemplify one of *wīsahkīcāhk*'s more novelistically endearing characteristics: his inability to follow instructions whose violation will bring disastrous consequences. In two versions (Curtis, Paget), *wīsahkīcāhk*'s transformation is only a ruse intended to lead the birds toward human hunters. *wīsahkīcāhk* becomes a swan rather than a goose in two versions (Skinner 1916, Curtis).

The Shut-Eye Dancers

Perhaps the most widely distributed trickster tale in North America, "The Shut-Eye Dancers" has been recorded from many Cree communities (Ahenakew 1929: 330–31; Ahenakew and Hardlotte 1977; Bloomfield 1930: 37–40, 1934: 283–85; Clay 1938: 48–51; Cresswell 1923: 405–06; Curtis 1928: 132; Dusenberry 1962: 240–42; Hamilton 1894: 202; Paget 1909: 188–93; Russell 1896: 212–13; Skinner 1911: 84–85, 1916: 349; Ray and Stevens 1971: 38–39; Vandersteene 1969: 50–52) and is regarded by many Rock Cree as *wīsahkīcāhk*'s apotheosis.

Although some versions (Linklater, Ahenakew and Hardlotte, Cresswell, Hamilton, Skinner 1916) are isolated from the rest of the cycle and conclude with the escape of the surviving waterfowl, most variants of "The Shut-Eye Dancers" continue into further misadventures. Two versions lead into "Squeezed by Trees" (Michel, Ahenakew); *wīsahkīcāhk* asks trees to squeeze him and his feast is stolen while he is held captive. Mrs. Merasty's account appears to be an attenuated form of a longer version which involves *wīsahkīcāhk* with Fox (Bloomfield 1930, 1934; Curtis; Dusenberry; Paget; Vandersteene) and appears to be limited to Plains and Thickwood Cree. While cooking his birds in an earth oven from which their feet protrude, *wīsahkīcāhk* encounters a limping Fox and proposes a foot race prior to a shared feast. Fox agrees and *wīsahkīcāhk* ties a stone to his foot to provide a handicap. Fox lags behind, sneaks back to the camp, eats all of the birds, and then positions their feet as before. *wīsahkīcāhk* returns, discovers the ruse, and angrily pursues the fugitive Fox. Finding him sleeping, he ignites the prairie grass around him; Fox awakens and escapes unscathed, except in a few versions where he is singed red or acquires patchy fur.

Another variant is found among Swampy and Severn Cree (Clay, Russell, Skinner 1911, Ray and Stevens). *wīsahkīcāhk* eats and then decides to sleep and appoints a body part, variously his side, back, or rear-end, as a sentry. The sentry awakens him when human or animal intruders approach, but *wīsahkīcāhk* cannot see them and chastises his body part for waking him needlessly. When the intruders finally steal the remainder of his meal, the body part remains silent. Upon awakening and discovering the theft, *wīsahkīcāhk* punishes the ineffective sentry by burning it. In three versions (Russell, Clay, Stevens and Ray), he proceeds unwittingly to eat scabs from his own burns and is ridiculed loudly by birds ("Scab Eater" infra).

The offending bird who discovers *wīsahkīcāhk*'s treachery in the dancing lodge is usually transformed in some way as punishment. Except in those versions (Curtis, Vandersteene, Ray and Stevens) where all the victims are geese, the offending bird is either a loon (Michel, Merasty, Linklater, Cresswell, Hamilton, Clay, Russell) or a waterhen (Ahenakew, Ahenakew and Hardlotte, Skinner 1916, Dusenberry).

Squeezed by the Trees
Other versions were collected by Ahenakew (1929: 332), Ahenakew and Hardlotte (1977), Bloomfield (1934: 291), Clay (1938: 86–87), Dusenberry (1962: 239), Russell (1896: 209), and Skinner (1911: 87). Like "The Shut-Eye Dancers," "Squeezed by Trees" enters into different combinations with other stories in the *wīsahkīcāhk* cycle. Essentially, the story involves *wīsahkīcāhk* requesting that two trees hold him tightly either to prevent him from eating too soon or, more characteristically, to make him defecate so he can continue to gorge himself. The trees treacherously refuse to release him and animals and birds steal his food while he is immobilized. The story presupposes a surplus of food and thus variously follows "The Shut-Eye Dancers" (Michel, Ahenakew), "Bear's Eye Medicine" (Clay, Skinner), an encounter with a sleeping bear (Russell), or a Plains Cree myth in which *wīsahkīcāhk* tricks and kills buffalo (Bloomfield, Dusenberry). The story is also interwoven with or contiguous to "Muskrat Cools Fat" in four versions. In Clay's version, *wīsahkīcāhk* brings bear fat to the muskrat to cool and then arranges for the trees to squeeze him. While *wīsahkīcāhk* is immobilized, the treacherous muskrat dives, spreads the fat in the water, and then summons other animals to the feast. In Skinner's version, the encounter with the muskrat immediately precedes the squeezing episode and the muskrat is rewarded with a new tail for its services. In two other versions, the muskrat encounter follows immediately the tree-squeezing episode but is not overtly connected with it (Dusenberry, Russell). As in Michel's version, the trees may be specified as birches (Ahenakew, Ahenakew and Hardlotte); the angry *wīsahkīcāhk* whips

them, resulting in marks on the bark, and decrees that they will grow in low-lying country. In two versions (Russell, Skinner), *wīsahkīcāhk* twists his antagonists, resulting in curved branches which are difficult for humans to split for firewood.

Tricks Moose and Squeezed by Birds

The passage describing *wīsahkīcāhk*'s farcical triumph over the moose has not, to my knowledge, been recorded before from Cree sources, but the remainder of the story replicates "Squeezed by Trees." *wīsahkīcāhk* asks two birds to squeeze him so he can relieve himself and they imprison him while animals steal the remainder of his feast. As he does with the antagonistic birch trees, he whips the birds with willows and produces characteristic markings on them.

wītikōw and Weasel

Other verions of this popular narrative were recorded by Ahenakew (1929: 352–53), Ahenakew and Hardlotte (1977), Bloomfield (1930: 293–95), Clay (1938: 68–70), Russell (1896: 211–12), Ray and Stevens (1971: 31–32), and Skinner (1916: 350). Russell's version substitutes a bear for the *wītikōw* and Michel labels the villain a *mistāpēw*. In all cases, however, *wīsahkīcāhk*'s rescuer is a weasel who crawls down the adversary's throat or up its anus and kills it by biting its heart.

The details of the weasel's transformation at the conclusion are variable between versions. All versions except Michel's have *wīsahkīcāhk* rewarding the weasel by changing its coat, and most relate that the transformer institutes the alternation between brown and white summer and winter coats, introduces the white winter coat, and/or establishes the black tip on the tail. Usually the method of transformation is unspecified, although two versions (Ahenakew, Ahenakew and Hardlotte) describe the transformer's use of different-coloured earth. In Mr. Bighetty's Rock Cree version, the original color of the weasel is not described; it emerges from the *wītikōw* black with blood and *wīsahkīcāhk* changes it to white while leaving a black tip on the tail "so the people in the future generation, they'll remember this story for a long time." Only the two Rock Cree versions state that the transformer instituted the name "*sēhkos*" for the weasel which had previously born the derivative epithet *apiscisākwīsis* "small mink."

Mr. Bighetty's version is rich in humorous and expertly performed irony. *wīsahkīcāhk* travels to a point thinking to cadge a meal and finds himself the potential food of a cannibal. Under the *wītikōw*'s hypnotic control, he is forced to collaborate in the project of his own culinary preparation and is sent out to cut the seven roasting sticks that the *wītikōw*, after ruminatively counting his victim's body parts, concludes will be necessary. Similar ironies are found in Mrs. Merasty's version in which *wīsahkīcāhk* encounters the *wītikōw* after vainly boasting that he will twist its neck and is forced to assemble his funeral pyre from the wood he has cut while breaking trail.

Eye Juggler
Another story of wide North American distribution, "Eye Juggler" has been recorded from other Cree sources by Ahenakew (1929: 347–49), Ahenakew and Hardlotte (1977), Bloomfield (1934: 285–87), Dusenberry (1962: 235–36), Russell (1896: 215–16), and Vandersteene (1969: 49–50). Mrs. Merasty's version parallels Vandersteene's in treating the eye-juggling power as a game or amusement that *wīsahkīcāhk* desires to learn; in other versions, eye-juggling is intended to cure headaches or sore eyes. *wīsahkīcāhk* learns the trick from birds except in one version where an elderly medicine man instructs him (Russell). The birds are variously tomtits (Ahenakew), kildeers (Ahenakew and Hardlotte), Candada jays or whiskey jacks (Bloomfield), and chickadees (Vandersteene). In two versions, *wīsahkīcāhk* impersonates an elderly man with a headache in order to persuade the birds to teach him the trick. Usually *wīsahkīcāhk* is told that the trick can only be performed two (Michel), three (Dusenberry), or four (Ahenakew, Ahenakew and Hardlotte, Bloomfield) times. In two versions (Merasty, Vandersteene), he attempts the trick on the spot and immediately loses his eyes. In Merasty's version, the comedy attending the knowledge that *wīsahkīcāhk* will try the trick one time too often is supplanted by his willingness to juggle his second eye after having already lost the first; here the birds egg him on, exhorting him to "Try the other one, older brother, you'll be sure to succeed."

Having lost his eyes, *wīsahkīcāhk* is in most versions teased by Fox who diverts himself by poking branches in the empty eye sockets. In three narratives (Michel, Merasty, Russell), *wīsahkīcāhk* manages to grab Fox and compels him to fashion new eyes for him out of spruce resin. In other versions, *wīsahkīcāhk* himself successively encounters trees and asks their names, finally making his own resin eyes when he encounters a spruce (Ahenakew, Ahenakew and Hardlotte, Bloomfield, Dusenberry, Vandersteene). In three versions, he attempts to revenge himself on Fox by burning him (Ahenakew, Ahenakew and Hardlotte, Russell). The attempted burning of Fox occurs several times as the final incident in "The Shut-Eye Dancers"; in two versions (Merasty, Bloomfield), "Eye Juggler" immediately follows that story and continues the hostility between the two characters.

The Startlers
Other versions were recorded by Ahenakew (1929: 333–34), Bloomfield (1930: 23–25, 1934: 281), Clay (1938: 12–13), Dusenberry (1962: 237–38), and Russell (1896: 211). In the three Rock Cree versions *wīsahkīcāhk*'s antagonists are identified as *piðīyak* "spruce partridges." In other versions they are identified as

"grouse" (Russell), "prairie chickens" (Dusenberry [Cree form "*pah-ha-yo*"]), "prairie chickens" (Ahenakew), "partridges" (Bloomfield [Cree form "*pihēwak*"]), or a conspiracy of "ruffled grouses," "willow partridges," "spruce partridges," and "sharptailed grouses" (Clay). In Mr. Umferville's version the bird's trick is unmotivated and in Clay's narrative they conspire against *wīsahkīcāhk* for unspecified injuries. In the other versions, *wīsahkīcāhk* encounters infant birds and demands to know their names. Upon repeated inquiry, he finds that they or their mother possess a name formed from verbs for "startle" or "frighten." Amused that birds should possess such names, *wīsahkīcāhk* disparagingly defecates on the birds, farts on them (Bighetty), or, more delicately, simply frightens them (Russell). The mother of the befouled chicks learns the perpetrator's identity and, either alone or with companions, flies up out of the brush and frightens *wīsahkīcāhk* as he is about to leap across a river; he winds up in the water, soaking his leather clothing. Mr. Michel's version is unparalleled in having the bird pour cold water in the transformer's ear as a prelude to his immersion. Rock Crees related the narrative to the propensity of spruce partridges to take flight and startle people who inadvertently flush them. The story often precedes "Fooled by Reflections" (Umferville; Linklater; Bloomfield 1930, 1934; Clay).

The Farting Hunter
"The Farting Hunter" has also been recorded by Bloomfield (1934: 291), Dusenberry (1962: 148–49), Paget (1909: 197–99), and Ray and Stevens (1971: 39–40). Two versions begin with *wīsahkīcāhk* following the sound of voices until he encounters clusters of *okinīyak* or roseberry bushes (Michel, Ray and Stevens). He asks what will happen if he eats them and they reply that they produce itching. *wīsahkīcāhk* stuffs himself and, of course, suffers itching in consequence. Undaunted, he disregards the advice from the next plants he encounters, usually lichens, and gorges himself upon them despite their warning that they produce uncontrolled farting. Soon, *wīsahkīcāhk* is breaking wind to such a degree that his prospective game is always frightened away. Angry with his rear-end for spoiling his hunting, he heats rocks and then sits upon them, burning the offending body part and finally silencing it. In two versions (Linklater, Dusenberry), this story immediately precedes "Scab Eater" (infra). In the Severn Cree versions (Ray and Stevens), *wīsahkīcāhk* throws his burn scabs onto poplar trees whose black markings they predestine. Paget's bowdlerized Plains Cree version has *wīsahkīcāhk* eat grass after simply being warned that it will interfere with his hunting. He is unable to shoot game and regains the ability to do so only after apologizing to the plants and enduring a moralistic lecture.

Bear's Eye Medicine
Other versions were recorded by Ahenakew (1929: 349–50), Clay (1938: 85–88), and Skinner (1911: 86, 1916: 347–48). As in Mr. Michel's version, the Clay version and a variant mentioned by Skinner (1911) have *wīsahkīcāhk* living with the bear in order to supervise its fattening before the berry trick is played; in these latter two cases he allays the bear's suspicions by claiming that they were once genealogical brothers. It is interesting to see in this "fattening" regime parallels with certain Cree techniques for harvesting rabbits. Jackpine trees, for example, are cut down and arranged in parallel rows for purposes of snaring rabbits, but it is only after rabbits have congregated at the site and become fat on the needles that snares will be hung over the runs. Similarly, cub bears were sometimes kept and fattened before butchering and consumption, although, as one would expect, some Crees became fond of the animals and ultimately released them in the bush instead. In the Skinner (1911), Ahenakew, and Umferville versions, the trick proceeds immediately after their encounter.

In the Michel, Umferville, and Skinner (1911) versions, the berry juice is intended to remedy sore eyes while in the Ahenakew and Clay versions it is supposed to produce a euphoric effect. In each case, *wīsahkīcāhk* kills the bear after disabling it with the berry juice. In two cases, the story is immediately followed by "Muskrat Cools Fat." Skinner's (1916) Plains Cree version reverses the roles of transformer and bear. *wīsahkīcāhk*, desiring to have small eyes like the bear, is fooled by the latter into putting glue in his eyes; the bear then abandons him. *wīsahkīcāhk* attempts to orient himself by identifying trees in a passage paralleling the ending of some versions of "Eye Juggler." Finally removing the glue in a river, he revenges himself on the bear by luring it into a sweat lodge and killing it. However, in a passage paralleling "Squeezed by Trees," he gets his hand caught in tree branches and is imprisoned while a wolf steals his bear meat.

Muskrat Cools Fat
Other versions were recorded by Bloomfield (1934: 86–87), Clay (1938: 85–88), Dusenberry (1962: 240), Russell (1896: 209–10), Skinner (1911: 86–87), and Vandersteene (1969: 48–49). Most versions follow Michel in having *wīsahkīcāhk* approach a muskrat with a bladder of hot grease and request that it carry the grease through the water to harden it. The muskrat agrees and in two versions (Skinner, Russell) *wīsahkīcāhk* rewards it by narrowing its tail so that it can swim more rapidly. Joe Michel's attenuated version makes no mention of the grease but contains the tail-narrowing episode; this account also appears to begin with a fragment of "Bear's Eye Medicine" in which *wīsahkīcāhk* keeps company with an intended victim in order to fatten it up. In three versions (Michel, Bloomfield, Dusenberry), the muskrat cautions *wīsahkīcāhk* not to frighten him and the latter,

of course, cannot resist doing so, resulting in the loss of the grease which is spread through the water. In other versions, the muskrat spills the fat, either accidentally (Vandersteene, Skinner) or on purpose (Russell, Clay). In two versions, the story is fused with "Squeezed by Birches." In Skinner's Swampy Cree version, *wīsahkīcāhk* is squeezed and imprisoned by trees after the fat is spilled and animals come to eat both his bear meat and the fat. Similarly in Clay's Swampy Cree version, the muskrat dumps the fat after the transformer is immobilized and then summons animals to eat the bear meat. Four versions explain the differential fat content of animals in terms of their consumption of or exposure to the spilled fat (Clay, Dusenberry, Russell, Skinner). In one case (Vandersteene), the muskrat burns the hair from his tail with the spilled fat and *wīsahkīcāhk* angrily decrees that hairless tails will endure among muskrats as a punishment.

Fly Transformation
Other versions were recorded by Bloomfield (1934: 287–89) and Dusenberry (1962: 249). These parallel Michel's version in most particulars, although they place greater emphasis on the flies' cautionary remonstrances about the transformation and *wīsahkīcāhk*'s characteristic disregard for advice.

Fooled by Reflections
Other Cree versions of this widely distributed trickster story were recorded by Bloomfield (1930: 25, 1934: 281–83), Clay (1938: 12–13), and Russell (1896: 281–83). Michel's version closely parallels that of Russell in having the transformer encounter a seemingly dead beaver who subsequently revives and disappears into the water with his game or fire bag. All the other versions have *wīsahkīcāhk*'s tobacco bag or loin cloth (Clay) wind up in the tree when he is frightened by birds in "The Startlers," and all dwell on his farcical attempts to retrieve the reflection in the water. Bloomfield's (1930) version adds a comical conclusion of the "spite your face" variety: having finally found and recovered his bag from the tree, and still greatly in need of a smoke, *wīsahkīcāhk* petulantly discards it.

Scab Eater
Other versions were collected by Clay (1938: 55–56), Dusenberry (1962: 148–49), Ray and Stevens (1971: 39–40), Russell (1895: 212–13), and Skinner (1911: 86, 1916: 350–51). With the exception of Michel's account, all other versions of "Scab Eater" follow either "The Farting Hunter" (Linklater, Dusenberry, Ray and Stevens, Skinner 1916) or the concluding events of "The Shut-Eye Dancers" in which *wīsahkīcāhk* angrily burns his back or rear-end for its failure as a sentry (Clay, Russell, Skinner 1911). In the longer versions, *wīsahkīcāhk* becomes confused about his whereabouts and doubles back on his path, encountering pieces

of scab that have dropped from his body. Thinking them to be pemmican or dry meat, he eats them and is observed by amused and voluble birds who announce publically that he is eating his own scabs. In three versions (Michel, Dusenberry, Skinner 1916), *wīsahkīcāhk* responds, evidently in earnest, that he is eating pemmican prepared by his mother or grandmother. This bit of dialogue is extremely humorous to Rock Cree although the import of the kinship reference is not clear to me. In three versions, *wīsahkīcāhk*, upon discovering the identity of his food, throws it against birch trees where it becomes the archetype of *posākan* or the birch fungus used by Crees to tinder fires (Michel, Skinner 1911, Russell). In one account (Skinner 1911) he then whips the trees, producing the cracks usually accounted for in "Squeezed by Trees." The Severn Cree version (Ray and Stevens) has him throw the scabs onto poplar, creating black markings on them. Clay's version is of interest both for the transformation of the red willow which is stained by blood from the burns and for the transformation of the scabs themselves into lichen or rock tripe. This is obviously a reversed form of "Farting Hunter" in which consumption of lichens results in the uncontrolled flatulance that prompts the burning (infra).

Moose Transformation
"Moose Transformation" parallels the "Goose Transformation" and "Fly Transformation" narratives in emphasizing *wīsahkīcāhk*'s inability to behave competently in his new form. The inventory of his inappropriate responses is juxtaposed humorously to that of the moose, a species regarded by Rock Crees as extremely intelligent and requiring considerable expertise to hunt.

Marries Daughter
Other versions were recorded by Curtis (1928: 132–33) and Skinner (1916: 350–51); Dusenberry (1962: 248–52) recorded two stories in a similar vein in which *wīsahkīcāhk* disguises himself in order to marry a chief's daughter and is later identified by his burn scars. Skinner's Plains Cree version parallels those of Michel, Linklater, and Merasty, although it includes a beginning in which *wīsahkīcāhk* fathers a daughter. Mrs. Linklater's version concludes with quoted speech nicely summarizing the *wīsahkīcāhk* persona: "It was that *wīsahkīcāhk* again. He was sleeping with his own daughter."

Imitates Baby
Two other versions (Clay 1938: 11, Ray and Stevens 1971: 36) are known. The Clay version involves a boy rather than an infant and the feat which *wīsahkīcāhk* tries to duplicate involves putting the foot over the neck. As Clay adds, "And the Indians very naively tell you that because a boy was once smarter than

wīsahkīcāhk, all boys are saucy!" The Ray and Stevens version, which is more detailed, has *wīsahkīcāhk* accepting a mother's challenge to duplicate all the activities of her infant. *wīsahkīcāhk* dutifully gurgles, sucks his thumb, eats objectionable substances, and soils his clothes; finally, exhausted and annoyed, he kills the infant task-maker. The punchline of the Rock Cree version was considered extremely humorous, the comedy proceeding apparently from the incongruity of the great *wīsahkīcāhk* using *nistīs* "my elder brother" to address a baby. In addition to the fact that use of this term can signal a measure of respect for the greater experience of elder brothers, it also contrasts with the ubiquitous *nisīmīy* "my younger sibling" with which *wīsahkīcāhk* addresses all animate and inanimate creation. *wīsahkīcāhk*'s insistence on these terms of address is exemplified in an interesting Plains Cree myth (Dusenberry 1962: 238) possibly influenced by Cree knowledge of Coyote as the comparable trickster-transformer character among some Plains and Plateau groups. *wīsahkīcāhk* and Coyote agree to a contest which will determine which of them is the oldest: they will sit immobile in the expectation that the youngest will die first. They remain there for years, each asking at two-year intervals whether the other is still living. When Coyote finally fails to respond, *wīsahkīcāhk* "triumphantly departs," but the Coyote subsequently rouses and addresses his opponent as "younger sibling":

> "Nobody must call me Me-sem [*misīm* 'younger sibling']," said Wi-sak-a-chak, "for I am the oldest." And the coyote ran away for he was afraid Wi-sak-a-chak would kill him.

wīsahkīcāhk Changes Frog, Bear, and Muskrat

I have been unable to locate other versions of this story, although Clay (1938: 80) obtained a somewhat similar etiological motif describing how the frog's originally short legs were lengthened. The story is of interest in representing animal transformations not as the random consequences of events but as linked to an implicit cosmic design to which *wīsahkīcāhk* refers in his climactic address to his victims. The animals' attempts to extricate themselves from the traps in which *wīsahkīcāhk* leaves them become, from this point of view, the means that produce preordained changes in their appearances.

CHAPTER 4
Other ācaðōhkīwina

Introduction: The *pawākan* and the *wītikōw*

Although both the *pawākan* and the *wītikōw* have already figured in several of the stories collected here, some amplification may enhance readers' understanding and appreciation of the narratives that follow.

pawākan, perhaps analyzable as "dream image," refers to the entity conventionally referred to as the "spirit guardian" (cf. Benedict 1923). Discussions of the *pawākan* in Cree culture can be found in Skinner (1911: 61–62), Merasty (1974: 15–27), Rossignol (1939b: 69–70), Mason (1967: 47–48; 61–62), Honigmann (1956: 71–72), and Cockburn (1985: 41–42). The information given below pertains specifically to the Rock Cree of northwestern Manitoba, although it is presumably relevant to related groups in Saskatchewan.

pawākan can refer to any animate nonhuman agency that enters into a relationship of reciprocal obligation and support with an individual human. People experience their *pawākanak* (plural) primarily in their dreams or in waking trance states, and the concept presupposes a Cree understanding of animals as spiritually complex, soul-owning creatures and of a vital or animating spiritual component to other objects and processes in the biophysical environment and also in the sphere of human manufacture. Formerly, the *pawākan* was acquired by men during a vision fast in the bush at puberty and subsequent fasting was sometimes undergone to acquire further guardians. Women sometimes underwent the fast but more typically acquired a *pawākan* in a less premeditated way by dreaming. Although some persons still fast in the bush, it appears to be more common today for persons of both sexes to acquire a *pawākan* through uninduced dreams. Formerly people fasted at sites associated with the beings they desired to communicate, although there appears to have been a generalized tendency to await the vision on tree platforms or scaffolds that removed the dreamer from the ground and placed him or her in contact with the upper air. These platforms were often built on the shores of lakes and rivers to facilitate communication with aquatic or underground beings.

The vision itself could be experienced either in a waking or dreaming state, both being glossed in English as "dream." The content of visions is difficult to interpret and doubtless also for the visionary to communicate. Typically, an animal or other entity manifested itself to the visionary, sometimes alternating between its conventional appearance and a human form. The entity addressed the faster, either telepathically or verbally, and provided songs, promises of assistance, and instructions relating to the dreamer's aspirations and objectives. In some instances, events which occurred in the dream were understood to prefigure events that would transpire many years later in the faster's adult life. In many cases, these dream experiences were understood to symbolize rather than literally replicate the wordly events they predestined, and all aspects of the dream or vision could be subject to interpretation. Rock Crees emphasized that boys were instructed to think very carefully about the content of their dream after returning to camp. The fast ordinarily lasted for three days with unsuccessful visionaries repeating the attempt thereafter until they succeeded. Most men possessed one or more *pawākanak* and many women were also said to acquire them. It was emphasized that a wide variety of objects including animals, the four winds, ice, snow, sunbeams, trees, lakes, rapids, topographic sites, and celestial phenomena could manifest themselves as a *pawākanak*.

Powerful individuals typically possessed multiple *pawākanak* and it is understood that a single agency is never simultaneously the *pawākan* of two persons. Success and skill in conventional tasks and occupations in the daily round were understood to be influenced by the *pawākan*, as were, of course, more specialized abilities such as extraordinarily successful hunting, use of the shaking lodge, curing, and the capacity to survive dangerous situations. Reciprocally, the human partner typically was obligated to make offerings of food and goods to his *pawākan* whom he addressed as *nimosōm* "my grandfather." Although the *pawākan* was usually understood as superior in power to its human patron, some powerful men were represented as superordinate over their nonhuman guardians.

A recurring theme in Rock Cree discussions of the *pawākan* is its capacity to substitute for the human patron in situations of conflict. Mr. Jeremiah Michel stated that "If you get into trouble with something, it will take your place and kill that thing" and that when two men were angry it would usually be their *pawākanak* who would fight. He concluded that "The owner wasn't strong but the *pawākan* was." Continuing discussion with Rock Crees underscores the fact that many aspects of the *pawākan* experience remain to be understood by non-Indians. Cockburn (1985: 41–42), for example, provides a text stating that animals possess *pawākanak*, although individual animals are usually themselves identified as being the *pawākanak* of humans by Rock Crees.

The text suggests that the *pawākan* relationship is extended such that animals themselves, and perhaps other beings, can also possess patrons. Another problematic issue concerns the transmission of the *pawākan* between generations. Sons were said to sometimes acquire the *pawākan* of their fathers. The *pawākan* is explicitly distinguished by Crees from the personal soul or *ahcahk* with which a person is born. However, Mr. Michel stated that a pregnant woman might pass on as a *pawākan* to her unborn child a being of which she dreamt during gestation; the infant was then born with a *pawākan* already in its possession.

The Algonquian understanding of the *wītikōw* or *wīhtikōw* (Ojibwa *wīntikō*) has engaged the interest of numerous scholars and the reader is referred to Teacher (1960), Fogelson (1965), and Marano (1982) for general discussions. The remarks below again focus on the category as defined by Rock Crees (cf. Smith 1976b).

The term *wītikōw* refers to a cannibalistic monster that was previously a human being; Rock Crees did not recognize a nonhuman "*wītikōw*-spirit" or any kind of *wītikōw* lacking human antecedency. In initial stages, *wītikōwak* may conceal their condition, but they inevitably degenerate into disfigured and mentally impaired creatures with torn and dirty clothing, long ungroomed hair, and lips and fingers stripped bare of flesh from autocannibalism. As Johnny Bighetty put it succinctly, "They don't look like a living thing. They look like they're dead." The gigantism ascribed to the *wītikōw* by Ojibwas and some Swamp Cree groups was not known to Rock Cree.

Rock Crees recognized four ways in which people could become a *wītikōw*. Practitioners of famine cannibalism were said to turn into them in some cases, although no stories of such events were collected and typical *wītikōw* stories deal with already transformed monsters. Secondly, transformation could follow possession by "some kind of spirit" associated with the north. On the strength of Nelson's (1823) data on Cree at Lac la Ronge, these beings were probably Ice and North Wind. A related etiology links the *wītikōw* to the spirit guardian fast; a person may inadvertently acquire Ice or an existing *wītikōw* as his *pawākan* and will then subsequently transform in later life. Finally, people who freeze to death in winter are said to become *wītikōwak*. It is said that persons "get cold air in their mind" when they freeze and that their brains continue to function although the rest of their body dies. With the warmth of spring, they become reanimated in a demented condition and seek human victims.

The most salient characteristic of the *wītikōw* is its voracious anthropophagy, and it is said that they usually consume their victims raw after first exerting a hypnotic or melancholic influence which immobilizes them. *wītikōwak* are understood as being nocturnal and as perceiving human beings as game animals. Their degeneration from human status is accompanied by a great increase in spiritual power over their victims and, as the narratives indicate, they are usually overcome only with the aid of the *pawākan* or spirit guardian. They reject conventional food: "And then if you feed him good food he won't take it. Never mind if you put food out, he won't touch it. It just wants to eat people. That's what it's hungry for."

The associations of the *wītikōw* with starvation and with cold weather will be obvious to the reader. The voracity of the *wītikōw* and its connection with famine cannibalism suggest starvation as does its period of maximum activity during the spring which, in earlier years and prior to open water, was the season when hunger posed the greatest threat to Crees. Other associations with cold weather include the connections with the malignant Ice and North Wind beings, the propensity of the *wītikōw* to approach its human victims from the north, its frozen heart and viscera, and death by freezing as a transforming agency.

During the period when these stories were collected, popular interest in Sasquatch or Bigfoot was high in both Canada and the United States. Crees tended to associate the two beings, but made clear that they were distinct. Sidney Castel emphasized that the sasquatch might be seen at any time of year and also that it didn't harm people. Similarly, Jeremy Caribou compared the two in the following words:

> That person [*wītikōw*] believes he's the supreme guy. He's the best guy, he can kill the other guy, he can even eat him up. It's just that evil spirit, that evil spirit in him that's conducting his mind. But I know there were some good guys in the [pre-Catholic] past. There were still some good people living. Like my great grandfather there, he was one of them. And he didn't believe in this evil spirit. Maybe he did but he still had enough reason in him that he could oppose these things. He used to go out there and kill those guys. There were still some good guys. Even though the Devil was in control of most of them. And I still think these *wītikōw* they had here, that's nothing compared to Sasquatch (nothing like the sasquatch). Sasquatch, Bigfoot, maybe that's an animal. They don't hurt people. That's different. They're shy from people. They don't hurt people at all. Not like that *wītikōw* they had here. They'd kill him. Eat him. That's like what you call cannibals in the north. Well, they had cannibals in the South Seas. It must be the same. He (sasquatch) must have been formed before like the animals. They're just a little bit different. They're just few.

Rock Crees differ as to the present existence of the *wītikōw*, although most people agree that they existed in the past in great numbers. The *wītikōw* disorder is often said to have been the only form of serious illness prior to the intrusion of the Whites. Joe Bighetty provided a "rational" explanation based on mental illness; he suggested that people who nearly froze to death in storms became crazy and cannibalistic after near-starvation. Today such people would be dealt with by doctors, but care would not usually have been available in the last century. Many persons still believe in and fear the *wītikōw* and encounters with them persist into the present. The disappearance of a child at Nelson House in 1975 was attributed to a *wītikōw* and persons may adjust their territorial movements in conformity to rumors or dreams locating a *wītikōw* in a particular area. One individual suggested that persons who laugh about or profess disbelief about *wītikōw* while in town do not do so if they're on the trapline. The term *wītikōw* is often used metaphorically to refer to insane, gluttonous, or dangerous individuals, but its central meaning continues to be that of a spiritually empowered cannibal monster that was previously a human being.

Other *ācaðōhkīwina*

The Origin of Animals
Narrator: Johnny Bighetty
I don't know any stories about how the animals were first made. They say that they were here before the human people. But my father told me something that the old people a long time ago learned in their dreams. The animals came into the Churchill River country flying from the four directions. Some kinds came from the south and some from the north and the east and west. All the dangerous animals came from the north. That happened in the time that *wīsahkīcāhk* was alive.

Discussion
Mr. Bighetty's account is typical in presupposing the existence of animals rather than directly describing their origin. The emphasis on the four cardinal directions is characteristic of Algonquian religion and philosophy and parallels an Ojibwa-influenced Cree cosmogonic myth (Brown 1977) in which different aspects of the biophysical environment are introduced from different directions by the four Wind brothers. Stories relating to the *origin* or creation of animals or of particular species are exceedingly rare and are predictably unstandardized between different narratives and different communities. Some Rock Crees speculate that bears might at one time have been human beings, paralleling a Saulteaux myth recorded by George Nelson (1811) in which beavers are explained as human transforms. However, another Ojibwa or Saulteaux account (Thompson 1962: 155) emphasizes that beavers were never human beings. Some hominid characters in myth are represented as transforming into the first or prototype specimen of a species. Thus *wīmisōsiw* becomes in different versions the first northern pike (Rock Cree) or Canada jay (Russell 1896: 205), and *ayās* and his mother (infra) become the prototypes, respectively, of the crow and woodpecker. Many stories focus on the

transformation or innovation of behavioral or physical characteristics of animals by the transformer. Paget (1909: 176–77) describes such transformations by *wīsahkīcāhk* after the flood and Clay's (1938) Swampy Cree collection is especially rich in such stories. Thompson (1962: 78) noted the belief that *wīsahkīcāhk* regenerated the different animal species from their bones after the flood. The only story known to the author that describes a generalized origin of animals is a remarkable Plains Cree narrative by Ahenakew (1929: 319–20) in which the transformer creates the different species from the bodies of the "Short Noses," or "Up-Standing Cattle," a class of anthropophagous animals that afflicted the early humans. Ahenakew's story parallels references in other myths to anthropophagous animals preying on early humans and/or to an unregulated regime of carnivorousness in which all animals ate each other (Bloomfield 1930: 19, Ray and Stevens 1971: 75, Vandersteene 1969: 43).

God's Oven
Narrator: Albert Umferville
Now I'm going to tell it again in English. When I was overseas the time of the war, there was a bunch of officers laying out on the lawn and I happened to be passing by there with just my shorts. And I had my shirt off and one of the officers called to me and he said, "Umferville, what do you want to get a tan for? You're black enough…"

So I turned around and told him. I says, "I don't burn like you guys. I'm natural." And I says, "You know when God made the world, he made men. He made a man. The first one he made of his image, he put in the oven. And while he was working he forgot all about it. When he did think about it, when he opened his oven and pulled his image out, it was burned black. Well, that was the Negro. So the next image of himself that he made, he put it in the oven. And he didn't leave it long enough. So when he pulled it out, it was still pale and that was the White man. So when he made the third image of himself, he put it in the oven. And went to work for awhile. He waited for awhile before he opened his oven. And when he did, it was just nicely browned. So that was me, I told my officer, "just nice and brown. I'm an Indian."

Discussion
Mr. Umferville here deployed to good rhetorical effect a Cree tradition of wide distribution and probably of pre-Columbian antiquity. The earliest eighteenth-century reference to human creation in Cree belief (Wales in Cooper 1934: 56) describes the molding by the creator deity "*Ukkemah*" (*okimāw* "leader"/"chief") of three figures from different coloured clays; the excessively dark and light colouring of the first two cause the creator to discard them and they become the

progenitors of the Black and White "races." The creator retains the aesthetically satisfying "brown" figure which becomes the first Indian. This polygenist account of creation, based either on different coloured materials or differential baking, occurs also in versions by Nelson (1823), Skinner (1911: 112), Ray and Stevens (1971: 24–25), and Rossignol (1939b: 68).

Like most versions, Mr. Umferville's account is not temporally situated relative to other mythological events. However, four accounts locate the creation of human beings as an event that transpires immediately after the flood and identify *wīsahkīcāhk* (Nelson 1823, Vandersteene 1969: 48, Ray and Stevens 1971: 24–25), or the creator deity (Bloomfield 1930: 19) as the architect. Nelson's (Brown and Brightman 1987) version describes the creation of a male and female pair but departs from other myths that account for both sexes (Bloomfield, Vandersteene, Wales in Cooper, Dusenberry 1962: 66) by identifying the Moon as the separate creator of women and of menstruation. In Nelson's account, the scriptural motif of female creation from a male rib is applied only to Whites; other versions (Bloomfield, Dusenberry) apply this element to Indians. In Vandersteene's version, *wīsahkīcāhk* creates two male and female figures and then removes their sides to create children. In Bloomfield's version, the creator being makes two men and then creates two women from their ribs. The Bloomfield and Vandersteene versions give the name of the first man ("Dugout Canoe" and "Crooked Canoe" respectively) and note that his first utterances were requests for food and water.

With the exception of Dusenberry's Plains Cree version, in which the creator animates two-dimensional figures outlined on the ground, all accounts represent humans as fashioned from earth or clay; this applies apparently also to Denig's (1952: 68) anomalous Plains Cree variant in which humans spring from multiple images that rise out of the ground and are animated by the rays of the sun. In Nelson's version, *wīsahkīcāhk* fashions the first image from stone but then substitutes clay after reflecting that humans would be too aggressive and long-lived. A related Saulteaux version (Simms 1906: 338–40) similarly describes the substitution of clay after a jealous bear ruins the first stone image.

Since human, or in any event, hominid characters appear in myths describing events prior to the flood, it might be inferred that the post-fluvial human creations are actually secondary recreations. Only the *wīsahkīcāhk* cycle in Ray and Stevens (1971: 21, 25) appears to specify that there were no humans on earth prior to their creation after the flood. Most Rock Crees state that there were humans or human-like beings in the world before the flood, although they emphasize that there were very few. As Hallowell (1955: 232–33) noted for the Saulteaux, a concern with the temporal ordering of mythological events is often absent. This lack of concern may indicate a genuine indifference to temporal ordering in Cree cosmogonic and cosmological thought or it may point to characteristics of this thought that have yet to be delineated by non-Indians. As indicated in an earlier section, some narrators possess ideas of sequential ordering that apply to certain of the *wīsahkīcāhk* stories.

Wolverine and Wolf
Narrator: Selazie Linklater
Translator: Caroline Caribou

Once then and long ago this happens in that time when the animals spoke and acted like human beings. One wolverine and he intends to marry the young daughter of a family of wolves. So he travels in the bush to where that wolf family stays and he asks the old woman, the mother of that wolf-girl, if she will agree to the marriage. Really, she thinks badly of it. "Really, I should not let them marry," she thinks to herself. But she consents. Then that wolf-girl went off to live with that wolverine. They have several male children. All of them are wolverines except for one only who is a wolf.

Soon that wolf family is starving. The wolves are not able to kill moose or caribou. "He [wolverine] intends for us to starve," that old woman thought about the wolverine. And really that wolverine was throwing bad hunting luck towards them. He curses them so that they cannot kill any animals; he intends that they should all starve [Mrs. Caribou observes that wolverines are always greedy and that the wolverine, being a poor moose hunter, wanted to secure all the game in the district for himself]. But she continues to send her sons out to hunt moose. Finally they kill one moose and they bring it back to their lodge in the evening. The old woman cooks all of that moose. She knows that the wolverine comes always to spy on their camp and she wants him to know that they have killed and cooked a moose. So really they feasted on moose that night. And then in the night they moved their camp some distance away.

In the morning, that wolverine comes to the wolf camp intending to spy on them there. But all those wolves are departed. He returns to his camp and wakes his wife.

He spoke falsely about them, "Really, I'm concerned about the welfare of our relatives. Perhaps they moved camp because they are starving." He sends those wolverine boys to look for the wolves. They find the new camp and they see that the wolves have much moose meat. Just there on the trail to that camp are scraps of moose meat. Really very greedy are those wolverine boys and they fight over the scraps.

The wolverine boys return to their father and tell him what they have seen. The wolverine has only a little beaver meat; he intends to visit the wolf family and trade with them for moose meat. "I will go on ahead to visit our relatives," he told them, his wife and sons. "Break the camp and follow after me." He goes on ahead of them to the new camp and offers his wolf brothers-in-law the beaver meat.

One wolf says, "our brother-in-law is hungry. We should offer him some moose meat."

To one side that old woman said to her son, "Why should we feed him? This is the one who tried to starve us all." Finally she agrees to feed the wolverine.

"If wolves are to hunt successfully, they must close their eyes when eating moose meat," she says to that wolverine.

"I also will close my eyes while eating," he said to her. They sit around the fire and the wolverine closes his eyes as he eats moose meat. The old woman picks up a stone from the fireplace and strikes him immediately on the head. That wolverine is unconscious, but he doesn't die; soon he begins to move around. Then she throws another rock and she kills the wolverine. Then they bring his body outside of the lodge and they bury it in front so that only the tail sticks up vertically out of the snow.

Soon they come there, the wolf-girl, she who married the wolverine, and also the children. They pull their toboggans into camp. They see the tail protruding from the snow and begin to weep.

The old woman said, "It was necessary for me to kill him because he was trying to starve all of us to death. And I have to tell you this also that we must kill your children because they will resemble their father in their behavior when they mature." And really the old woman kills all of those children except the boy who looked like a wolf. That boy was generous and would always bring a little meat to the old woman when they were starving. That is finished.

Discussion

"Wolverine and Wolf" is one of a number of myths that represent characters identified as animals in hominid terms; they speak, arrange marriages, practice sorcery, exchange food, live in camps, and use toboggans. In other myths, hominid animal characters interact with what appear to be human beings as in the story of *ayās*. Additionally in many other narratives, animals converse with humans (the *wīsahkīcāhk* cycle, "*maskōkosān*," "The Woman Who Married the Bear"), although it is not clear that their hominid characteristics are foregrounded to the degree found here. It is interesting that these hominid animals in "Wolverine and Wolf" are conceptualized as at least partially zoomorphic, evidenced by reference to the wolverine's tail, and also that they prey on beaver and moose, herbivores who are not themselves described here in hominid terms. Implicitly, such myths suggest that animals, subsequent to the mythological age, underwent transformations in which they became less hominid and lost the facility for conventional communication with humans. Some Crees speculate that the differences between humans and animals, as they are manifested to conventional waking perception in the present, are in some sense illusory and that animals continue to possess human characteristics that are not available to ordinary human awareness. In dreams and in the shaking lodge ceremony, animals in the present continue to manifest infrahuman characteristics.

Another version of this story occurs in Ahenakew's (1929: 322–24) *wīsahkīcāhk* cycle where it recedes "The Flood and the New Earth." In this version, *wīsahkīcāhk's* lupine brother departs to rejoin his wolf family and discovers that his wife has been killed and his mother-in-law and son left impoverished by a wolverine. There is no mention of a marriage of the wolf woman to the wolverine and consequently no "hybrid" wolf and wolverine children, although the wolverine's sons are represented, like the lupine son in Linklater's version, as generous and are consequently spared. The two versions are parallel in having the old wolf woman lure the wolverine to her new camp with moose meat and then dispose of him with the shut-eye ruse. An additional version from the Swamp Cree has been recorded (Skinner 1911: 98–100).

The Bear Abductor
Narrator: Johnny Bighetty

There was a hunter who was always being helped by a bear in his dreams. But this man broke promises that he made to the bear. He didn't do what was right for the bear. So this bear told the man in a dream that he was going to take away his son. And then that man's son disappeared. The bear took it away and kept him in his den all winter. That hunter grieved for his son and was always weeping. Finally, that bear felt sorry for the man. After a long time, the bear talked again to the man in his dreams and told him how to find the den where his son was staying. He told that hunter to go into the bush in a certain direction until he crossed a moose trail. He was ordered not to follow that moose trail or to try and hunt that moose, eh? He has to keep on going until he finds a rabbit trail. Then he has to follow that rabbit trail.

The next day at sunrise, the hunter goes out. He does just what he tells him, eh? Just what the bear tells him. He crosses the moose trail but he doesn't do nothing. He finds the rabbit trail beyond and he follows it along until he sees snow piled up and yellow snow there. That's the bear's house there. So then he began to dig at the snow. And from inside he hears his son calling, "Papa! Papa!" Finally he gets all that snow cleared from the entrance and he called to the bear to come out. The bear came out of the den and he lectures that man, eh? He tells him from now on he has to keep the promises he makes to animals. He can't waste the meat of bears or other animals. Then he lets that man go home with his son.

Discussion

Although I have located only one other Cree version of this story (Bloomfield 1930: 255–56), the story of the boy abducted by a bear is apparently widespread among boreal Algonquians as witnessed by Southwestern Ojibwa (Jones 1919: 271–79) and Mistassini Cree (Tanner 1979: 148–50) versions. As is well-known (cf. Hallowell 1926), Algonquians and other Subarctic Indian groups define bears as the most intelligent and spiritually empowered of animals. This definition may derive both from the anthropomorphic behavior and morphology of bears, witnessed by the Rock Cree term *āpīhtāwiðiniw* "half-human," and also from their capacity to invert the conventional hunter-prey relationship by killing and eating Indians. Bears are understood to exert controls over other animal species, and unusually competent or successful hunters and trappers are sometimes said to possess a bear as a *pawākan* or spirit guardian. Although traditional Rock Crees extend to most game animals such observances as special forms of address, butchering, offerings, and bone disposal, these practices are most elaborated with respect to bears. Mr. Bighetty's narrative exemplifies both the religious proscription of the waste of animal food and the propensity for animals to communicate with humans in dreams and thereby indicate their location. Also characteristic of other communications between humans and spirits or animals are the precise instructions issued to the father; these often take the form of self-abnegations which must occur before a primary objective is achieved.

mistāpēw
Narrator: Jean-Marie Merasty
Translator: Pierre Merasty

mistāpēw ("Giant") lived alone in a lodge in the bush. He was very strong and powerful. One night while he was sleeping, another man possessing great strength came to the camp and looked down at *mistāpēw* while he was sleeping. Even when asleep *mistāpēw* always wore a hat upon which was written, "I kill twelve men with one blow." That man was scared by what he read on that hat. He wanted to make sure of what it said and so he woke *mistāpēw* and asked him. *mistāpēw* said that it meant that he was strong enough to kill twelve men with one blow. That other man concealed his own strength from *mistāpēw*. He desired to find out how strong *mistāpēw* really was. The next day when they were travelling through the bush, *mistāpēw* said that they would need firewood that night at camp. The man took a dry tree and pulled it out of the ground by its roots. *mistāpēw* said that one tree wouldn't give them enough wood for their fire. He said that there was lots of dry wood there and that he was strong enough to carry it all back. The man, not wishing *mistāpēw* to learn of his lesser strength, convinced him that one log would be sufficient. They brought the tree to camp and cut it into firewood.

The next day, two more men came to that camp. *mistāpēw* told all his guests that there wasn't very much food and that three of them would have to go out hunting. The first man who came decided to stay and watch the camp. That day and the next, *mistāpēw* and the other two men returned at night-fall and related that while they were hunting they became too sick to kill anything. On the third day, the three again went hunting and the man who stayed behind detected a noise at the edge of camp. He hid himself and observed a bearded dwarf sneaking into the camp. He grabbed the dwarf, took him to the cache platform, and hung him up by his whiskers. When the others came back, he told them that he had found out why they were getting sick. The dwarf had been throwing bad medicine at them. *mistāpēw* went to the cache rack and took down the dwarf. He released it but told it never to come near the camp again or they'd deal harshly with it.

Discussion

Among Rock Cree, *mistāpēw* is glossed into English simply as "giant," and it was not possible to discover any shared knowledge of a class of beings referred to by this term. Mr. Michel, in the transformer story "*wītikōw* and Weasel", substitutes *mistāpēw* for *wītikōw* as the cannibalistic antagonist, but this appears to be an individual innovation. The *mistāpēw* of Mr. Merasty's narrative is a heroic figure, and the reference to killing twelve men with one blow ("The Brave Tailor") together with the presence of the bearded dwarf suggest obvious Euro-Canadian influence. Among Eastmain Cree, Montagnais, and Naskapi, cognates of *mistāpēw* refer to the spirit guardian and occur as a proper name for a spirit being associated with the shaking lodge (cf. Preston 1975: 105–06, Tanner 1979: 113–16); the name has no comparable associations among Rock Cree.

The Thunder Women
Written in Cree syllabics and English
by Henry Linklater and Angelique Linklater

Once upon a time long ago there were two brothers living together without mother or father or sisters or brother. Maybe *wītikōw* had eat them. All except the two brothers.

So one of them asked his brother if they could go and stay somewhere where there's beaver. So they went and stay where there's beaver and build a *wīkīwāp* from there so they could hunt. So the next day they went hunting beaver. Next morning they went again. They come home and find out someone had cut wood for them so they went in their place and find out all the beaver they killed before, someone had cleaned them and all stretched and the inside camp was nice and clean. But they didn't know who had clean it, they wonder who come to their place. Because there was no human round long time ago. So they went back again to hunt beaver, they come back in the evening.

When they come home to their camp, they went in and see two women sitting in their bedding. The oldest brother was happy to see a nice-looking woman sitting in his bedding and the young brother looking at the other woman, he didn't like it too much. I suppose he was jealous of his brother because the woman was nice-looking. His woman was not the same looking.

They stay for awhile with them. So one day they went hunting again. They come to beaver house and the young brother asked his old brother if he could stay where those beaver was and try and kill them. So the oldest brother telled his brother to come along [home]. But the young brother didn't want that way. So the oldest brother went alone and left him.

But the young brother had in his mind to kill his brother's wife. So he went back to the camp instead. After he got there close up, he saw her cutting wood. So he took a shot at her with his arrow and hit her on the rib and the woman run to her sister crying and screaming. So the other sister pulled the arrow from her rib. So she talked "From now on, in the near future when there will be humans around in this world, with this arrow, if anyone hit the animals on the ribs he will not be killed."

The brothers didn't know where women come from. But later they find out after this happens that they were thunderbird women. So the thunder women went back to their home, and when the oldest brother got home, the other brother went away that day. But he know what happen before he get home, his brother had done it. And when the brother got back, he asked him what he did. But he denied it. So his brother talked him he is going to leave him.

"I am really mad at you, I know you did it. But I will try and look for them." On his way he come to a place and see a wikwam standing so he went in and saw a old woman sitting alone inside. So he asked the old woman if she seen someone. The old woman answered yes. But one of the women was very sick. So he asked the old woman if she could help him.

"Yes, son, I will." Now she told him what to do. She told him he had to go to the Rocky Mountains. "The first thing, just put this squirrel nails [claws] on you. Because it's a hard place to get there and when you wear them you can climb that steep Rocky Mountains. And then put this Thunder Hide on you. So he did it. Then he flew on that Rocky Mountains, the very top.

He seen a house right on the mountain. When he went in, he seen the two Thunder Women staying there with their whole family. The women recognize him and they're very happy to see him again. When he was ready to come home, the old folks of the thunderbirds told the girls to come home with him. Just before they leave, the old Thunder Bird tell him his "brother was just about dead crying for you." So they left for their camp and when they got home, his brother was still crying. So his brother told him to get up. He told him that "we got home, back again. But let me tell you, don't do this again, what you been doing."

So they stay together again and happily they went hunting and killed lot of beaver and moose. And one day the Thunder Bird Women asked them to go together somewhere in the bush and stay there for awhile. So the women went back and got the arrow. She come back with it. "This is the arrow that my sister was shot with it and this arrow from now on if anyone uses it to hunt there will be good luck with it.

That's it. End.

Discussion

At least three other Cree versions of this narrative have been collected. The Severn Cree version (Ray and Stevens 1971: 88–92) most closely parallels Mr. Linklater's in having two isolated brothers approached at the outset by two nubile thunderbird women. Versions recorded by Bloomfield (1930: 229–36) and Skinner (1916: 353–61) from Plains Cree are considerably longer and more detailed. Both begin with ten coresident brothers who discover a single elusive woman caring for their camp; she marries one of the younger brothers and is subsequently approached by *macihkīwis*, the eldest brother and the counterpart of the morally chaotic and jealous younger brother in Linklater's version, who shoots her with an arrow when she rejects him. Her husband pursues her to the domain to the thunderbirds and after several adventures returns to his brothers accompanied by his wife's nine nubile sisters. The character of *macihkīwis* possesses the malice and folly that are important facets of the trickster-transformer *wīsahkīcāhk*, motivating, apparently, a passage in a version of "The Startlers" (Ahenakew 1929: 333) in which the latter claims to possess three names: "Wesakaychak, Nanaposo [the Ojibwa trickster-transformer], and Mutchekwis." A cognate of *macihkīwis* occurs also among the easternmost branch of the Plains Cree as the name for the west wind (Hamilton 1894: 203).

ayās
Narrator and translator: Caroline Dumas

ayās stayed with his grandfather. One day his grandfather asked him to go out in the lake to look for some seagull eggs at a big island. So away they went, they went to a big island in a large lake. That's where his *omosōma* ("his grandfather") took him. So his grandfather told him to go ashore, to go and see if there were any seagull eggs. So *ayās* got off and started running.

"I'm here, *nimosōm* ("my grandfather")," he called back. And the old man said, "Farther! Farther!"

"I'm here, Grandpa."

"Farther! Farther!" So *ayās* went farther and farther in that big *mimistiks* ("island"), and there were many eggs. And the next time *ayās* said that, he could hardly hear the *omosōma* shouting, "Farther ! Farther!" And the next time he called out to his *omosōma* he couldn't hear him any more. And he turned around from there and started running. He ran up to the top of the hill and then he looked. He saw his *omosōma* far out in the lake already going home. He left him there. So he went to a hollow rock and went inside and cried and cried until he fell asleep.

So he slept and slept in there and towards evening he was waking up and he heard someone making noise in the rocks. So he looked where the noise was and he saw a big snake in there and he screamed and he was going to run away. So the *misikinīpik* ("great snake") said, "Don't be scared of me, *nōsisim* ("my grandchild"). I'm your *kōhkom* ("your grandmother"). That old man thinks that I'm his *pawākan* ("spirit guardian"). He thinks that I'm going to eat you up, that's why he came and left you here. He left your mother to his *opawākana* ("his spirit guardian") too. But you'll find your mother. So he thinks the same thing is going to happen to you, but I'm not going to do anything to you," she said. "So, *nōsisim*, if you do exactly what I'm going to tell you, you're going to find your mom." So *ayās* got up and he looked around and he saw a cloud coming. It was getting toward evening already. So his grandmother told him, "You're going to sit on top of my back and I'll take you across the lake." So he got on his grandmother's back and he held onto horns. (Mrs. Dumas explains that giant snakes possess two horns on the top of their heads). So his *ōhkoma* ("his grandmother") told him, "If you hear thunder and lightning coming, you let me know right away." [Mrs. Dumas explains that thunder and lightning don't like giant snakes "and other animals like that."]

So away they went after he got on her back. So while they were going, *ayās* heard the thunder coming. So the old snake knew right away and she asked *ayās*, "*nōsisim*, what's that I hear?"

So *ayās* said, "It's nothing, *nōhkom*, it's only your body moving in the water. (Mrs. Dumas explains that *ayās* is lying because he wants to cross the lake and fears the snake will submerge if thunder approaches). So they were going and going and he could see that they were getting closer to where she was going to take them. The cloud was coming closer and closer to where they were going. So they hear the thunder coming. The old snake told him that it was thunder that was coming, but *ayās* wanted her to take him where he wanted to go. So he told her a lie again and said, "It's only your body moving." He hit her horns again and they traveled fast through the water. So, as they were coming real close to shore, then the lightning and thunder came down. So *ayās* jumped off her back and jumped ashore. When you see a hollow space in the earth along the shore at a certain place, that's where *ayās* jumped ashore. So that lightning stunned him and he couldn't hear anything right away. He couldn't hear his *ōhkoma*. So he went to sleep in there. The clouds blocked the sunlight. There was a big storm with lightning, thunder, and rain. So *ayās* camped in there because it was too late to keep traveling.

So he got up in the morning and he was all wet from the rain. And he started going down to the lake where lightning had hit them. There was blood all over the shore and water. So he went to the bush to go and get some *waskway* ("birchbark") and he started making *kakwayēwatsa* ("birchbark baskets"). He came down and he went down to the shore where he saw the blood and he scooped up the blood with the two baskets he had made. And then he went to some trees and hung the baskets of blood on *watīkwana* ("branches"). So after he did that, he went in the bush to hunt partridges. So he killed a partridge and came down and cooked it for himself. So after he finished eating his meal there, he went to bed to rest.

Just toward evening he woke up. So he went and checked those baskets he'd hung in the tree and he saw *kinīpikosisa* ("little snake") swimming around in the blood. That's his *ōhkoma*. So he took the little snake to the lake to wash it out. And it was his grandmother. So he brought his grandmother back to life. So his grandmother told him, "You saved my life so if you do what I'm going to tell you, you're going to find your mother. You're going to keep going. The first thing you'll see along the way is a *mīkīwāpis* ("small three pole lodge"). That's where your grandmother *aðīkas* ("frog") lives.

So he walked into the *mīkīwāp* and he'll see his grandmother the frog in there. His *omaskisina* ("moccasins") will be broken. So he'll tell his grandmother to sew them up for him. So his *ōhkoma* fixed his moccasins for him while she was eating. So when he finished eating he picked up his moccasins. The frog had sewn the moccasins the way he jumps and so the stitches were too far apart. So *ayās* was angry at her for not doing a good job on his moccasins.

So he started walking again as his grandmother *kinīpik* had told him and he was looking for another little wigwam where his grandmother *apakosis* ("mouse") lives. So he kept on going and he was looking ahead and he saw a little *mīkīwāpis* so he starts running down the hill. And so he walked in and saw his grandmother the mouse. It was getting late already so he camped there. He had supper and gave his moccasins to *ōhkoma* mouse to sew them and he went to bed. The mouse sewed up the moccasins the way they walk. Real close together like mouse tracks. So when he got up in the morning, his grandmother gave him the moccasins. He was very happy because she had done a good job on them. So he put on his moccasins and started travelling again.

His grandmother had told him that he would come to another *mīkīwāpis*. That's where two old ladies live, the old ladies called *okīnipocoskwanīsiwak* who sharpen their elbows to points like knives. When they've sharpened their elbows, they sit on either side of the doorway with their elbows out. And when someone goes and visits them, they don't mind when someone comes in. But when someone wants to go out again, they have to know because that's when the pointed elbow old ladies stab people with their elbows. Because they want to kill them. *ayās* came to their wigwam and went inside. He was eating and the old ladies kept telling him, "Tell us when you want to go out." They intended to stab him then. *ayās* was eating pemmican and berries. So when he finished eating he lifted up the side of the wigwam in order to go out the other side. Those old ladies couldn't see him because they were kind of blind. They were going to start stabbing as soon as he said he was going out. So when he was going toward the door they heard him coming and *ayās* said, "I'm going out now." But he went out the other side of the tent. So when they heard that, they were standing on either side of the door and they started stabbing with their elbows and they stabbed and killed each other. They didn't kill *ayās* but they killed each other.

So *ayās* started going again. That was the last thing that he had to do that his grandmother had told him about. "If you get past the pointed-elbow old ladies you'll be able to reach your destination."

So *ayās* started going again. There was one more thing that he's going to do that his grandmother told him about. She told him, "If you get past the last one, you'll be able to reach your destination. So when you get into this little teepee, that's where an old lady lives and she has a sore leg. Whenever anyone visits, she tries to poison them. While you're travelling, try to run into a little *makīsis* ("fox") and pick it up and put it under your jacket. So when you get into where she'll be it will be getting around evening already. Don't let her kill you, look after your welfare, and keep an eye on her. Don't eat anything that she gives you. Tell her that it's late. She uses that sore leg of hers to kill people. After they're asleep, she moves it little by little and if she puts it on top of you, you'll die. And she'll try to poison you also."

So *ayās* kept going. It was getting late in the evening already when he saw the *mīkīwāpis*. And he walked in and he saw an old lady with her sore leg held out. And he had that little fox under his coat as his grandmother had told him.

So when he walked in, she said, "*ayās takosin*" ("*ayās* arrives"). She knows him.

ayās said, "It's me, *nōhkom*, I'm here."

So the old lady told him, "Fix yourself up and I'll feed you and then you can go to bed."

"Grandmother, I'm not hungry because it wasn't far back that I made a fire to have a meal." *ayās* didn't eat and he went to bed. And he had the fox under his coat and he had one eye open to keep an eye on that old woman. So this old lady kept looking at *ayās* to see if he was moving and she didn't see him move so she started moving her leg little by little toward him. *ayās* moved when he saw her do that.

"Grandson, you're not sleeping," she said. "I can't sleep, grandmother," he said.

"If you sleep, I'll wake you up early so you can go." But *ayās* couldn't go to sleep because he thought of what his grandmother snake had told him about what she'd do to him. So *ayās* didn't sleep. It was getting toward morning so he got up and his grandmother told him she was going to feed him.

"Because you're leaving, I'm going to feed you for the last time," she said. So she started fixing up the poisoned food that she was going to give him. So when he got that food from her, she was looking at him eating. *ayās* pretended that he was eating, but he was feeding the food to the fox that he had under his coat. The fox was eating the food and it got sick from the food because of the poison.

So the old lady said, "When you're ready to go out, tell me." The old lady couldn't see well, and *ayās* did the same as he'd done with the pointed-elbow old ladies. As he was going out, he told her, "I'm going out," and he threw the little fox at that old lady and the fox killed the old woman because he had eaten that poison. So *ayās* was safe from all the dangers that the snake had told him about.

ayās started going again. All of a sudden while he was walking he heard someone cutting wood in the bush. So he started going toward where he heard the noise. There were big trees there and he approached slowly, hiding from tree to tree. And when he got very close to that noise, he saw an old lady cutting wood there. And when he was looking at her, he could see that she was covered with scabs on her face and hands. So while she cut wood a bird flew to where she was and sang, "*ayās takosin kikōsis*" (" *ayās* he arrives your son").

She said, "Oh, the poor bird is saying this to me and long ago my son was eaten by *kinīpikwak pawākanak*" ("snakes spirit-guardians"). The bird sang again that *ayās* was back.

"Don't say that to me, little bird," she said to that bird.

So *ayās* came very close and he said, "Yes, I am here, mother."

The old lady said, "*ayās nikōsis, ayās nikōsis!*" ("*ayās* my son"). She grabbed him and kissed him. *ayās* began crying and asked his mother why she had all those scabs on her hands and face. So the old lady said, "Those people I stay with abuse me. Whenever I finish cutting wood and go home and make the fire, they take burning wood and burn my hands and face."

So *ayās* said to his mother, "Mother, I'll go home with you. You're going to take the wood home so I'll go with you. And when we get there, you'll make a big fire. I know that the people you are staying with have a baby. After you finish making the fire, the woman will bring the baby there to change him because it will be warm there. So when she does that, you ask her to give you the baby. Tell her that you're going to kiss the baby. I'll wait for you outside."

So the old lady took her wood inside and *ayās* was waiting for her outside.

ayās was hiding on a cache platform. So the old lady made a big fire and the woman did just what *ayās* thought. She brought the baby by the fire to change him.

So the old lady said, "Bring the baby here, I would like to kiss him." The old man said, "Don't give it to her. She'll throw it in the fire."

The woman said, "*nē*, you always say that when the old lady wants to love the little baby."

So the old man said, "Give it to her, then. She'll throw it in the fire." So the woman gave her the baby and the old lady played with the baby. At the same time, she was watching those people to see if they were watching her. When she was sure no one was watching she suddenly threw the baby into the middle of the fire. The woman ran there to grab the baby from the fire. *ayās'* mother ran out of the lodge and she was calling, "*ayās nikōsis! ayās nikōsis!* ("*ayās* my son").

"You don't say that for any reason," the old man said. "Where do you think you have seen your son, since I fed him long ago to *nipawākanak*" ("ray spirit guardians"). And then *ayās* came out from hiding.

"See if you are able to abuse my mother now that I am here," he said. That old man went to his cache platform and he took all the beaver hides down from that *akōcikan* ("platform"). He spread them on the ground and said, "Really, your feet must be worn out [attempt at formal hospitality]."

And *ayās* said, "Go away (disparagement). Really, I would have worn my feet out a long time ago with all the traveling I've been doing to come and get my mother." Then *ayās* told them that he was going to do something.

"If you want to live," he said to the old man and his family, "make a big hole in the ground so you can take all your food and all your possessions in there with you and your family. Do this if you want to live because *wī-pasitīw askīy*, there will be fire all over the earth." They didn't believe him. So *ayās* made a great big bow and large arrow. When he finished making them, right there he told his mother, "I'm going to shoot this arrow up in the air and I'm going to say 'Let there be fire on the earth'." So he shot the arrow. And when he shot, fire sprang up and burned all over the earth.

So *ayās* and his mother departed from there. *ayās* became an *ahāsiw* ("crow") and his mother became *pāpāskīw* ("wood-pecker"). That's why when you see a woodpecker it has black on its back and white on its front. That's that old lady. She was wearing a white apron. And when you see a black crow, that's *ayās*. That's the end.

Discussion

Other Cree versions of *ayās* were collected by Petitot (1886: 455–59), Skinner (1911: 92–95), and Ray and Stevens (1971: 112–20); a Montagnais version

(Basile and McNulty 1971, cf. Bauer 1973: 1–9, Savard 1979: 12–14) resembles Skinner's version which was known both at Moose Factory and the Eastmain Cree community of Rupert's House.

Mrs. Dumas' version is unusual in its delineation of family relationships in the myth. In most versions, *ayās* is abandoned by a jealous father or stepfather after the latter's younger wife claims falsely that *ayās* has approached her. These other versions culminate with *ayās* returning to the camp of his family and revenging himself on his step-father and the younger wife. In Mrs. Dumas' version, *ayās* is abandoned by his grandfather with whom he has been living and finds his mother living with the latter and his wife at the climax. The grandfather's motivation appears to be that of offering relatives as sacrifices to the Giant Snake that he mistakenly believes is his guardian spirit. The Snake, assuming the benevolent relationship of grandmother toward the abandoned *ayās*, tells him that long ago his grandfather had tried to abandon his mother there for the same purpose.

In all versions, *ayās* is helped by animal or spirit beings who aid him in escaping from the island and prepare him for the ordeals he must encounter as he travels to rejoin or find his mother. The Ray and Stevens Severn Cree version contains an amusing interlude on the island in which giant seagulls, duped by *ayās* into thinking they are his spirit guardians, carry him out over the water and defecate on his stepfather. This exactly parallels one episode in Mr. Michel's "Contest with *wīmisōsiw*," and the evil stepfather possesses in the Severn version a name cognate to that of *wīsahkīcāhk*'s comparably malignant father-in-law. In most versions, *ayās* is subsequently carried through the water to the shore by a Giant Horned Snake, although a walrus plays this role in Skinner's version. Similarly, most versions exemplify the antagonism between such water entities and the thunderbirds by having the Snake destroyed by thunder and lightning when a storm blows up just as they reach shore.

In the Dumas and Ray-Stevens versions, *ayās* reanimates his benefactor. In the Dumas version he does this by gathering its blood, suspending it in a tree, and then placing the resulting small snake in the water where it expands to its original size; this passage again exemplifies the Rock Cree association of trees with animal rebirth or regeneration. In the Ray-Stevens version, the resurrection occurs when *ayās* places tobacco in a scrap of snakeskin hanging from a branch and then places it in the water.

In all versions, *ayās* is instructed by the Snake or another subsequent benefactor concerning his ordeals. An interesting aspect of the story that pertains to at least three versions is the relationship between *ayās*'s instructions or revelatory dreams and the subsequent acting out of the foretold events. Mrs. Dumas, for example, makes a transition between the Snake's instructions and predictions and the actual exploits that *ayās* successively undergoes (cf. Petitot 1886: 457,

Ray and Stevens 1971: 113). *ayās*'s subsequent benefactors include two old women (Basile and McNulty), a fox (Ray and Stevens), and anthropomorphic frog and mice women who sew his moccasins (Dumas). *ayās*'s dangerous obstacles vary from one version to another, although the memorably nightmarish *okīnipocoskwanīsiwak*, old women with pointed and knife-like elbows (cf. Speck 1925: 8–9), figure in three other versions (Basile and McNulty, Skinner, Ray and Stevens). Other perils include a lake of boiling spruce gum and swinging pointed shoulder blades (Basile and McNulty); a monster who crushes victims with his leg (cf. the poison-legged woman of Dumas's version), treacherous sky hooks, a cannibal hag, and women with toothed vaginas (Ray and Stevens); rattling bones that alert fierce dogs (Skinner), and a crevasse (Petitot).

All versions culminate in *ayās*'s reunion with his mistreated mother and his destruction of the earth by fire. In two versions, *ayās* tricks his villainous relatives into taking refuge in a grease-filled pit where they are deep-fried in the conflagration. The blaze is created by *ayās*'s fiery arrow except in the Skinner and Basile-McNulty versions where he sings the fire into being. Although the Petitot version has *ayās* and his mother survive the fire unchanged, other versions describe their permanent transformation into birds. In different versions, they become respectively a crow and woodpecker (Dumas), a Canada jay and robin (Skinner), and a toad and a robin (Ray and Stevens). Brassard (1980: 187–202) provides an interesting structural analysis of the Montagnais version of this myth.

maskōkōsan
Narrator: Catherine Merasty
Translator: Lorna Cook
Long ago in the past, a group of women traveled out into the bush to pick berries. There was one woman already out there picking alone and she joined the others after she met them. All at once, a bear appeared. The women were frightened and ran away, all except the one who had been out by herself. She stood her ground. To her the bear looked like an attractive man. She didn't think it was a bear. She went with that bear and lived with it for a long time as its wife. At length, the bear decided to return her to her people and he brought her back to that place where they were camping. When they had almost reached the camp, the bear told her that she was going to have a baby boy. He instructed her not to tell the people that he was the father. He predicted that the little boy, when he became a man, would see many bears, but he said that the boy should be instructed not to hunt and kill them. Only if someone who desperately needed meat asked him to kill bears would it be acceptable for him to do so. The boy's name would be *maskōkōsan*.

When the boy grew up he was very strong and could perform many feats of strength. He announced to his mother that he was going to leave home and go out traveling. He traveled for a long time and eventually he met two other men who were also traveling about. They told him that they were looking for a man called *maskōkōsan* and that they wished to compete with him and overpower him. *maskōkōsan* told them that he had never heard of such a person. The three traveled together through the bush and finally came to the camp of an old man who was known to the other two.

The next day, *maskōkōsan* and one of the men went out to hunt and the third man remained at camp. None of them had seen the old man who stayed at that camp. When they returned to the camp after hunting, they found the one who had stayed there stretched out on the floor and groaning. They asked him what was wrong with him and he said that he didn't know. They put him to bed and eventually he began to recover. The next day, *maskōkōsan* went out to hunt with the one who had been sick and the other man stayed in camp. Again the one who stayed behind became ill and was unable to identify what was wrong with him. They put him in bed that night and he felt better. *maskōkōsan* didn't know what was happening, but the other two whispered together and prophesied that *maskōkōsan* would be killed the next day.

The next day, the two men went off to hunt and left *maskōkōsan* alone at the camp. *maskōkōsan* was making a pot of tea. Suddenly the old man entered and demanded to know what *maskōkōsan* was doing in his camp. *maskōkōsan* told him that he was staying at the camp with two other men while they hunted. The old man kept going near the tea kettle and bothering it [trying to put poison in it]. *maskōkōsan* warned him to stay away from the kettle. The old man kept bothering it. Finally *maskōkōsan* grabbed the old man by his beard and told him not to move around or he'd kill him. He took the old man outside and tied him up in the bush by his beard. When the other two men came back to the camp, they were surprised to hear *maskōkōsan* whistling instead of groaning. After they finished eating, *maskōkōsan* told the other two that it had been the old man who had been making them ill. [The complicity of the two companions in the old man's sorcery remains unclear.] He took them out in the bush to where he had the old man tied up in his beard.

He untied the old man. The old man said that *maskōkōsan* did not know where he really dwelt, whereas the other two already knew this. Then he told *maskōkōsan* that he would take him and show him where he lived. They travelled out into the bush to a place where there were many flat rocks. On one of the flat rocks handles were attached on two sides. The old man took hold of it, picked it up, and slid it over. Beneath, there was a great hole leading down into the ground. Attached to that rock was a rope. The old man scurried inside the hole and then pulled the rope. The flat stone slid over the hole, leaving the other three outside. The two men each attempted to lift the rock off but were unsuccessful. *maskōkōsan* asked them if they remembered telling him about the man called *maskōkōsan* and how they wished to compete with and overcome him. He told them his identity and then said that he would remove the rock that was blocking the entrance to the tunnel. He easily lifted the stone off the entrance and set it to one side.

Leaving the other two on the surface, *maskōkōsan* crawled into the tunnel. The rope hung loose over a deep vertical hole and *maskōkōsan* descended into the earth by climbing down the rope. Finally he came to the bottom. There was another world under the earth there. *maskōkōsan* found a path and began following it. The path led to a lodge and *maskōkōsan* saw that it was the home of the old bearded man who had attempted to poison him. That old man was really surprised to see *maskōkōsan* because he thought that it was impossible for anyone but himself to lift the rock covering the entrance. Then he told *maskōkōsan* that there were three *wītikōwak* ("cannibal monsters") living some distance away in a region of barren land. One *wītikōw* had one head, the second had two heads, and the third had three heads. These three monsters had kidnapped the three daughters of a White man and carried them away to their home in the treeless land underground. *maskōkōsan* said that he intended to rescue those three women. The old man then gave him a medicine called "old-man-medicine" which was to be used for wounds and cuts. When the medicine was placed on a wound it would heal it instantly. He warned *maskōkōsan* that the *wītikōwak* were very dangerous and that they killed their victims with knives rather than with guns. The *wītikōwak* lived in three separate lodges. The old man instructed *maskōkōsan* to go first to the house of the one-headed *wītikōw* and that he would then call the others. He said that the *wītikōwak* would offer him three knives and ask him to choose one before fighting. Two of the knives were new and one was old; *maskōkōsan* was to take the old one.

maskōkōsan travelled across the treeless barren lands and came finally to the lodges of the *wītikōwak*. He entered one lodge and found one of the White women sitting there. She told him that the one-headed *wītikōw* would soon return. *maskōkōsan* concealed himself and waited. That *wītikōw* couldn't tell ahead of time that *maskōkōsan* was hidden there and was surprised when he stepped out [ordinarily a *wītikōw* would sense the presence of human prey]. Immediately, this *wītikōw* called the two others into his lodge. The two-headed *wītikōw* was reluctant to kill *maskōkōsan*. He desired to be friends with human beings but the other two would never permit this. They brought out the three knives and told *maskōkōsan* to choose one. He chose the oldest knife. The *wītikōwak* tried to stop him from taking that one, but he held onto it and refused to change. Then they all three attacked him. For a long time they fought there and the *wītikōwak*, unable to kill *maskōkōsan* easily, became frightened. At length, *maskōkōsan* killed all three of them. The White woman who had been held captive went and called her two sisters from the other lodges. As a reward for saving them, they gave gifts to *maskōkōsan*: a ring, a pin, and a scarf. *maskōkōsan* guided them along the road through the barren grounds, past the old man's house, and back to where the rope led up to the outer world. They each climbed up to the top along the rope.

When the first woman reached the surface, the two men who were still waiting there began to fight over her. She told them not to fight because her sisters were also ascending and that there would soon be three women there. After the other two women reached the top, the two men maliciously cut the rope leading into the hole. *maskōkōsan* was already climbing near the top when the rope was severed and he fell back into the underworld, striking his head when he fell. For four days he lay there unconscious. Finally he regained consciousness and returned to the old man's house. The old man told him that there was no way that he could help him if the rope had been cut. But the old man told him that there was an eagle who would carry him to the top if *maskōkōsan* provided him with food. *maskōkōsan* found the eagle and the bird agreed to carry him but insisted on being fed at intervals during the ascent. When they were nearing the top, *maskōkōsan* ran out of food and the eagle threatened to swallow him if no food was forthcoming. *maskōkōsan* cut strips of meat off his leg and fed them to the eagle.

They reached the top and *maskōkōsan* climbed out of the hole. He was searching for those three girls but didn't know where to go in search of them. He transformed his appearance so that he looked different and then began walking. Finally he reached the village where those three girls were staying with their father. None of the women recognized *maskōkōsan* because of his transformed appearance. *maskōkōsan* tore the knee of his pants and then knotted the scarf he had been given over the tear. The girl who had given him the scarf then recognized him. She asked him if he was the man who had rescued them from the *wītikōwak* and he said that he was.

The father of three girls lived in a large house which he had built for all the people to use during their dances and feasts. That evening, all the people of the village came there. Also present were the two men who had cut the rope and abandoned *maskōkōsan* to the underworld. They got up in front of all the people and lied, telling everyone that it was they who had rescued the three women. The old man believed them and he intended to let them marry his daughters. Then *maskōkōsan* stepped forward and accused them of lying. One of the two recognized the voice of *maskōkōsan* and became frightened. He attempted to flee from the dance house, but the girl who had recognized *maskōkōsan* secured the entrance so that he couldn't escape. *maskōkōsan* recounted the whole story and the woman confirmed all he said. The father knew then that the two men were lying and he decreed that one of them should be imprisoned and the other should be hung. As a result, *maskōkōsan* was given all three of the women to be his wives.

Discussion

Like *"mistāpēw," "maskōkōsan"* blends Euro-Canadian with Cree characters and events; it is probable that the essential plot of the story derives from European sources and again there are obvious relationships to "The Brave Tailor." References to the White father and his three abducted daughters, to the bearded old man who is successively antagonist and benefactor, and to the punishments of *maskōkōsan*'s duplicitous companions (imprisonment and hanging) are all European. Identifiably Cree are the human-animal marriage with which the story begins, the hero's sororally polygynous marriage with which the story happily concludes, his trick for feeding the eagle, and perhaps also the multi-headed *wītikōwak*, although the latter possess a certain European flavor. In contrast to the story of "The Woman Who Married a Bear" (infra), *"maskōkōsan"* is of interest in representing a heroic character who results from a marriage between human and bear. The story also parallels other Algonquian animal marriage myths (cf. Jones 1919: 251–57) in having the human spouse perceive the animal suitor as a human being.

mistacayawāsis
Narrator: Angelique Linklater
Translator: Henry Linklater

Two brothers were married to two sisters and they lived together in a camp in the bush. Greatly they loved each other, those four people. The youger brother and the younger sister had two children. But one day when the brothers had gone out to hunt the elder sister transformed into a *wītikōw* [No explanation for the transformation is provided].

"I'm hungry," she said to her younger sister.

"We have plenty of meat for you to cook if you're hungry," her younger sister said to her.

"Oh, no," that older sister said, "that's not the kind of food I'm hungry for." Then she grabbed those two young children, those two sons of her sister, and killed them. Only halfway she roasted them and then really she ate them. The younger sister, their mother, could do nothing to stop her. Soon the younger of the two brothers came back to the camp. Really very strong was that *wītikōw* woman. She threw him to the floor and killed him. Then she half-roasted him only and ate him. Only her little sister did she spare because she yet loved her.

Later that night, the eldest of the two brothers, the husband of that *wītikōw* woman, returned to the camp. He was one who was able to know before he came to a place what had happened there. He entered the lodge and told that *wītikōw* woman, his wife, that he knew exactly what she had done. She attacked him and tried to wrestle him to the floor. Three times he threw her to the ground; he was stronger than that *wītikōw*. That *wītikōw* woman begged her younger sister, she whose children she had eaten, for help. Her sister did not help her.

Then he said, "I could kill you now, but you've already killed those I loved in this world, my brother and my brother's sons, so I'm going to allow you to overcome me and kill me." So she killed him and again she only half-roasted and ate him.

Nearby were camped the parents of the two sisters and the sisters' three younger brothers who were yet children. The older sister could command the younger sister to do anything because she knew that she might be killed. So now she told her that they would travel to the camp where their parents were staying. When they came there, her parents asked about them, her husband, and her brother-in-law, and the children. The older sister, that *wītikōw*, said that they had gone hunting for two nights. The younger sister was not able to say anything because she thought her older sister would kill her.

The next day, that *wītikōw* woman told the eldest of her three younger brothers to come out in the bush with her and their sister to shoot spruce partridges. Really that little boy was excited and happy to be doing this. He brought with him a small bow and small arrows that his father had made for him. When they saw a spruce partridge, the older sister pointed the arrow at it for him. Really very excited was that boy about killing that spruce partridge. Just then, she grabbed him around the neck, strangling and killing him. And, as before, she built a fire and only half-roasted her younger brother and ate him. Still there was nothing that her younger sister could do. When they returned that night to the camp, the older sister told the people that the boy had been lost and that they had searched long and hard for him with no success. Those people believed her and they were very sad about it that the little boy was lost. There was nothing that the younger sister could say.

The next day, that *wītikōw* woman asked the next oldest brother to come out with them to shoot spruce partridge. The same thing happened. When the boy aimed at a spruce partridge, the woman strangled him, half-roasted him, and ate him. This time they were observed by one man from the camp who was suspicious of the woman's story and thought that something evil might have happened. He followed them out into the bush and he watched everything she did while he was concealed. He went back ahead of them to the camnp and he told all of the people that the woman was a *wītikōw*. The people took bows and arrows and spears and went together into the bush to that place where the two sisters were. And then together they fired on those two sisters with their bows and arrows and hurled spears at them. Immediately, that young girl, the younger sister of the *wītikōw* woman was killed. They killed her because she always stayed with that *wītikōw* woman and they thought this about her, "She also is a *wītikōw*." But the older sister, truly the arrows and spears bounced away from her body; really all of her body had become hard ice. And really those arrows didn't frighten her at all.

"I'll fight and kill all of you," she said to them. "But only after I've finished eating the body of my younger brother." After she finished eating, she fought all of those people, eight or twelve people, and killed them all. But before the fight, her mother had hidden her youngest son, that *wītikōw* woman's youngest brother, in the spruce boughs piled up against the walls of their lodge. This is the one who is called *mistacayawāsis* ("Big Penis Child" or, colloquially in English, "The Big Cock"), although his first name was *mākacās* ("Big Stomach"). That *wītikōw* woman knew how many people there were in those camps and when she counted the bodies she realized that one was missing. Just then, her consciousness returned to her and she reverted to a human condition. She looked at what she had done. Really, she was sorry about it, that woman. She returned to the camp and found *mistacayawāsis* in the spruce boughs in the lodge.

"Really I regret all these things that I have done," she said. "There is only one way for you to kill me and I will tell you exactly how it must be done." She gave him a small axe and told him to chop off her little finger. In her sickness, her heart had become small and had come to be in her little finger. "Don't be frightened," she told him, "if you strike a blow and I scream because the blade does not right away sever my finger but only glances off of it." He struck at her finger with the axe and the blade glanced off because the finger was hard like ice. Just as she had said, she screamed and *mistacayawāsis* was frightened; he jumped back and dropped the axe.

"You will have to strike one more time," she said. Again, he struck her finger and this time really he cut off the finger containing her heart. Immediately then he killed her, that *wītikōw* woman who was his oldest sister.

mistacayawāsis travelled to another camp where his grandmother and grandfather were staying. [He apparently accelerates rapidly in growth and age at this point]. Very proudly *mistacayawāsis* walked into that camp and told all the people that he had slain a *wītikōw*. None of the people believed him; they all laughed at him. In that camp, the grandfather and grandmother of *mistacayawāsis* were from two different branches of his family. He stayed with his grandmother.

In those camps, the people were frightened of *mistahōðōwatim* ("Great Howling Dog"), a Great Wolf that would kill and eat whole camps of people. The grandfather of *mistacayawāsis* knew that the Great Wolf was traveling towards their camp along a certain trail that it always used. This road passed over a lake near the camp. Along this trail where it traversed the lake the people chopped out three holes in the ice and covered them over with snow. Really they hoped to drown that Great Wolf. When the Wolf came, it fell through the snow into the water at the first hole but it was able to climb out and dry itself by rolling in the snow. At the second hole again it was the same. Again at the third hole the Wolf crawled out and dried itself. It looked toward the village and traveled closer.

mistacayawāsis announced to the people that he would go out and meet the wolf on the ice and kill it. All the people laughed at him. "He will be eaten in one bite," is what they said about him. *mistacayawāsis* took out a small knife and told the people that he intended to use it to kill the Wolf. Again they all laughed at him. He marched out of the camp and met the Wolf who was approaching on the trail. He took out his knife and the knife enlarged and became three feet long. He struck the wolf lightly on the rib with the knife and immediately he killed that Wolf. All the people in the camp were happy to know that that Wolf was dead.

At a camp nearby there was a beautiful young woman whom *mistacayawāsis* desired to marry. In order to do this, he watched to see where she urinated and then he would go there after she left and urinate in the same place. Everytime she went to that place, he would follow after her and urinate there. So the woman became pregnant from that. All the men from those camps met in one house in order to determine who the father was. They would discover who the father was by handing the baby around in a circle. When they did this, the one the baby urinated on would be the father. One man, *macikaðawis* ("Good for Nothing") disliked *mistacayawāsis*. Although he was already married, he wanted that woman as his second wife and so he dribbled spit onto himself because he wanted to be named the father. The others saw him try to trick them and said, "He's not the father." *mistacayawāsis* was standing outside at the door to the lodge watching. His grandfather saw him and jokingly said they should give the baby to him. *mistacayawāsis* sat down in that circle of men and they handed the baby to him. The baby began urinating even before he had a full hold of it; it urinated all over his chest. Then they all knew that he was the father. But nevertheless that woman didn't want *mistacayawāsis* as her husband. That woman didn't like *mistacayawāsis* because he was short and fat. Always *mistacayawāsis*' grandmother would ask that girl to come and stay with them, but she refused because she said that *mistacayawāsis* was ugly. Then *mistacayawāsis* built a *matōcisan* ("sweat lodge") and entered it. He carried a big drum into the sweat lodge with him. Inside he built a fire and heated rocks.

He called out to his grandmother, "What does a good man look like?"

"Kind of stout with blue eyes and brown hair," she called back to him. So really he transformed himself into a handsome man. He went out of the sweat lodge and his grandmother was surprised about the way he looked. Right away she went to the camp where that woman was staying.

"You should find a way to come to our camp and see the new man who is staying there." That woman was curious. She went to their camp and saw the way *mistacayawāsis* looked with his new body. She really liked the way that he looked and she stayed there as his wife.

That old man, *mistacayawāsis*'s grandfather, did not like his grandson; also that *macikaðawis* did not like him. "He will be incapable of hunting," they said about him to the others. They were close to being out of food at that camp. So they left *mistacayawāsis* and his wife and his grandmother there and moved to make a camp at a lake some distance away. They left no food behind them. *mistacayawāsis* asked them for twelve beaver tongues.

"Really, he doesn't ask for much," the old man said. "Give him the tongues if he wants them." *mistacayawāsis* brought those tongues back to his lodge. Just there he dug a hole in the lodge flooring and put the twelve beaver tongues in the hole. For some time he waited there. Presently water began to appear in the hole. Up and down the water moved just as the water in a chiseled beaver lodge moves up and down when a beaver is swimming. The grandmother of *mistacayawāsis* was nearly crying because they had had no food for so long a time. Then, all at once, *mistacayawāsis* pulled twelve beavers out of the hole. "We will be able to feed ourselves now," he said.

Time passed and *mistacayawāsis* knew that the others of the camp, those who had abandoned them, were starving to death. He told his grandmother to pack much dried beaver meat into a skin bag. So he took that bag of dry meat and travelled to the place across the lake where the other people were staying. When he was very near to their camp, he stopped and hung the sack in the fork of a tree. The first lodge he came to was that of *macikaðawis*. That *macikaðawis* looked very pitiful. He sat with his head leaned forward and held in his hands. He was close to death from starvation. He looked at his genitals. "I wonder if I could eat them in order to live," was what he thought about them. He didn't recognize *mistacayawāsis* in his new body and wondered who it was who had come to the camp. *mistacayawāsis* went next to the lodge of his parents-in-law. They didn't recognize him at first, but finally the old lady said, "It's our son-in-law, *mistacayawāsis*." He told them that things were good back at his camp and that meat was plentiful. He told them about the bag of dry meat he had brought and told them to send someone to retrieve it. *macikaðawis* went to get that bag but was so weak that he could hardly walk. He wasn't able to lift it down but finally he pushed it off the branch. He reached down to pick it up but was so weak that he fell over. Finally, he struggled to his feet and dragged the bag back to the camp. All those starving people at that camp ate the dry meat. *mistacayawāsis* told them that he would go back to his own camp that night. He told them to eat the dry meat so that they would become strong again. Then he told them to come back to his camp where there was plenty of food.

Very slowly those people recovered their strength from eating the dry meat that *mistacayawāsis* brought them. Finally they were strong enough to travel and they crossed the lake to the camp where *mistacayawāsis* stayed with his wife and grandmother. *mistacayawāsis* had many cache platforms filled with beaver meat. Finally those people had eaten most of the meat. When the food was nearly gone, *mistacayawāsis* told the others that he intended to go out and drive caribou.

"Build a long brush fence for the caribou," he told them. "Assemble there near the end of the fence with your spears and bows and arrows. Many caribou will pass through. But the first caribou will be a large male that is leading all the others. Don't shoot that lead caribou because that will be me, *mistacayawāsis*, leading the caribou." All the people listened to him and agreed except *macikaðawis* who thought this about *mistacayawāsis*, "I intend to kill him."

The people did what he said and built a brush fence and waited with their weapons. Just as *mistacayawāsis* had said, many caribou came through the fence with a large male in the lead. All the people waited for the lead caribou to pass except *macikaðawis* who took his bow and shot that caribou through the side just below the ribs. The arrow passed through one side and the point protruded from the other side. *mistacayawāsis* was still living but he fell to the ground. His wife, who was standing near with their baby in a *tikinākan* ("cradleboard"), ran to where he had fallen. She kneeled there and pulled the arrow from the caribou's ribs. She held the arrow up in front of the people and said, "In the future when there are many human beings in the world, hunters will shoot caribou there behind the ribs and they will never kill the caribou when they strike them there." That caribou transformed back into *mistacayawāsis* who was uninjured.

The men killed many caribou and for a long time there was plenty of meat in the camp. Finally they had eaten almost all of the meat. *macikaðawis*, who was always jealous of *mistacayawāsis*, told all the people that he would do what *mistacayawāsis* had done. He gave the people all the same instructions and then transformed himself into the lead caribou and brought caribou into the brush fence. *mistacayawāsis* thought this of him, "He will always try to harm me. I intend to revenge myself on him." So he shot him with an arrow. The wife of *macikaðawis*, who was carrying her baby in a cradleboard, ran down and removed the arrow. But when she removed it there, the caribou did not become *macikaðawis*. Really, that caribou became a *wiskacānis* ("grey jay").

Discussion

To my knowledge the *mistacayawāsis* narrative has never previously been recorded or published and Mr. and Mrs. Linklater's narration and translation constitute a significant contribution to the record of Cree oral literature. The passages describing the girl's impregnation, the identification of the father, and the hero's physical transformation (this time in a shaking lodge) appear consecutively in a Severn Cree story about a dwarf found in a tree (Ray and Stevens 1971: 64–65), but there are no further resemblances. The Plains Cree story of "Mis-ta-ta-o-wa-ses" (Dusenberry 1962: 260–66) shows no relation to the Rock Cree story despite the cognate name of the hero. Mrs. Linklater's performance is of sufficient length and complexity to indicate that an interlinear translation will be necessary to unpack many of the stylistic and narrative details; this free translation is provided as an interim compromise. It is useful to note in passing that the *wītikōw* character here possesses such typical attributes as indirect references to her own cannibal proclivities ("That's not the kind of food I'm hungry for"), a frozen physical condition (usually ascribed to the viscera and not, as here, to the external body), and a period of lucidity during which the monster expresses horror and remorse and requests execution. The narrative repeatedly points out that the *wītikōw* woman only half-roasts her victims, a variation on the conventional image of the *wītikōw* as eating its human prey raw. *wītikōw* characters are usually said to possess frozen hearts; the image of a shrinking heart that shifts into the monster's finger appears to be unique to this narrative.

Regarding the unusual circumstances of the woman's impregnation, Mr. Linklater stated that children during the mythological period were often said to be conceived by a man urinating repeatedly at the same spot as a woman. Sexual intercourse was, it is said, subsequently introduced among humans by *wīsahkīcāhk*. George Nelson's manuscript (Brown and Brightman 1987) on Cree religion at Lac La Ronge contains a story in which harmful medicine is sprinkled at such a site in order to harm women; no reference is made to impregnation. The idea that a baby will urinate on its father and thereby establish paternity is apparently of wide distribution. Mrs. Elizabeth Brunette (personal communication), a Minnesota Ojibwa born at White Earth Reservation, stated that she was familiar with this conception.

The hero's physical transformation in the sweat lodge exemplifies the association of that structure, and of the drum which here augments it, with *mamāhtawīsiwin* or the exertion of spiritual power. That *mistacayawāsis* should take on the phenotypes of a White man is a curious detail which Mr. and Mrs. Linklater found amusing.

The transformation incident near the end refers to a portion of caribou anatomy, unfortunately not specifically identified, which is said never to produce a fatal wound when struck either with an arrow or a bullet. Discussing the narrative with Henry Linklater provided the opportunity to observe the possible genesis of a new explanatory element which might appear in subsequent narrations. Mr. Linklater pointed out that transformation of *macikaðawis* into a grey jay at the end explains why that personable and voracious bird is often referred to by that name today, as a humorous synonym for *wiskacānis*. He then noted that the grey jay eats all day, often by pillaging food lying around camp, and never gets fat. This state of affairs, he suggested, may relate back to the fact that *macikaðawis* was starving after he abandoned the hero.

At a more complex level of interpretation, Mr. Linklater regarded the myth as containing disguised and symbolic references to varieties of human misfortune. This kind of interpretation parallels that applied to images in dreams and to unusual events in waking life. All of these can be something other than or additional to their manifest appearance and their decipherment is said sometimes to result in knowledge useful or critical for practical affairs or emergencies in the daily round. Mr. Linklater stated that the story contained three great disasters: the *wītikōw*, the Great Wolf, and the abandonment of the hero. He conjectured that these symbolized the three major diseases of the Cree people, respectively *wītikōw* illness (thought to have been the only pre-contact disease), tuberculosis, and cancer. When asked whether there were words or phrases in Cree for stories or images possessing such symbolic or allegorical refererence, Mr. Linklater said that people would use the phrase *ēkosi itāpiminākwan* "thus it-sounds-like" to talk about such interpretations.

The Hairy-Heart People
Narrator: Selazie Linklater
Translator: Caroline Caribou

Once then and very long ago this happened. There were then in this country Hairy Hearts. You would say of these that they were without hearts or goodness. Then at this time there are two of these Hairy Hearts: a father and his son. They travel between the camps of the people, and they kill and eat the people. At one camp there is an old man, a "dreamer" himself, who had spiritual power. He can know before it happens that those Hairy Hearts are coming to his camp. He tells this to the others, his relatives and the people that stay with him. Really, very quickly they then break their camp and travel to a place there where the old man intends to hide. They have with them a moosehide. They use this hide by filling it with grass and then just there they hang it on wooden poles. It looks like a living moose. Then I suppose just there they dig a hole under the snow. Over the hole they position this "moose." The head of the moose faces north from there. "Truly they will not look for us here," he says, that old man. "Those ones who are coming are not interested in moose. Only people they intend to eat." A long time they will stay in that hole so that the Hairy Hearts will not find them.

This Hairy Heart old man owns a staff. Straight up and down he aligns this staff, placing one end in the snow so it stands upright. Then, if he sings, this staff is able to incline toward that place where people are hiding. He sings to his staff, this Hairy Heart. But the human old man, he who hides in the snow, uses his "power." Then truly that staff inclines in the opposite direction. For a long time they hunt the human beings, those Hairy Hearts, and the old man (Hairy Heart) uses always his staff. Always that old man in the snow uses his "power" to overcome them. Finally, then, those Hairy Hearts leave that place there and travel to another lake. When they are gone, those (human) people come out of their place in the snow. They intend to warn the other people around that lake that these Hairy Hearts are going around.

Truly almost starved to death now are those Hairy Hearts. "Near us there are people in a camp," that Hairy Heart old man says to his son. "Go and hunt for us. Bring from that camp two children. Run through them rawhide cordage so I can roast them." Then he catches them, two children who are playing outside of that camp. They scream with fear those two children. He brings them to the old man. Then really that old man roasts them, those two children. The people at that camp hear those children screaming. Greatly they are frightened. Then they break their camp, and move from there, towards where the others stay at the lake.

That old man warns the people that they should stay together in a large camp. "We should not be in small groups," he says to them. They all travel together to a bay just there. Just there they will be able to see what might come towards them from across the lake. That old man is able to know that the Hairy Hearts will again hunt them, that the Hairy Hearts will transform into trees. In this way, they will stalk them (the people), those Hairy Hearts. He (old man) says to the children, "Always watch the ice on the lake. Maybe soon you will see something coming towards us from there. You will see trees. They will be closer to us each time you see them. When you see them, these trees, say loudly, 'Trees are on the ice'."

Soon those children see trees on the ice. Each time that they look, they are a little closer to the camp, those trees. Those children were very frightened. Very close to the camp those trees approached. And then: "Trees on the ice" they say. Just then, there those Hairy Hearts stopped.

That old (human) man does not act frightened. He tells those Hairy Hearts to come inside the lodge. Inside the lodge, they are eating beaver meat. And then really when they come into the lodge, they become human beings. They lose all their powers and the ice in their bodies melts. Truly, those Hairy Hearts would be frightened of fires and heat because it melts the ice in their bodies and they lose their "powers."

They stayed there then with the people in that camp. Always they would eat animal meat like the others. That old man and his son both marry women in that group of families just there. In the winter, the young man goes out hunting with his brothers-in-law. He brings back to the camp every kind of meat. But he stays a long time outside the lodge; seldom does he go in and stay by the fire. Really, he is still wicked, that young man. By staying out in the cold, he is getting "stronger." Again there begins to be ice in his body. He stays out in the bush because he doesn't want to be warm.

It becomes spring there. Still that young man goes hunting with his brothers-in-law. Then really: "When I hunt with your younger brothers, they resemble animals to me," that young man says to his wife. In the morning, he will go out hunting again with his brothers-in-law. They are preparing, outside the lodge. Then she hides the snowshoes of her brother, that woman. He comes inside the lodge to look for them. "There is something wrong again with my husband," she tells her brother. "Be careful when you hunt with him. Watch out for the welfare of our younger sibling."

They leave and go to hunt animals. Never is that young Hairy Heart staying with his brothers-in-law. He follows behind them, looking at their snowshoes tracks. He walks ahead of them through the bush. Then just there, he jumps out and grabs him. Then just there, the other one chops off his head.

At the camp, those two old men are sitting in the lodge. Immediately, he knows it, that his son has been killed, that old Hairy Heart. Truly he says to all of them there: "You killed my son. Now, if you don't kill me I will destroy all of you." They took sticks and tried to kill that old man. He is too powerful for them, always he overcomes them. One woman stabs him in his arm with a sharp roasting stick. There is bone marrow on the stick. "How does it taste to you?" she says to him, that woman. "It is good meat," he says. Then just there, he seizes her with his other arm and kills her. Now the others are frightened that they cannot prevail over him. They run from the lodge. Just then those two men return to the camp. They enter the lodge and see that old Hairy Heart sitting by the fire. With their clubs, they strike him until he is dead. Only because he is near the fire, are those brothers able to kill him.

kayānwī Kills Hairy Hearts at the Beaver Lodge
Narrator: Cornelius Colomb

That's this *kayānwī*. So it so happens that he went and looked for his nephew. The guy killed his brother, so he went and looked for him. That nephew was staying with the *mīmīðītīhīsiwak* ["hairy heart beings"]. Married to a Hairy Heart woman. Because these Hairy Hearts, they wereīkill people whenever they run into them. Kill all the men and take the women. Take all the women for later. He feeds on all the kids and they kill all the men. Because the men were dangerous to them. Might kill them. The women couldn't kill them. But this time they kept one guy. That nephew of *kayānwī*'s [now in league with Hairy Hearts]. Those Hairy Hearts eat those women. That's their feed. Some Hairy Hearts, they married the nice-looking women. Have them for wives. Well, they each have five or four wives.

And it so happens that he found the guy he was looking for, that *mīmīðītīhīsiw*. He runs into the old man. He [*kayānwī*] had his father-in-law's pants. Well, of course, old people, they had moose hide pants. Old man always kneeling—well, back then it was in the wigwams. Well, first thing you know, his knees are sticking out of his pants. Because he's always kneeling. When he stand up, the hide will be worn away. So he had his father-in-law's pants and bow and arrows and a jacket.

Oh, he was dressed kind of funny. That old man [Hairy Heart], he wanted to pack *kayānwī* home and kill him right away but he was scared of his knife.

He goes back to where the Hairy People are camped. "I was going to pack him home but I was scared of his knife. And his cheeks were like this—there were marks on his face like a burn mark. Kind of a dangerous looking guy." So that Indian [nephew] they were living with said, "Oh, that's my uncle. He's going to kill us. Sure as hell he's going to kill us. He's a dangerous man." "Oh hell," the old man says [addressing his sons], "you're brother-in-law [nephew] is turning out to be a coward. We'll kill that *kayānwī* this time with all the rest of them."

So early morning they went back where they had met this *kayānwī*. The Hairy family move in there. They were supposed to—they had a beaver house in there. And *kayānwī* was there already. He had these poles cut to block the runways. That's what they used to do. Break the house and chop it [after blocking the runways under the ice] so the beavers don't go anywhere. You just have to catch them by hand and throw them on shore. So everything was ready. The Hairy Hearts come there, the old man and his two boys. *kayānwī* says to him, "Let your boys go cut poles in the bush." So they go off on the side-road. So he told the old man, "Taste the water and see how many beavers." They can tell by tasting the water if it's a big family. *kayānwī* tasted the water first. And the old man just about hit him with the chisel on the head. And *kayānwī* looks at him and he said, "Boy, I think you just about did something to me." "Oh," that Hairy Heart said, "No. That's just this *patamikan* ["trail over ice"]. Hard packed. Just about slipped."

Ha! And this *mīmīðītīhīsiw*, he was the next to taste the water. And he kept looking at this *kayānwī* and *kayānwī* said, "What the hell, I wouldn't kill you." Ha! The Hairy Heart believed him. As he was kneeling over to taste the water, *kayānwī* stabbed him and hit him on the back of the head and shove him under [the ice]. He broke [up through] the ice and he said, "Someday, there'll be people later on. I want them to do one set of beavers for me sometimes [sacrifice beavers]." "Oh," *kayānwī* said, "you've had enough of them Indians. You've eaten lots. So nobody has to do one set of beavers for you." So he killed the old man in there. The Hairy Heart wants—like a guy will kill one beaver house now and then, every now and then. Like one set of beaver, one whole beaver house. And he wants—like you kill them and maybe you throw them in the fire or whatever. That'd be for the old man. He want it that way. So *kayānwī* didn't want it that way. He said, "The hell with you. Nobody's gonna' take one set of beavers for you." So he had him there and he drowned the old man.

So *kayānwī* picked up his bow and arrow where he left them on the side there where he'd been cutting those logs [runway poles]. He went along the side-road until he saw one Hairy Heart packing logs. He shot him with his bow and arrow and he got him in the ribs [killing him]. So to the next one, the last one. The Indian guy was still up in the bush. He didn't want to come down because he knows—he didn't even say hello to his uncle because he knows he's after him. So finally he sees him coming and he said, "Thanks for killing them all [Hairy Hearts]. I've seen them killing people all the time." *kayānwī* said, "You think you're going to pull through? I made a special trip for you. You killed my brother. You're not going to live." Then that Indian began throwing poles at him until they were gone. Until there was none left. So he shot his nephew in the ribs and killed him. So he goes back down to the beaver house.

And the [Hairy Heart] women were coming down. They're surprised because they only see one guy [*kayānwī*] down there by the house. They keep stopping and talking about it. And he holler at them, "Hurry up! I killed out your whole family!" And the old lady misunderstood him. She said, "I think all the Indians are dead." They figure that's that old man [Hairy Heart] over there by the beaver house. So they came. They were coming to the beaver house. And now they see it's *kayānwī* there. The old lady comes up close to him and says, "Where's the old man?" He was coming out, he was sticking up out of the hole in the ice. His ass stick out after he was drowned. *kayānwī* said, "You can see his ass sticking up over there." She said, "Where's my boys?" "They're in the bush, here and there, laying dead."

The old lady got angry. She said, "You think you're going to live?" Oh, *kayānwī* never answered. She took her pack and she had this rock for pounding meat with. The old ladies used to have that rock all the time. So she had that rock. "You're not going to pull through," she said. "You kill all my family and I'm going to kill you." She gets ready to throw that big stone. "*tapascin*! ["run from me in fear"] Run away!" she keeps saying. "Run away!" Oh, *kayānwī* knows when she's going to throw the rock. And as she throw the rock, he duck into that hole in the beaver house and come up the other side. Well, the beaver house, it's pretty strong. Old lady threw that rock right through that beaver house. Then she took off, the old lady took off. Because she had nothing else to fight with. *kayānwī* ran after her. He had a spear and he speared the old lady in the back and killed her.

He went to the Hairy Heart where they were keeping those [Indian] women. So he told the women, "Take all whatever they got, those *mīmīðītīhīsiw* women. Take all the axes." He said that to those Indian women. They went back, trailing those Hairy Heart women. They catch them and *kayānwī* took everything off of them. After he took everything off from those other women, he told them [human women] to start killing them. So they kill all those *mīmīðītīhīsiw* women. All killed.

And that was the end so he took all the women home. All that was left. A few kids too, I guess. That's one story. That's the end of it. That's the one who used to hunt those Hairy Heart people. That was his trade. He wanted to wipe out every one of them. So finally he did.

kayānwī Kills Hairy Hearts with Trees
Narrator: Cornelius Colomb

One time *kayānwī* was coming to a lot of wigwams. That was a big village of Hairy Hearts. Well, all the men were out hunting yet. First wigwam he come into, there was two old guys who were in there talking. In the wigwam. This one old man was saying he had a swell time last spring. They run into a big family of Indians. They kill all the men and they take the women for later to eat. And they were eating some small kids too. They were making those birch canoes. Instead of using—for front keels, they use the back of a small kid. They just bend the backbone and use that for making canoes. He said, "We had a swell time last spring. We were eating a lot of people."

And *kayānwī* was listening and he come in the door just then. And he said, "What did you say you were eating, old man?" And that Hairy Heart understood it was an Indian, it wasn't his kind. He just about said "Indians" and then he said "beaver houses." He said he was talking about beaver. "Oh, I don't think you said beaver house because I was listening outside." So he grabbed the old man from the head and put his head into the fireplace in the wigwam. He does the same to the other one. So he takes off from there. As he's going through the bush, every time he sees a tree hanging down—you see those trees in the wintertime. They're bent under all the snow in the branches. *kayānwī* jumps over those trees. Every time he jump over a tree, he said, "Grab him!"

So that old Hairy Heart in the wigwam. He didn't want anyone to do anything about his burned face or the ashes on him. "Don't bother," he said to them. "I want my son to see me like this." So his son comes in that night. He sees his father is badly burned in the face. He ask him, "Who did that to you?" Oh, he said he had a visitor, an Indian guy come visit. So his son take off after *kayānwī*. Takes his partners with him. The others tell him not to go, but he takes off. So later they go after them to check what happened. So they went on the trail and about a hundred feet away they see him hanging there in the tree. Well, the ones that go on ahead, they see guys hanging from the trees all along the trail. All dead. They had no idea to go around the tree because they got to stick close on his trail.

This guy *kayānwī* had more guts than the other guys, I guess. So that's how he come to wipe out the *mīmīðītīhīsiwak*. He kill 'em all. Because there's none now. That's this guy and he kill every one of them. Ah, it was his job, hunting them until there was none left. That was the end of *mīmīðītīhīsiwak*. No more Hairy Hearts.

Discussion

Both the *mīmīðītīhīsiwak* and their opponent *kayānwī* are widely distributed and little-known characters in Subarctic Algonquian oral literature. Although the first and third of the preceding narratives do not, to my knowledge, occur in published sources, versions of *kayānwī*'s duel with the monsters at the beaver lodge have been recorded from Cree, Ojibwa, and Montagnais sources.

Rock Crees translate *mīmīðītīhīsiwak* as "Hairy Hearts" or "Hairy Heart People" and define them as an autochthonous race of cannibal beings who fed on humans in the remote past. Henry Linklater defined them as "a kind of *wītikōw*," but stated that they had not previously been human beings, that they ate animal food in addition to people, and that they could speak and might otherwise appear normal to humans. They are understood literally to have possessed hearts covered with hair, an attribute that recalls the frozen viscera of the *wītikōw*. Since Crees, like Europeans, associate the heart with kindness, the hairy hearts themselves are tangible symbols of cruelty and inhumanity. Caroline Caribou explained that "It's like they don't have any hearts" and Henry Linklater stated that the name connoted "no goodness, no feelings."

The earliest reference to the Hairy Hearts that I have located is in Nelson's 1823 letter journal (Brown and Brightman 1988). Nelson's Saskatchewan Cree sources represented them as a bellicose and primitive race who contested with Indians for control of the earth in the remote past. Nelson recorded the name "o-may-mi-thay-day-ace-cae-wuck" [*omēmīðētēhēsiwak*], clearly cognate to modern Woods Cree *mīmīðītīhīsiwak* in which /ī/ and /ē/ have fallen together in many positions; he glossed the form as "hairy breasts" and also used the term "ancients." Nelson preserved a narrative recounting the deliverance of humans from the Hairy Hearts by the hero *nēhanīmis*, here represented as the son of *wīsahkīcāhk*. The hero determines to make an end to the monsters lest they exterminate humans, and, after a dispute over the ownership of beaver lodges, the opponents engage separately in competitive eat-all feasts that prefigure the victory of those who eat the most. The chief Hairy Heart tries also to divine his success with a rattle that remains ominously silent. In the subsequent battle, *nēhanīmis* kills one band of the monsters and, in a passage recalling Mr. Colomb's narrative above, instructs their female captives to kill the Hairy Heart women. Subsequently, the hero insults two older Hairy Hearts by shoving their heads in the fire, again a motif reproduced in the second of Mr. Colomb's stories. He then destroys the monsters by enticing them into a pitfall trap in which they are impaled or clubbed.

Although hostile to human beings, the Hairy Hearts of Nelson's account are not cannibalistic and it remains unclear whether this is an error or whether the category is regionally or temporally variable with respect to this feature. In Nelson's time, the Hairy Hearts were summoned into the shaking lodge from whence their voices could be heard, boasting of their strength and their prowess with the pre-European technology. In these respects, Nelson's Hairy Hearts resemble the *kayāsiðiniwak* ["ancient people"] in modern Rock Cree tradition, a primitive race of "cave men" who occupied the Churchill drainage before the Crees.

The Hairy Hearts figure also in a Plains Cree *wīsahkīcāhk* myth (Ahenakew 1929: 339–43) where, as in all other sources, they are represented as cannibals. Like *nēhanīmis* in Nelson's narrative, *wīsahkīcāhk* determines to destroy the monsters before they exterminate humans. After playing various tricks upon them, he lures them into a trap, clubs them to death, and then burns their hearts; the ashes become the first rabbits. Reminiscent of the old Hairy Heart's staff in Mrs. Linklater's "The Hairy Hearts" is a staff on which human victims are compelled to impale themselves. As in Nelson's description, much is made of the stupidity of the Hairy Hearts, an attribute not developed elsewhere.

Two versions of *kayānwī*'s duel with the monsters at the beaver lodge were recorded from Montagnais groups. Skinner's (1911: 108–12) Rupert's House version identifies the hero as *"kanweo"* and his opponents only as cannibals; the encounter at the beaver lodge follows an earlier battle and, as in Nelson's story, a competitive eat-all feast. Speck's (1925: 19–20) version identifies the hero as *"känowéo,"* and the name is glossed as "he who kills at a great distance with an arrow." His opponent is named *mamilteheo*, "he who has a hairy heart"; it is unclear whether members of the monster's family were known generically as Hairy Hearts. Both Montagnais versions add the grisly resolution of the villain's body being used as a pole to stake the runways from the beaver lodge.

The character of *"guy-an-way,"* cognate to *kayānwī* and to the Montagnais names given above, appears in a cycle of narratives known to the Severn Ojibwa of Sandy Lake (Ray and Stevens 1971: 136–42) where he is represented as descending to earth from another world in the sky. As among Rock Cree, he is explicitly identified with a period of the world during which cannibalistic beings are gaining ascendency over humans. The version of the duel at the beaver lodge makes no explicit reference to Hairy Hearts but the leading cannibal possesses waist-length hair as a distinguishing feature. The story also contains the motif of rattle divination that figures in Nelson's Hairy Heart narrative. Both the hero character and the Hairy Hearts are known to the Lake Winnipeg Saulteaux as indicated by manuscripts by Hallowell in the American Philosophical Society collections.

Wolverine, Wolf, and Fire Medicine
Narrator: Cornelius Colomb

There's this wolverine and the guy who's with him, Wolf, and they were out hunting one day. The wolf was the one that had the "matches." They make a magic fire. They just jump over the dry wood and that thing explodes and they make fire.

And the wolverine never had that kind of/of power. So he asked that wolf to have some of the powers.

Oh, wolf said, "That's right, brother, I'll give it to you." Because, of course, he was a brother of the animals. So wolverine tried it and the damn thing exploded. "Oh," wolf said, "You're alright, brother. As long as you don't just play with what I gave you."

Oh, wolverine said, "No, no, I wouldn't do any such thing. I need the fire."

So later wolverine is monkeying around the shoreline. Sometimes old beaver houses, that's where you see lots of dry wood. Every time wolverine sees dry wood he wants to make fire. Pretends that he's cold. Throw a few sticks, jump over it, jump over 'em, and it explodes. Few minutes, he's done with the fire and away he goes again. So every morning, wherever he goes, you see about five or six fires. That's wolverine. Making fires all morning for nothing.

So the wolves got mad at him. Said, "I guess our little brother is making fun of our medicine. Every time we see him going he always fires all the way. Gotta' cut off his 'match'."

So happens, the next fire, wolverine couldn't make a fire. Tried it again. No. So one cool morning he went up in the hill. Seen lots of fires. All different kinds of animals making different fires. All kinda different smoke from there. One of them's got different smoke from the other. And him, he had nothing. He was cold. So he hollered, "Brothers! Sisters! I don't have no lights, no match, no way of making any fire. But there'll be people years ahead. They'll be wanting to make fire. But all they'll do is start hunting us when they see our fires. Best if we don't have any fire. That way we'll make it. But if we have fires, they'll clean us out. Best if we share it with them." Oh, all the animals agreed with him. "I think that'll be true," they say. "If there's gonna' be any people, they gonna hunt us out." So they holler at him, "Okay, brother, no more fires!"

So that's how come there's no fire for the animals. Otherwise, they'd be hunted out [laughs]. It would be lots—people would be making lots of money as fire fighters nowadays. Animals would be putting on all the fires like wolverine.

Discussion

This is the only Cree myth I have encountered that accounts for the origin of fire and human proprietorship over it. Of particular interest are the differentiation of types of fires by animal species, the fact that the wolverine is the only proto-animal to lack fire, and the broadly Darwinian rationale used by the latter to persuade the others to relinquish fire to human beings. The ability of some *opawāmiwak*, "dreamers" or "spiritually empowered persons" to start fires by leaping over the firewood is recalled by some Crees and parallels the technique that the wolves teach to wolverine.

wīhcikōsisak
Narrator: Cornelius Colomb

These *wīhcikōsisak* were small people but they were *wīhtikōw*s. They were the ones who were eating people. But they were in bunches. Different with *wīhtikōw*. *wīhtikōw* is alone, eh? He eat the whole village. He eat the whole thing. But these *wīhcikōsisak*, they were different people. They were in families but they used to eat people. I guess that's those—what you call them down south? Cannibals. Cannibals used to eat people, eh? That must've been them. Well, they used to eat people. And this one man was always hunting them. Trying to kill them all. Finally he did kill them all.

This one time, this one *wīhcikōsis* was chasing him all over the place. This is in early fall. Freeze up. So it was getting dark. So he went up in a tree. The man went up in a tree. He was tired. And the *wīhcikōw* couldn't find him. The guy's gonna quit, the small *wīhtikōw*. Thought, "I'll spend the night here." And it to happens the man was up in the tree above. And him, the *wīhtikōw*, it so happens the *wīhtikōw* camped right under the tree. Was waiting for daylight so he can track that guy, wherever he's going. The man in the tree wanted to piss late at night. He know that *wīhcikōw* was sitting there. So he pissed on this *wīhcikōsis*. And the *wīhcikōsis* said, "Hell, it's not warm enough. It couldn't be raining. Not warm enough." So he waited 'till morning. And it was daylight already and the *wīhcikōsis* got up from where it was sitting all night. Said, "Now I'm going to look for that moose." Used to call them [humans] "moose," *mōswa* ["moose"]. "Hah!" he said, "I'm going to look for the moose now in the daylight." And he was stretching out. He was looking at the sky. "It was raining last night." And here the man was sitting on the top of the tree. "You son of a bitch, you pissed on me last night! Well, I'm going to pack you home, moose! After all, you piss on me last night!" So he climbed up the small tree. He had spears with him all the time. He had a hard time climbing the tree with the spears. He was getting close to the man.

"Oh, you might drop your spear," the man said. "If I was you, I'd give it to the moose to hold for me."

"Ah," he said, "you're going to trick me, moose."

"No," he said, "I wouldn't trick you." So, I guess this man—I guess he overbrained the guy. Like a guy wants to say something to you. He looks through your eyes. Like you're playing poker, eh? You can't tell what I got in my hand. If I bet and I'm trying to bluff you—if I know you got something and I'm trying to get your money—I'm trying to bluff you—you might pass with a pair. This way I haven't got nothing, just the big cards on top. Same thing with the little *wīhtikōw*.

Finally, he said, "You might be true." He gave him the spear. "Here, hold it. Hold on. Hold onto the spear and I'll get to you." Stupid guy.

And after he's just about coming up, the man said, "Don't look up. Because I'm moving lots. Something might get in your eye."

"Don't move around," the *wīhtikōw* said. And he was just right close to him and the man speared him. Somewhere in here [indicates back of head]. Away he went. Down. After he got up he was looking at the man who was holding the spear and he said, "You son of a bitch, I figured that's what you were going to do." So he went home. Got home.

He said, "I seen a moose last night. But it threw my spear into me when he was on top of the tree. Told me to give him my spear and after I got to him he speared me."

So the other *wīhcikōsis* said, "What are we going to do with the guy?"

"Well, pull it out," another *wīhcikōsis* said. "He'll be alright." Well the guy hollered lots when they wanted to pull the spear out. Oh, he hollers loud.

"Now what are we going to do?" They asked the medicine man to come around.

And the old [medicine] man said, "Get a big stick. Hit the spear in further and we'll cook him." So they hit the spear into him and they killed him. They cook him. That was the end of him.

So he went back to the [*wīhcikōsis*] village again, the same man [*wīhcikōsis* slayer]. Went and visited the tent. Oh, right away, they all jumped up yelling, "Moose! Moose!" They started chasing him. But he'd seen—like around Churchill River, you see potholes [on the ice] where it's not frozen, eh? He check all those good places as he was coming to the village. So the *wīhcikōsisak* were chasing the man. He was zig-zagging as he was running. That must've been here in Churchill River because you can see a lot of bad spots where you can go through the ice. And the *wīhcikōsisak*, they just went straight, running after him. And they keep falling through the ice. Until there was none left.

So again they were hollering for help. They had no rope in them times. There was no rope. They tried to catch them with a stick but the ice was too weak.

Oh, one of them ask the old people, "What are we gonna do?"

Oh, the old man say, "Spear them." Like you can throw on the smooth ice, eh? You can throw a sharp stick to something. That spear will slide into that thing, eh? So they keep sliding sharp sticks and they had them, every one of them. "We'll eat them," the old man said. So after the ice was solid enough, they went and picked up those guys. About seven there to cook afterwards. And the ones that got them, they feed their cocks to the *wīhcikōsis* women. The old man said, "You feed the women the cocks. Feed those women so they'll have a last feed out of their men." And those *wīhcikōsis* women, they keep crying because they didn't want to eat the cocks. Makes them remember their old man [husbands]. Oh, the medicine man got mad. Said, "What the hell they crying for? You kill 'em. We'll cook them tomorrow." So they kill the women. They had a great feast the next day. They were strict people.

So that's how this man, he wiped them out. He was hunting them all the time. There was none of them left. He was a smart man. He kept hunting them. Well, they kill themselves. If one of them is sick like that one with the spear, they kill him because he's no good anymore. Can't hunt. Oh, they'd eat him. No use feeding him all winter to get well. These *wīhcikōsisak* are different people. Hairy [Heart] people are different. These are small *wīhtikōw*. That's how there are no more of these now. He cleans them out.

Discussion
Although Mr. Colomb made clear that the *wīhcikōsisak* are distinct both from the solitary *wīhtikōw* and from the Hairy Hearts, the trickster episode in the tree occurs in a Plains Cree myth (Ahenakew 1929: 341–42) describing *wīsahkīcāhk*'s encounter with the latter. The small stature and endocannibalism of the *wīhcikōsisak* appear to differentiate them from other cannibal monsters. It is interesting also that the stupidity ascribed to the Hairy Hearts in some Cree narratives (Ahenakew ibid., Brown and Brightman 1987) is here attributed to a distinct class of beings.

The cannibals' reference to potential human victims as "moose" parallels the perceptual distortion or orientation ascribed to *wīhtikōws* which are said to experience human beings as conventional game animals. It is unclear in the case of the *wīhcikōsisak* whether the reference is literal or nomenclatural; whether or not the cannibals perceive humans as game animals, the myth emphasizes the homology between the cannibal/human and human/animal relationships.

cahkāpīs Kills Giants and Snares the Sun
Narrator: Cornelius Colomb
So this *cahkāpīs*, those *mistāpēw*ak ["giants"] killed his dad and his mother. *cahkāpīs* was a kid then. They were hiding, him and his sister. So he come to be a man and he went and look for those giants. He went and look for the giants.

So he see they were chopping beaver houses. So he went up to them and they said, "Well, *cahkāpīs*, we've blocked everything [runways from beaver lodge] there. Go take those beavers." *cahkāpīs* took his jacket off. He threw two beavers out and hit [killed] them. He had two big beavers. That was all he wanted. Didn't bother the rest. So he took the string from his bow and tied them up. He was going to leave and the giant said, "Aren't you going to give us one? We did all the work." *cahkāpīs* threw down the two beavers again.

Said, "Go ahead. But only if you can untie my string." They couldn't do it. Oh, he said, "Too bad you can't do it. So you get nothing." Oh, the giants got mad. They went back and looked for *cahkāpīs* next day. So he knew they were going to come for him. He had this—clam. You see them in the water. They open up. And he took one of them home. And the giants were coming so he got into the clam and shut himself in. He got inside. He told his sister not to go out, to stay inside.

Oh, those giants came there. "Where's *cahkāpīs*?"

"Oh, he's right there in the clam," the sister says. So they pound the clam with an axe and rocks but they couldn't do it. Couldn't get it open. Then they made a big fire and threw the clam in the fire. Oh, the damn thing wouldn't burn. So they couldn't do nothing.

So they said, "The hell with him. We'll take his sister." So they took his sister. They left. They were crossing the lake. *cahkāpīs* came out of the clam. Seen them going. So he had a big arrow with a big head [point]. He had one special.

So he said to his arrow, "You see those two big men. Not the little one [sister], the two on each side. I want you to hit 'em." So he shot at them. He shot the arrow. Seen the one falling [dead] and then the other one. And he hollered to his sister. He said, "Come back." So that was the end of it. That was the end of the giants.

So he was always hunting. He seen a road hard-packed [snow] like a guy had been going there steady. He didn't know what the hell was that. So again he took his bow string and made a snare wire and laid a snare and then he goes home. It was always daylight in them days. There was no night, nothing. So finally all of a sudden it got dark. No daylight for a long time.

So the woman [sister] asked *cahkāpīs*, "What the hell, did you do anything again the last time you were out?"

"Oh, yeah," he said, "I snare somebody who was using a packed road. I put a snare out there."

"I bet you snared the sun," the woman said. "You better go and try and get him out." So *cahkāpīs* went out in the dark where was setting his snare. So he come into the place and he seen he couldn't go close to the sun. Too hot. Couldn't do nothing. So he hired this little mouse. This one mouse that we see in wintertime. Stupid mouse. On the trail, if he comes into the trail—well, the snow stiffens [forms crust] right away. He doesn't have no idea to punch a hole in the side to get into the warm [soft] snow. He stays in the bottom. Once he gets on the road, he got no idea to get off the road. So he freezes. You see lots in wintertime. It's brown as if it's burnt. Looks like it's burnt. But that's the only one. The rest of them, you don't see these mice like the ones that stick around the house. Big ears. Kind of brown light-colored ones. And the ones with long tails. The ones with long noses. You don't see those freeze in the road. But this special one, it looks like its burnt. Brownish color in the back. It's got a small tail. That's the one. That's the one that went and cut that rope.

cahkāpīs said, "Don't worry. I'll pull you through. See if you can cut the rope [snare holding the sun]." So he went and cut the rope but he was burnt on the back. So he put him back to life. "But every time," *cahkāpīs* said, "after this, every time you run into a trail you'll die." So everytime you see that mouse, he comes into the road and you'll see him laying there dead, frozen. That's the story of the mouse and the sun. That's why it's dark at night now. Before it used to be straight daylight. After *cahkāpīs* snare the sun, that's how it comes to—the sun is weaker. It stops now and then because its—not enough energy to make it. He's got to stop to rest every twelve hours. Every twelve hours he stops to rest. That's why you see dark. Because *cahkāpīs* wanted to have it that way.

Discussion

cahkāpīs [Swampy and Plains Cree *cahkāpēs*, Ojibwa *jēkabēš*] figures as the hero in a cycle of recurring narratives extending from Quebec-Labrador to at least as far west as Manitoba. A preliminary tabulation of the character's exploits appears below based on Montagnais and Eastern Cree (Skinner 1911: 100–02; Speck 1925: 3–6, 12–16, 25–27; Savard 1979: 4–11; Bauer 1971: 58–64), Swampy Cree (Skinner 1911: 102–04, Cresswell 1923: 404–05, Clay 1938: 28–33), and Severn Ojibwa (Ray and Stevens 1971: 101–10) sources. Solar and lunar associa-

Table 4. The *cahkāpīs* Cycle

	Skinner E Cree	Skinner S Cree	Speck	Savard	Bauer	Cresswell	Clay	Ray & Stevens
Parents killed by monsters	+	+		+	+	+	+	+
Lives with sister								
Slays killers of parents	+	+		+	+	+	+	
Fights giants at beaver lodge	+	+		+	+		+	
Conflict with female giant	+	+	+	+	+		+	+
Acquires wives	+		+	+	+			
Swallowed by fish	+	+		+	+	+		+
Conflict with sorceror								+
Outwits giants on ice								+
Transforms into stone								+
Snares sun			+	+	+	+		
Snares moon	+	+	+					
Becomes sun			+					
Becomes man-in-moon			+		+		+	
Defeats cannibal women with swing			+					
Transforms mink			+					

tions, co-residence with his sister, and small stature are recurring attributes of the character.

Mr. Colomb's version of the hero's conflict with giants at the beaver lodge is unusual in identifying them as the slayers of the parents since these characters and the revenge upon them typically form a distinct story. Mentioned in other versions is the fact that the monsters are engaged in trapping giant beavers which they expect will pull *cahkāpīs* underwater when he attempts to remove them from the lodge. The Clay version simply terminates with the hero breaking the giants' arms. In the Bauer and in Skinner's Eastern Cree version, the hero, rather than retreating into a clam, protects himself and his sister from the giants by transforming his lodge into stone. Skinner's Swampy Cree version most closely parallels Mr. Colomb's narrative since it contains the episodes, missing elsewhere, in which the giants abduct the sister and the hero shoots them with a verbally instructed arrow. The recurring motif of the hero's use of a hard barrier to confound the giants occurs in the Severn Cree version to bring the cycle to a melancholy close: *cahkāpīs* transforms himself and his sister into stones but is then unable to resume hominid form.

cahkāpīs's exploits with the sun and/or the moon figure in all accounts of him and, like other versions, Mr. Colomb's narrative explains the alternation between day and night as a consequence of the sun's temporary imprisonment. The hero's associations with the sun and moon are, in some versions, intensified to identity or near-identity. In one of Speck's versions (1925: 53–54), the hero is appointed to substitute for the sun he has snared; elsewhere he ascends into the sky-world with his family at the end of his career (Skinner 1911: 101–02) and/or becomes the man in the moon (Speck 1935: 56, Clay 1938: 32–33, Bauer 1971: 64–65). Mr. Colomb's evident concern with the mouse (the redback vole, *Clethrionomys gapperi*) that bites through the snare and releases the sun exemplifies the interest often taken by Cree narrators in the etiological aspects of their literature. Mice also figure in the Ray and Stevens and in the Bauer versions; a shrew (Speck, Skinner) and a mole (Cresswell) figure as the liberators in other versions. It is clearly significant that from among all possible animal characters small burrowing and/or subterranean animals should re-establish the connection between the earth and the sun. It is also relevent to suggest a possible parallel between the trail of the sun across the sky and the terrestrial foot trails through the snow within which the mouse freezes because it cannot escape by burrowing through the crust.

Levi-Strauss (1979: 390–98) has placed *cahkāpīs*'s snaring of the sun within the context of cognate Algonquian and Siouan myths, emphasizing that the snare material identified as the sister's hair (Speck 1935: 55–56, Cresswell 1923: 404) is more narrowly specified as pubic hair (Bauer 1971: 64) in some versions. Aside from the evident parallelism between solar/lunar and menstrual periodicity, Levi-

Strauss's comparative discussion demonstrates the association of the pubic hair trap with the disjunction between earth and sun that it inaugerates. It is worth noting, in this connection, another dimension of hair symbolism that occurs in different versions of the hero's revenge on his parents' killers. In three versions (Skinner, Bauer), *cahkāpīs* retrieves his parents' hair from the stomach of the monsters and brings it home to his sister, an obvious reciprocation for the hair with which she continually provides him. In a significantly differing Swampy Cree version (Cresswell), *cahkāpīs* plucks hair from the bear that had killed his parents and, rather than presenting it to his sister, forbids her to look at it before suspending it in the lodge in a birchbark covering. Subsequently, they hear shouts in the bush but are unable to locate anyone. *cahkāpīs* then accuses his sister of looking at the hair and begins weeping. There is no elaboration but inferentially the sister interferes with the regeneration of the slain parents by gazing excessively at the hair while menstruating. From this perspective, the bear's fur, metonymically and metaphorically associated with the ingested parents, potentially functions to create a conjunction between life and death while menstruation is represented as disjunctive and antagonistic to the project of regeneration.

The Dog Council
Narrator: Caroline Caribou

A story about a dog council meeting. Well, one day the announcement came. It said there was going to be a dog council meeting. But before all the dogs could come in, they all had to hang their rear-ends in the doorway. So while they were all in the middle of their stories, somebody shouted "Fire! Fire!" And they all ran out and they pick out any rear-ends that were hanging there. They all ran out and scattered around the village. So when you see a dog today/everytime you see a dog, you know, they run up to each other and smell behind their tails. They're still looking for their rear-ends. That's why today when you see a small dog with a big rear-end—big around its behind/that means it took the wrong rear-end. End of my dog council story.

Discussion
Mrs. Caribou narrated this story deadpan, her voice registering the heroic suppression of involuntary laughter. No other published versions are known to me. Other persons in the Pukatawagan community recalled versions in which *wīsahkīcāhk* figures as the instigator.

Wolverine Defeats Great Skunk
Narrator: Cornelius Colomb

Animals used to travel in bunches like humans. They had their—all mixed animals: squirrels, rabbits, foxes, coyotes. All the animals. They were scared of this *misisikānātōs*, this big skunk. They were trying to run from him, but the skunk was behind, tracking them. They didn't know how far behind he was so the mink decided he'd wait for him. Pretend that he was dead.

So here comes that big skunk. He was ready to shoot it. Shoot his poison at the mink from that machine he has under his ass. Thought he was sleeping. Well, he had his poison. Was going to shoot the mink if he takes off. So anyway the mink pretended he was dead. So he grab the mink and look at him, try to figure out what happened to him. "I don't see nothing wrong with him." Oh, he was turning him around and finally he come to his ass side. Looks at the ass. "Oh, son of a bitch, someone shot it with a bow and arrow. They guy must have pulled an arrow." [The Great Skunk, because of its gigantic size, is unaware that it has an anus and that other animals also possess them; consequently, it misidentifies the mink's anus as an arrow wound.] He hung that mink in a tree. He said, "I'll eat it on my way back." So after he was gone, the mink took off and went ahead and told the animals, "He's two days behind." He was coming close to catching them. He wasn't too far from them, eh?

So again this weasel did the same thing after two days. Pretended he was dead. Acted dead there on the road. The same thing happened. The big skunk checked that weasel. Looked at the weasel to see what happened to him. How come he was dead. He come to it and look at his ass. "Oh hell," he said, "someone shot it with an arrow. I don't know what the hell happened. Maybe he got into an argument and got shot. I'll hang it up here. Pick it up on my way back."

So they weren't too far. Another three days' time. They were camping across a lake. He [skunk] was crossing the lake and he can hear the ice breaking because he was so big. Ice keep breaking as he was going. Anyway, they weren't too far. They were tired because they were running away from this big skunk. They had no time to hunt or nothing. It was travelling, just straight travelling. So they were getting scared because the guy is catching up on them. So they ask for whoever can do something to that skunk. So finally they come to this wolverine.

They say, "Brother. You're the brother he [skunk] was given. [Mr. Colomb points out that both species smell bad.] You should know what to do."

He said, "Oh, well, if we see a beaver house tomorrow, you pass the house and I'll chop [open] the house. I'll wait for him there." Well this wolverine knows stories. He likes storytelling. And his tail was his chisel. That's why its short. He broke it one time, that's why his tail's so short now. Well, I guess he had the whole tail then at that time because he was chopping a hole in that beaver house. He was making holes here and there.

So this skunk come there and he says, "You guys are really travelling. What the hell are you travelling so fast for?" He said, "I'm tired trying to catch up with you guys."

And the wolverine said, "Oh, they're scared of *misisikānātōs*." Well, the guy didn't know his name. Supposed to be "*sikāk*" but they call him *misisikānātōs*.

He said, "Who's that guy? What the hell they scared for?"

Wolverine said, "It's your stink. That's what they're scared for, your stink." Well, the guy was bitching, wolverine. "They're scared of your stink."

Ha, the guy got mad right away and said, "You're not a friendly guy. You sure talk rough. This is the first time I see you. You're not a friendly guy." The skunk said that to wolverine. So, "I'll face you on it," he said. He turned around and he wanted to throw the stink on him, eh? The wolverine ducked down into the hole [in the beaver lodge]. Ha! Skunk looked back and the wolverine wasn't there. He was coming out from another hole. He dug holes where he can dig in and duck under and come out from another hole. That's what he was doing when he was chopping that beaver house.

He stick his head out from another hole and he said, "You miss me!" Oh, the wolverine got mad. He made another shot. Well, he seen it coming and he duck again and come out from another hole. "Ha! You miss me again!" Oh, the guy was really mad then. Went around and gave him another shot and the wolverine ducked again. First thing you know, he was out of—he had nothing left. The skunk, he was out of his medicine. He couldn't shoot any more. So the wolverine grab him, grab him by the asshole. And he holler on one side of his mouth to his partners, "I got him. Come on over and give me a hand."

So they all came down and said, "Cut him into all small pieces and throw them all over the place so he wouldn't be that big." That's how you see a small skunk now. They tear him up in small pieces and scatter him. Until there was just little pieces. He was too dangerous being the size of a moose. So after there was just the ass left. "Well, it's all gone," they told the wolverine so he let go. Well, he was blind then [having received a final blast of "medicine" from the anus when he released it]. So he told them to put a rag on his face. "Point me to the ocean," he said. "Because if I wash my face around this country here, people won't be able to drink it. I'll go wash my face in the ocean." So they point him toward the ocean side and away he went.

So as he was travelling he run into a tree. This was a spruce. He grab it and he said, "What kind of tree are you?" "Spruce." "Oh," he said, "usually spruce up on top of the treeline." He knows the area where he was. Up on top, in the middle of the bush. Ha! He was gone again. Well, he run into another tree. Grab it and he said, "What kind of tree are you?" "A jackpine." "Oh." Again he knows this. When you come down to the shoreline you see jackpines as the earth turns facing south, eh? It's always jackpines. So he said, "Jackpines. Well, that's halfways, now. Halfways to the ocean already." Oh, he started running again. Again he hit a tree. Run into a tree and he grab it and say, "What kind of tree are you?" And this was a birch. "Ohhh," he said, "not far from the ocean. If you see a birch, not far to the water." Away he went. Hit another tree and grab it. "What kind of tree?" "Poplar." "Ohhh, that's a shoreline tree." He start running again. He hits willows. "What kind of little sticks are you?" "We're willows." "Oh hell," he said, "I'm home. Not far from the ocean now," he said. Oh, he started running again. Finally he noticed there was hay; he was running on top of the hay. Keep going and then he start to notice there's a little bit of water until he hit the ocean. He wash his face and take that rag off his face. And that's how he happened to see the stripe on his back, eh? The time he had this—the time he grabbed that skunk, after he let go, there was a little bit of that stink left on that skunk. That stuff came out and it happened to go along his back. That's why that white stuff is on his back. So he wash his face over there in the ocean. I guess that's why the ocean is salt and you can't drink it. So ever since then the skunk is changed to small skunk now. They put him in small pieces. Scatter that skunk. It was too big. Dangerous. That's the end of it.

Discussion
The myth of wolverine's conflict with the great skunk exists in several other published versions and figures twice as a component of longer narratives. The most unusual of these is a syncretic Plains Cree version in which the victorious wolverine, after killing the skunk, takes up residence with wolves and reveals himself as *wīsahkīcāhk* (Skinner 1916: 341–46); despite their similar characteristics, the two characters are not elsewhere, to my knowledge, associated in Cree literature. A Swampy Cree version from Albany leads directly into "Wolverine and Wolf," a narrative represented in this volume by Mrs. Selazie Linklater's version. Another Swampy Cree version (Russell 1896: 217–20) parallels Mr. Colomb's in most respects. All except the Plains Cree version account for the saltiness of the ocean [identified as Hudson Bay in the Albany version] and all relate the contemporary skunk species to the dismembered corpse of its monstrous predecessor. The story is known to Severn Ojibwa at Sandy Lake (Ray and Stevens 1971: 78) and probably in other Saulteaux and Northern Ojibwa groups. The same story occurs among Eastmain Cree (Bauer 1971: 51–55) with raccoon replacing wolverine as the hero.

Wolf and Dog
Narrator: Cornelius Colomb
So it happens in the time when people start to—before there was no people. Well anyway people start to—well, there happen to be people in these times [human beings are appearing on the earth]. There was just animals before. Way back there was no people, just animals. Well, I guess the people move into our country, this side of the country. So they [animals] notice there was people. There was just

wolves and the dog was—oh, he was bigger than the wolf. But they used to call him—they didn't call him a dog like "*atim*" in those days. They used to call him "Narrow Tail." That was his name. Because his tail was narrow. Not bushy tail like a fox. "*cīcīhkwāðōs*." That was his name. And he was—at that time, he was bigger than a wolf. And his name was *cīcīhkwāðōs*.

So they had a race. So of course the dog won the race because he was a lot bigger and slimmer. So anyway after the race, he said—the wolf got a little mad. He was left behind.

Said, "You're too big to stay with the people. You're gonna eat twice—you eat twice as much as me."

Oh, the dog said, "I wouldn't be this size. I'll be way smaller than your size. So that way I won't eat that much."

Oh, the wolf said, "Good." "But remember," the wolf said, "everytime I see you, I'm gonna' kill you. Because you beat me in the race." That's why you hear—if you camp and there's wolves close by, they'll holler. As if they're crying. They're crying because a dog is there, not working for himself. Not hunting. He's just fed without worrying about what he's going to eat next. Indians—trappers, they look after their dogs. That's why a wolf, everytime he get a chance to get ahold of a dog, he kill it right away. That's his punishment. And you hear wolves hollering, they're crying because they got to hunt for their feed. Well, that's the story. That was those days.

Discussion

Although the contest between wolf and dog is widely distributed in Subarctic and Woodlands mythology, I was unable to locate other Cree versions. Of particular interest here is the representation of the sled dog's not always enviable condition as a sought-after objective by proto-animals in the mythological period.

Wolverine, Wolf, and Dog
Narrator: Cornelius Colomb

Wolverine, wolves, and the dog. They were in a bunch like. So of course the wolverine was the brother of the animals. They treat their brother nice and they told him not to chase the moose but just to run behind him and the dog and some other wolves. The older hunters [wolves] were chasing the moose. So they [the stragglers] happen to see a wolf shit.

And the dog said, "Brother, grab that fur coat."

"Oh, hell," wolverine said, "that's just wolf shit. I don't wanna' go and dirty my hands." "What's our brother saying?" The wolves said that to each other. They grab the shit and swung it. And then it was a fur coat.

Wolverine said, "Oh, I didn't know it was a fur coat. I thought it was a wolf shit." And not too far from there they seen this wolf tooth that got stuck on a tree. And again the dog say, "Pull that arrow, brother. Good bow and arrow. Oh, the moose wasn't too far. I guess the hunter miss it. Hit the tree." Oh and again wolverine try and pull it. And wolverine say, "Oh, it's just a wolf tooth. Why should I be bothering with it?" And the guy behind him grab that—pull that bow and arrow. And the wolf brings it and wolverine said, "Oh, I didn't know it was a bow and arrow. I thought it was just a wolf tooth."

Oh, the wolves already had that moose. They skin it and bury it under the snow. When they got to where they kill the moose there was just a little bit of blood, here and there.

Oh, of course wolverine, he was new with those wolves. He took a little bit of that—whatever it is—he eat that blood. He was talking to himself. "Crazy wolves," he said, "They eat every damn thing before I got here."

Oh, again one wolf said, "What's wrong with our brother, talking to himself."

Oh, wolverine said, "Nothing much." So they took the moose out and they started to divide the moose between themselves.

"Well, what do you want?" a wolf says to wolverine. "What are we gonna' give to our brother? Hindquarter?"

Oh, he says, "No, that's too bony. It's all bone. And the back end of the hindquarter is too thin and dry. There's nothing much there. It's dry. It's all solid meat [referring to absence of fat]. I don't want that."

"The ribs?"

"Oh, too many bones." Wolverine want that—I don't know what you call this part in English. We call it *osōkan* ["rump"]. Anyway, he want that part. So, he said, "Chin-chin-chin-chin-chin-chin" [wolverine's characteristic interjection]. You should have said that a long time ago." That's what he want. The best part of the moose. So anyway he had that. So he started eating. Mostly fat. After he had the best part of the moose—the best part of the meat—he drag it a little ways off and piss on it and bury it [behavior perpetuated by contemporary wolverines]. Went to sleep. Well, the wolves already had this wigwam set up already. So he went inside and sleep inside.

When he get up he seen this *akwāwān* ["drying rack"]. He was so full. All this time the wolves were making this *akwāwān*. Hanging the meat. Make fire inside, and him, he was sleeping always. Anyway, he got up and the wolves were finally sleeping. So he figures he's gotta go and do a little bit of that too. So he went and dug his meat. What's left is a little piece of meat and he hang it. Next thing you know, they were pounding the meat and they were boiling the bones. We boil the bones for a long time. Get that grease from the bones. It's nice. Good taste, you know. So wolverine, he didn't do much. He eat the bone like that and he threw it out. He didn't mind.

So anyway, after they take off, two days after, the meat was dry. Pounded meat—everything. Grease in the bag—everything. Ready to start travelling again. Oh, everytime they made camp, they were eating this dry meat, pounded meat.

And him, he only has a little dry meat. Little chunks. He had it in his coat and he'd take a little bit of it. Oh, of course, he eat all he's got the first few days they were there. Anyway, that's the end of it. He quit those wolves after that. Couldn't keep up with them. The wolverine's a small animal. Wolves travelling all the time. He said, "The hell with the guys, I'm going on my own."

Discussion

"Wolverine, Wolf, and Dog" is one of a number of myths exemplifying the incompatibility between characters belonging to different animal species, and humorously contrasts the greed and prodigality of the wolverine with the generosity and industry of the wolves. The myth also makes use of the Cree philosophical premise that different classes of beings, because of their innate characteristics, differently perceive the same phenomenal objects. The wolverine successively perceives as feces and as a wolf tooth what the wolves identify as a fur jacket and a bow and arrow. Similar cases include the identification of humans as moose by the *wīhcikōsisak*, the generalized perceptions of humans as animals by *wīhtikōw* monsters, and perceptions of animal spouses as hominid by human beings.

CHAPTER 5
kayās ācimōwina

okimāw acāhpīy Kills a Caribou With Snow
Narrator (English): Johnny Bighetty
okimāw acāhpīy was my great-grandfather. He was one the old men who had a lot of power. One winter, snow was piled up and there were no animals anywhere. No moose, no beaver, nothing. And they have no bullets and powder for those old muskets they used. So the whole family is starving, eh? And after looking for a long time, he finally sees a little herd of *sakāwatik* ("woodland caribou"). But no way to kill them, eh? So he begins to dream. He begins to pray to his *pawākan*. "We're really hungry, grandfather," he says. "We need those caribou to live," he says. He had that old Hudson's Bay musket with him. Well, the *pawākan* is talking to him...begins giving him a lesson. "Just fill up the barrel of your musket with snow. Don't be afraid of anything." So the old man did that. And it's just like moose shot in that musket. His *pawākan* made it like bullets. So he killed all those caribou.

Discussion
Johnny narrated this memorat with evident solemnity and respect. The verbs *pawāmi-* (intransitive) and *pawāt-* (transitive) can be translated as "dream" but include in their reference also waking conditions during which communication occurs between humans and spirit agencies. The use of "grandfather" to address the *pawākan* is typical. *okimāw acāhpīy* was a skilled hunter and fur trapper, mentioned in several contexts in post journals and censuses of the Hudson's Bay Company in the 1820s and 1830s.

mīmīkwīsiwak
Narrator: Sarah Bighetty
My grandfather *mīsīl* (Michel Dumas) paddled his canoe past the point over there (Granville Lake) in autumn during a moose hunting trip. He made camp on the

shore by the point and went to sleep. But he just continues to sleep. It gets to be winter and the snow covers him over but he's still sleeping there. Then something woke him up. Those *mīmīkwīsiwak* brought him inside the big rocks at the point. Everything was like glass in there. All the walls and all the things they had were made of glass. The *mīmīkwīsiwak* told *mīsīl* to sleep in there until the end of the winter. So he slept more. And when he woke up they said, "There's something that we're going to tell you now that you've stayed in our house. They told him what was going to come in the future when the White man came into the Churchill River country. They said the White man was dirty and made too much noise talking and with machines. They were going to harm everything, pollute the water and the land. "You won't see us anymore," they said. "We're going to leave here and go to Manitou Island where the Whites won't bother us." *mīsīl* knew all that years before the Whites came around here.

Discussion

Conceptions of the *mīmīkwīsiwak*, a small race of furtive hominid beings associated with water and/or riparian rocky cliffs, appear to be shared by most boreal forest and plains Cree and Ojibwa groups. The Crees at Granville Lake confirm the account given above; the dwarves once lived in the rocks at the point across from the settlement but removed to Manitou Island in order to avoid human beings and specifically White men. The *mīmīkwīsiwak* are about the size of a five year old boy, are covered with hair, and lack noses; the latter feature is particularly disgusting to some Crees. They live in families and eat fish. Several people reported having seen them in peripheral vision, but the dwarves vanished before a better view could be had of them.

Although the *mīmīkwīsiwak* are said to be shy and harmless, some persons avoid Manitou Island because it is known that dwarves prefer to be left alone. It was thought that an overnight camper might disappear for a long time like *mīsīl*. Johnny Bighetty discussed the *mīmīkwīsiwak* with little solemnity but with evident interest. He joked about camping overnight at Manitou and dreaming about the dwarves, mentioning at the same time that he would have his boat ready for a rapid departure if necessary.

The aversiveness of the dwarves to White men is reported not only from other Rock Cree communities such as Southend, Saskatchewan but also in narratives collected from Severn (Ray and Stevens 1971: 97) and Nipigon Ojibwa (Morriseau 1965: 25). Although this attribute may have diffused rapidly over the Subarctic and Plains, it appears more likely that different Algonquian bands independently ascribed to the dwarves some of the ambivalence and dislike they felt both for intrusive Whites and the social innovations the latter introduced.

manicōw
Narrator: Johnny Bighetty

A long time ago, the *opawāmiwak*, the men who had a lot of powers, used to get together in the bush and challenge each other. They'd settle on a place and meet there in the summer and demonstrate their powers. This happened up north of Granville. The *maskīkōwak* ("Swampy Crees") would come up and the Crees would always beat them.

There was one meeting with thirty or forty people there and there was one Cree called *manicōw* who could do more than any of the others. There were six gangs of them there, each with its leader. *manicōw* was the chief of one bunch. When they were about to separate, *manicōw* got up and said to the others that they were always throwing bad medicine from a distance because they were afraid to do it when their enemy was around. He said he was willing to fight [with sorcery] anyone who was on the spot. Then, to show them how much power he had, he suggested that they try to kill a caribou for their last meal together. There were no caribou around there and no one there knew how to get one. They were within sight of a large lake and *manicōw* began using his power to make a caribou come to them. Then, far away in the water, the others could see a caribou swimming towards them. *manicōw* asked the others if anyone of them had the power to kill that caribou. None of them could do it. *manicōw* pressed on his throat with his fingers. He opened his mouth wide and a bird with a sharp beak flew out of his mouth, went across the lake, and struck the caribou in the head, killing it. They went and brought the caribou into camp. Then they began to cut roasting sticks and they wanted to build the fire on clay where it would be easy to plant the sticks in the ground. *manicōw* told them to build up the fire on solid rock. So they built six separate fires on the rock. *manicōw* took the roasting sticks for his group and planted them in the solid rock just like it was clay. Then he asked the others if any of them could do that. No one could and the others became frightened. *manicōw* was doing that to frighten the other men.

When they all went off and left camp no one was talking which meant that they were angry. The six parties paddled off in their canoes in different directions. Those other medicine men were mad at *manicōw* and they began sending things at his canoe through the air. Only *manicōw* could see what they were sending at him. He protected the others by raising his canoe paddle and intercepting those things. Everytime he raised the paddle, something would hit it and stick in it. Finally there were forty things sticking to that paddle: little spears, eagle claws, bear claws, fish hooks. They couldn't strike him so the ones who were sending those things gave up.

Discussion

The story eloquently attests the arrogance and competitiveness of some Cree religious specialists, epitomized by *manicōw*'s repeated demand that others duplicate his achievements. The attack at the conclusion exemplifies one aspect of Cree disease theory, the idea that health disorders can be caused by intrusive objects shot into the victim's body from a distance by malevolent sorcerors. The discussion of shamanistic gatherings at the beginning suggests occasions comparable to Midewiwin meetings among Ojibwa and some Cree groups. No Rock Cree with whom I discussed it was familiar with a Cree cognate of the Midewiwin society, although some had heard of it among the Saulteaux to the south. The word *mitēw*, noted by Honigmann (1956: 71) as a Swamp Cree term for shaman or religious specialist, was also unknown.

The Rival Suitors
Narrator: Pascal Bighetty

There were two men who wanted to marry the same woman. The woman was already sweethearts with the younger man. The other man was much older and knew a lot of things [sorcery] so the younger one didn't want to go up against him. The old man went to the girl's parents and asked them if he could marry her. They asked the girl about it and she said she didn't want to do it. So the old man said that he would be fair. He challenged the younger man to a foot race and he promised him in front of everybody that he wouldn't do anything bad to him if he lost. That old man was really fair. He lost the foot race and he abided by his promise. Because the younger man won the foot race he got to marry the woman. The old man became more and more despondent over losing the girl. He kept asking his brother to hang him. He kept asking and asking until finally his brother agreed and hung him.

Discussion

This melancholy tale exemplifies a different side of shamanism in traditional Rock Cree society, an older man gifted with spiritual power who refrains from using it in a competitive situation and who ultimately seeks death rather than acquiring the woman he desires via threat or bad medicine. Since powerful men were said to have used threats of sorcery to press their advantage in courtship, this story possesses particular cogency in dramatizing a shaman who behaved correctly and honorably.

Medicine Woman Defeats *wītikōw*
Narrator: Mrs. Philomene Umferville

There was one old *maskīkīyiskwīw* ("medicine woman") who knew a lot of medicines including love medicines. She had long braids, wore a shawl, smoked a pipe, and was scary-looking. All the parents told their kids not to bother her.

One time a bunch of women and girls were paddling by an island and they were hungry so they stopped to cook their meal there. That old woman was there too, sitting on the grass. The women began to cook but all of a sudden the old woman told them that they had better keep quiet or something was going to happen to them. All of a sudden the wind began to blow very hard and storm clouds began to darken the sky. The girls went into the tent that had been set up. They could hear something outside, something that was coming towards them through the water. The little kids were crying. They felt cold. They looked outside the door of the tent and they saw a *wītikōw* coming through the water towards the shore. All they could see of it was its head. It had long hair floating behind it in the water. The old woman came up to them and told them to stay in the tent. She said that she intended to go and fight with that thing. The old woman went down to the shore carrying only a little hatchet. She made the thing turn around and go away. Then she came back up the shore and told everyone that they were safe now.

Discussion
Mrs. Umferville's narrative may perhaps refer to the same events reported in a narrative by Marie Merasty (1974). Characteristic are the climatic changes that auger the approach of the *wītikōw*, the latter's long, uncut hair, and the children's sensation of freezing. As in many other stories, the *wītikōw* is turned away by the intercession of an older individual with superior power endowments.

Repulsing a *wītikōw*
Narrator: Johnny Bighetty
In the old times every camp of Indians had to have a man who had the power to beat *wītikōw*. If there was nobody like that there in the camp, *wītikōw* might come and eat every person there. These old men could tell when a *wītikōw* was coming. My great-grandfather *okimāw acāhpīy* was one of those men. When a *wītikōw* was coming toward a camp, the old man would just…we call it *i-pawākwāmit* ("s/he is in a waking trance state"), they're awake but they won't talk or move.

Their mind is away somewhere else travelling. So *nitānskotāpan-nimosōm* ("my great-grandfather") is in the camp at night and he becomes like that. And then finally he comes out of the trance and announces that a *wītikōw* is forty miles away but coming towards them. The old man begins to give instructions to the other people. First he asked for an axe handle and head and he cleaned that handle very carefully with a scraper and then sharpened the blade. Then he asked them to bring him charcoal and he mixed it with water and removed all his clothing and painted himself black all over. Then he put on a special shirt he had made out of caribou hide. Then again he's *pawākwamiw* and he stayed that way for a whole hour. During all that time he was calling and talking to *opawākana* ("his spirit guardians"). And when he comes awake again, he announces to them all that his spirits were coming there and that they would lift him up and carry him through the air to where that *wītikōw* was coming. He went outside the lodge by himself. The people could hear the *pawākanak* coming towards the camp, moving through the air. These *pawākanak* are animals or things he dreams of. The *pawākanak* are all talking at once. They sound just like the radio when the reception is no good and four channels are coming in at once.

Those *pawākanak* picked the old man up and carried him away and he was gone for four hours. Then they bring him back and they land him not by the camp but about a quarter mile away at the frozen lake nearby. They could see by the marks on the snow there how they had landed him. There were marks on the snow like the Cessna coming in from Lynn (Lake). Or like willow ptarmigan when they land, leaving the strip of roughed-up snow. The old man walks into camp from the lake. When he came inside, he slumped over and lost consciousness. He had told his brother to rub him all over with grease when he came back and that's what his brother did. Then he came awake again and told what happened. *wītikōw* was forty miles away. His *pawākanak* put him in a tree beneath which the *wītikōw* had built a fire. [Q: "Those *wītikōwak* can make fires?" A: "I guess some of them can do that."]. In the fire that *wītikōw* was roasting an old mitt. I guess he was going to eat it. He must have found that old skin mitt somewhere. The old man sent his *pawākan* to frighten that *wītikōw*. They tell that *wītikōw* to go off in the opposite direction. And they scared him so that he went off and didn't come to where they were staying.

Discussion

Mr. Bighetty's narrative exemplifies the importance of *pikisīwin* "cleanliness" or "purity" in dealings between humans and nonhuman agencies. The significance of the old man's black paint remains obscure aside from the conjecture that it instances an association of the color black with dangerous or death-like states. After a death, Cree children in the 1700s were painted black (Graham 1969) as also among Minnesota Chippewa (Elizabeth Brunette, personal communication); the intent was that the lonesome dead would perceive only ashes and a deserted household and travel elsewhere. The importance of the number four as an organizing device and sacred number is evidenced in the story several times.

Flight from a *wītikōw*
Narrator: Johnny Bighetty

My mother's dad and his family were out in the bush trapping. They were at a camp by the shore of the river. One day while he's checking his traps, the old man has a feeling that something is watching him or looking at his family. He had a feeling that something bad was going to happen. He hurried back to the camp and told his wife to break up the camp and get the kids into the canoe. This was in the spring time and there were narrow channels of water along the shore. They packed everything up real quick and loaded into the canoe and paddled away from the shore.

There in the bush along the shore, the old man could just see someone pacing along with them, keeping up as they paddled, keeping pace with the canoe. So he said, "We won't go on shore." So they continued to paddle as far as they could but then they finally came to the portage where they'd have to carry the canoe over to get to more open water. The *wītikōw* was right there at the portage, waiting for them to come up onto the land. So the old man began dreaming and asking his spirit for help. And his spirit heard him and began speaking to him, telling him that he would open up a channel to open water through the ice. He told him that he would have to paddle very fast and very hard to get through because he could only hold the ice open for a short time. There in that ice a channel opened up and the old man paddled the canoe through it as fast as he could. He followed that channel across the river ice and they came to the opposite shore. He knew that the *wītikōw* was still going to follow him so they pulled the canoe up and got out and ran as fast as they could through the bush. Pretty soon behind them they heard the sound of bushes snapping and rustling. *wītikōw* was following close behind them as they ran. My mother told me she remembered being pulled along by her mother, just rushing through the bush, and hearing the old man say, "We've got to live. We have to run really fast if we want to live." And the noises behind them get closer and closer. Suddenly [Mr. Bighetty lunges forward with grasping hands and contorted face] that *wītikōw* comes right up behind them at arm's length. He grabbed the kids and they screamed. Then that old man turned and reached into his hunting bag and pulled out a moose antler knife that he always carried. He looked right at that *wītikōw* and told him, "If you'd left us alone, you'd be able to live. But I have to kill you because of what you've done to my children by frightening them and trying to kill them." And he stabbed that moose antler into the *wītikōw*. The *wītikōw* begins to die, and the old man cut off the head, the arms, and the legs, and they lay there on the ground still moving back and forth. He only killed it because it was going to harm his family.

Discussion

Mr. Bighetty's performance of this narrative, unfortunately not taped, constitutes a Cree approximation of Hitchcock whose excellence is only marginally reconstructable from the notes I made of it. Again, the potential victim's spirit guardian is called upon for assistance, and the story also exemplifies the use of special objects or techniques, in this case the moose antler knife, in combating the menace. Very characteristically Cree is the old man's careful explanation to the *wītikōw* of why and how it brought destruction upon itself. It is an interesting feature of many *wītikōw* stories that the monster is driven away rather than killed by humans capable of destroying them.

wītikōw and the Big-Rock *pawākan*
Narrator: Johhny Bighetty

This is a true story of an old woman who lived here and who died sometime back around 1960 or 1965. Together with her brother and another woman she stayed out in the winter trapping at Watt Lake. Then they went to Suwanee Lake for early spring trapping but they left their canoe at Watt. Right before open water, she and the other old woman went back to Watt Lake to get the canoe while the brother stayed at Suwanee. As soon as they left, the brother began dreaming that this sister was in trouble. He dreamed that there was a *wītikōw* somewhere around Watt Lake waiting for them. So he went out after them.

When the women got to their old winter camp at Watt, that *wītikōw* was away off somewhere, but those women could sense that it had been there and that it was going to come back. They were scared so they loaded their canoe up on the toboggan in a big hurry and got their dogs and headed back to Suwanee. That *wītikōw*, it come back to their camp right after they left. He saw that the canoe was gone so it started out after them. It's not far behind. Meanwhile, her brother is travelling towards them from Suwanee. And they met each other at the narrows call *mistasinīy* ("big-rock") just halfway between Watt Lake and Granville. Just after they met, they began to hear the *wītikōw* travelling closer and closer behind them. That brother had a rock as his *pawākan* ("spirit guardian"). Right away he begins dreaming about Rock. He asks Rock to put a big stone wall right across the narrows between them and this *wītikōw*. Well, that Rock helped his partner. All the rocks crashed together and made a wall across the narrows at *mistasinīy*. The *wītikōw* couldn't find a way through so he turned around and went back in the bush. So they went on to Suwanee and told the people there what had happened.

Discussion

Aside from the characteristic invocation of the *pawākan* for aid, this story is also of interest in focusing on a winter hunting-trapping group composed of a brother and sister with another woman. Although it is the brother who ultimately defeats the *wītikōw*, the story makes clear that all-female groups sometimes functioned in contexts of production and winter travel.

CHAPTER 6
kayās-ācimōwina: *manitōkīwin* and Catholicism

Introduction

Concentrated missionary activity initiated by the Oblates of Mary Immaculate Order began in the Pukatawagan and Granville Lake areas in 1878, although it is unlikely that Crees in the region were entirely unexposed to Christian religious beliefs prior to that time. Some traders (cf. Thompson 1962: 79) were inclined to propagate Christian ideas, and certain concepts may have entered the area by diffusion from neighboring Indian groups. Some information pertaining to the introduction of Catholicism in the area is contained in the *Codex de la Mission du Sacré-Coeur, Pukatawagan*, and the author acknowledges the assistance of the Oblate priests who permitted him to consult it.

By the 1870s, a church of the Oblate order was already established in the Rock Cree community of Pelican Narrows (Pelican Lake) upstream along the Churchill from Pukatawagan. Pelican Lake had long been a summer fishing site and was also the location of trading establishments since at least the early 1800s. Desiring to convert the Crees who gathered around Pukatawagan Lake in the summer, Father Bonald arrived by canoe from Pelican Narrows in 1878 and assembled the people on an island where they reputedly heard the teachings of Catholicism for the first time. According to the *Codex*, the entire population was anxious to embrace the new religion. Accordingly, Bonald planted a cross on the island and built a log cabin which served as a church for annual services over the next decade. For at least a sizable part of the population, Catholic officiation at baptism, marriage, and death became customary; polygyny was prohibited for converts, but marriage to first cousins in the *-tim* (opposite-sex cross-cousin) category was permitted with special dispensation. Most of the early and later Oblate personnel appear to have opposed categorically beliefs and practices connected with *manitōkīwin* or the traditional religious system. It was probably the priests who introduced the equation of traditional religious practice with worship of the scriptural Devil and his minions.

In 1886, a more permanant church was built at the parishioners' request and the community was served by such visiting priests as O. Charlesbois, N. Guilloux, and M. Rossingnol until M. Renaud took up year-round residence in 1913. Rossignol possessed interests in the culture of his parishioners and wrote three short but informative articles on Rock Cree religion, cross-cousin marriage, and property concepts (1938, 1938a, 1939). In 1926, Father Emile Désormeaux replaced Renaud and served the community until his retirement in 1981; after his death in 1985, he was buried at Pukatawagan in accordance with his own wishes. In addition to constructing the present church building, Desormeaux functioned variously as doctor, dentist, fur buyer, and advisor during the fifty-five-year period of his residence. The mutual respect and affection shared between Desormeaux and many of his parishioners was evident even to an outsider, and between him and many Cree elders there existed a fraternity based upon advanced age, shared experience, and attachment to the earlier and more nomadic period prior to the increased sedentism of the 1950s. The last time that I saw Desormeaux, he was standing in front of the Bay deep in conversation with three elderly Crees about dog teams and winter travel.

As in any community, diverse religious orientations exist in Pukatawagan, Granville Lake, and Brochet. Many individuals are deeply committed to the teachings of Catholicism and disparage what they know of *manitōkīwin* as pagan superstition or worse. A very few individuals openly reject Catholicism and profess *manitōkīwin*. Primarily secular or agnostic opinions are expressed, especially by younger persons. Many persons have creatively synthesized or compartmentalized aspects of Catholicism and *manitōkīwin*, although this is an intellectually and perhaps emotionally challenging enterprise since all but a few of the resident priests have sought to discredit the traditional religion. When speaking English, for example, some individuals will state that "there was no religion here before the Fathers came," implying that the indigenous beliefs and rituals are something else again. Apparently, a precondition for conversion to Catholicism was overt rejection of the traditional religion; in the early years of the mission, "pagans" were buried in a separate cemetery and individuals desiring baptism were required to burn their drums and religious effigies. Syntheses of *manitōkīwin* with both doctrinal and folk Catholicism include the belief that the indigenous creator-being *kicimanitōw* is identical to the scriptural deity, that the *wītikōw* is a manifestation of the scriptural Devil, and that the *pawākanak* are equivalent to saints or guardian angels who intercede in human affairs. Other persons, less involved with Catholicism, deplore the attenuation of *manitōkīwin* and identify specifically the shaking tent, the sweat lodge, the vision fast and the traditional complex or ritual involving hunting as practices that should be perpetuated:

Usually it was the older people who knew how to do all these *mamāskāc* ("wonderful") things. When the religions—all different kinds of religionsīcame up north, people stopped doing the old things. The priests scared them so they stopped...scared them by telling them all about Hell. At that time people didn't know any better so they did what the priest said. They should have kept on. Mostly they didn't hurt anybody. Mostly they used it for hunting and for doctoring sick people.

God gave that *mamātawisīwin* to the Indians because they didn't have all the machines and guns that the White man has. When the priest came, he told everyone to quit everything and believe in Jesus. Especially, he told everybody to get rid of their drums. So they stopped talking to their dreams [spirit guardians] and they lost all those powers they had. Indians would have a lot of money and be a hundred percent if they still kept their drums and kept up the old powers. I heard this story about G.N. at Pukatawagan. It was a bad winter there and they didn't have any meat. Couldn't kill anything. So the priest tells G. to throw away his drum and pray to God for food. G. stayed in his cabin for a week praying to God. Nearly starved to death. He went back and gave that priest Hell.

The authoritarianism of some priests is recalled with bitterness. It is said that one priest used to break up Cree dances with a whip: "He could get away with it because the people were scared of him. People didn't know much at the time. Priest couldn't get away with it today. They used to try to run everything." Aside from the interference in traditional religious ritual, the proscription of polygyny is remembered by some men and women as an arbitrary and authoritarian stricture.

The Arrival of the Priests
Narrator: Matt Sinclair

At Granville Lake there was a certain island where the young used to go out to dream in order to get a *pawākan*. Usually they would go to do that in the spring. And one year a young man told his father that he was going out here alone to try and dream. So he paddled to the island and stayed there by himself for a long time. But nothing came to him. So finally he went back to Granville and told his father that he had tried to succeed in dreaming but that he couldn't. He said that it was as if something was telling him to leave and go back home. Whatever was talking to him was telling him that there was a new religion coming to the area and that the people should all accept it.

It was just shortly later that the priest first came to Pukatawagan and they heard about it in Granville. The priest had the first mass out on the island in Pukatawagan Lake. After it was over, the priest made everybody throw their drums into the water.

Discussion
Mr. Sinclair's account presumably refers to events shortly before the arrival of Bonald in 1878 and exemplifies the prophecy of impending events that often figures in visionary experiences. Premonitions of the arrival of Whites and/or the introduction of Christian religion are part of the oral historical traditions of other North American Indian groups (cf. Nabakov 1978: 1–18).

mīsīl Kills a wītikōwak
Narrator: Selazie Linklater
Translator: Caroline Caribou
mīsīl [Michel Dumas] was a very spiritually empowered man and possessed many *pawākanak* ("spirit guardians"). With their aid he was sometimes enabled to fly through the air. If something bad was happening at his camp while he was away in the bush, he could call his *pawākanak* and fly back there. Once while he was trapping beaver in the spring something told him that someone was watching his kids and that they were going to be in trouble. He summoned his *pawākanak* and with their aid he was able to fly over the trees back to his camp. His sons told him that they had been gathering wood and that they had suddenly become aware of something watching them. mīsīl told his whole family to go into the house. He said that two *wītikōwak* were coming toward them, a man and a woman. mīsīl felt strong enough to fight those things so he went out to meet them.

From inside the lodge the family heard sounds as though a flock of birds was coming toward them from the sky. Those were the sounds of mīsīl's *pawākanak* coming when he called them. Maybe those *pawākanak* of his were birds. They attached themselves to mīsīl and pulled him up vertically into the air. And they carried him to where the two *wītikōwak* were approaching. They lowered themselves around the male *wītikōw* and, still carrying mīsīl, pulled him high up into the sky and then dropped him to the ground. They did the same thing with the female. When the *pawākanak* returned mīsīl to the ground he was so weak that he was almost dead. His sons brought him inside their cabin and they positioned a rock in the fire and poured water on it to throw off steam. The steam began to warm mīsīl and slowly the old man became conscious. He instructed his sons to assemble a large pile of wood to burn the bodies of the *wītikōwak*. They build a great fire and threw the bodies into it. Those *wītikōwak* were filled with ice and the water from the melting ice extinguished the fire. It was necessary for them to rebuild the fire twice more before the bodies were finally burned. It was necessary to burn the bodies because otherwise the *wītikōwak* would return to life.

Later mīsīl communicated with his *pawākanak* and chastised them for not appearing more rapidly when he summoned them. They told him that they had finally agreed to come to his aid but that they had been reluctant because he had been baptized.

Discussion

The story is included in this section because of the concluding passage that succinctly expresses the conceptual antagonism between the indigenous and introduced religious systems. To the degree that the priests represented *manitōkīwin* and Catholicism as mutually exclusive religions, an individual's *pawākanak* were experienced as hostile to or frightened by the institutions of the Church. Both in the past and in the present, attempts to reconcile the two traditions, or to move between them, produce subjective conflicts. In the words of Andrew Flett:

> The burden of puagan [Andrew says] was great. Particularly was this true when a person got baptised. He had seen such old men, baptised late in life, who would strike at their foreheads and make motions as if to pluck out the dominant puagan. (Cockburn 1985: 41)

Simulated Crucifixion
Narrator: Jean-Baptiste Merasty
Translator: Pierre Merasty

When the priest first came he instructed the people about religion but many people did not understand what they were supposed to do. One old man was named P. and he told the people that he would be their god. He instructed the people to build a great cross out of logs and so the people built this great cross. Then P. told all the people that he wanted to be crucified so that he could become god. He told the people to cut willow sticks and to strike him with them while he carried the cross around. So P. carried the cross around and the people hit him with willow sticks just as he requested. One man who understood more about religion came there from some other place. This man saw what P. was doing. P. was dragging the cross around and falling down. He asked that newcomer why he didn't join in with the others in hitting him. That man went and cut a thick willow and he whacked P. real hard with it. P. complained to him. "That's too hard," he said.

Then a canoe came with the priest and the people recognized him. P. was carrying his cross towards the priest. Then he fell down again. People started hitting him with the willows again, saying, "Get up! Get up!" By this time P. is tired from dragging that cross around and getting hit all day. Finally he got up. The priest ran over to him and told him he should never pretend to be Jesus. Then the priest shoved him to the ground again.

Simulated Crucifixion II: Jesus at Highrock
Narrator: Johnny Bighetty

This story happened way back around 1910. There was an old man named P. When the priest came to Pukatawagan, he told all the people to throw away their drums or they'll go to Hell and burn forever. He really scared those people telling them that. If they threw away their drums, he said, the Indians would get to go to Heaven and be angels.

This old man was crazy. He began to think that he was Jesus and then he wanted to act like Jesus, to do all the things that the priest told the Indians about Jesus. He dressed up like Jesus in a white robe and then he got twelve Indians to be the twelve apostles. And then he travelled around trying to make miracles. He travelled around in four canoes with his twelve "apostles". Finally he decided to go to the village at High Rock with his apostles and preach to them there. P. told all the people to go into their cabins and tents and then he walked in a circle, singing and praying, around every house. Then he told them all that he was going to die for all the people at High Rock. He was really crazy. He made his apostles make a big cross out of logs and then he told them to crucify him. They tied him to this big cross with rope and then they planted the cross in the ground right by the shore of High Rock Lake. P. hung up there on that cross singing. Finally it got to be late at night and the Apostles and the other people there fell asleep. All the dogs in the camp kept fooling around by that cross.

That night a big wind storm blew up by the lake. The wind blew the cross over into the water and P. was almost drowning. He yelled for help but his mouth kept getting full of water and he made gurgling noises. Finally the people heard him and came out to look. P. was thrashing around in the water trying to get free of the ropes. All the dogs were excited and were fooling around, biting P. and barking at him. So they pulled him out.

Discussion

Presumably both of the preceding stories describe the activities of the same individual. Both stories were perceived as being extremely funny by their narrators, although from varying perspectives. Mr. Merasty, a devout Catholic, appeared to find humor in the imposter's presumptuous impersonation of Christ and in his ignorance whereas Mr. Bighetty, less partisan to the religion being simulated, thought it amusing that the priest's message could have had such an effect on an individual's behavior. The slapstick elements themselves were a source of laughter in both versions. I was unable to discover more information about the mock-Christ, but it is interesting to speculate that under appropriate circumstances his activities might have resulted in a syncretisitic religion comparable to that described by Brown (1982: 142–43) among the Westmain Swampy Cree.

Flying to Heaven
Narrator: Jean-Baptiste Merasty
Translator: Pierre Merasty

When the priests first came into the country they travelled around and visited the Indians at their winter camps. Many people didn't understand about the new religion right away. They thought that they could get food and trade goods just by praying for them and without doing any work. The priests would tell people that they should pray for food. The people prayed and they didn't get anything. They finally decided to select one man who would travel to Heaven in the sky and get all this food and all these trade goods from God. So they built wooden wings for this man and he put them on. Then he climbed up on top of a little spruce tree. He's going to fly off the top of that tree and go up to Heaven. All the people on the ground are yelling up to him what things he should bring back from God. One old lady asked for a knife. Finally he jumped up off the tree and fell down onto the ground. After that those people were mad at the priest. They said, "The heck with that. We aren't going to pray anymore."

Discussion

Mr. Merasty's narrative suggests parallels with certain aspects of Melanesian cargo movements as well as addressing the interesting question of how Crees during earlier periods ultimately explained the existence of trade goods introduced during the fur trade. Some context for the behavior described is provided by the understanding, shared by some traditional Crees, that metal knives, axes, and other manufactures antedated the arrival of Whites and were obtained originally from the *pawākanak* ("spirit guardians"). The fact that Whites possessed trade goods, and/or the knowledge permitting their manufacture, was sometimes explained in terms of spiritual powers or endowments from spirit beings (Robson 1965: 53, Petitot 1886: 462–65). In some cases, the White monopoly on these goods is explained within the context of Cree cosmology, as, for example, when *wīsahkīcāhk* is said to have instructed the Whites in the knowledge underlying their material culture. Similarly, two Cree myths represent the introduction of trade goods by Whites as part of the cosmic design intended by the creator being (Petitot 1886: 467–74) or East Wind (Brown 1977: 46). In Mr. Merasty's narrative, immediate access to food and trade goods appears to have been understood as one possible consequence of communication with the scriptural deity, or at least of prayer within the Catholic idiom. The idea that Catholic prayer might secure its objectives without practical activity occurs elsewhere in Cree narratives and attests the confidence that at least initially was placed in the introduced religion. Although traditional ritual conventionally accompanied rather than supplanted technical activity in the daily round, narratives in which powerful dreamers or medicine men secure food or exert other effects without physical effort provide a precedent for belief in the sufficiency of Catholic prayer. The expedient of "flying to Heaven" appears as an additional empowerment associated with Catholicism, although the ability to fly through the air with the aid of spirit guardians figures in other narratives without Catholic associations. As with the hunter who "gave a priest Hell" after praying for food and receiving none, the actors in this narrative are rapidly disillusioned when Catholicism does not immediately yield up the anticipated benefits.

Eskimo in Heaven
Narrator: Jean-Baptiste Merasty
Translator: Pierre Merasty

Long ago there were some Eskimos up in the barren grounds who hadn't heard about God or about praying. Finally a priest came to where they stayed and instructed the Eskimos in Catholicism. One old man was very glad to hear about this and listened carefully to everything that the priest told him. The priest told him that if he prayed he would go to Heaven where everything would be good and there would be angels all dressed in white. That old man was happy when he thought about that.

Later on, that Eskimo hit his head and knocked himself unconscious while he was out trapping. He didn't come around for a long time so finally they brought a plane in and they took the old man down to the hospital in Edmonton, Alberta. It was the first time he'd ever been out of the barren grounds. When he finally regained consciousness, he was lying on a hospital bed. That was the first bed that he'd ever been on. Then a nurse with a white uniform came up to him with a plate of food. That old man thought that the nurse was an angel and he thought that he had died and gone to Heaven. Later on his son came to visit him. The old man grabbed his boy and said, "Oh, my son, are you dead too?"

Discussion

Like other narratives in this section drawn from Mr. Merasty's repertoire, the often saturnine humour derives from the naivete or ignorance of characters who misinterpret or otherwise misunderstand the religious teachings introduced by the priests. Although the story is told as a joke, it possesses sufficient plausibility to derive, in whole or in part, from some northerner's first experience with an urban hospital.

Last Offering
Narrator: Jean-Baptiste Merasty
Translator: Pierre Merasty

Before the priest came and taught the people about God and praying, the people used to have different things as their gods. They would dream about these things and they would believe their dreams. They would pray to different things, to trees, animals, and even to rocks. There was one old man who had this big rock that was at a certain place along the river. And he prayed to that *mistasinīy* ("big-rock") *pawākan* ("sprit guardian"). That *mistasinīy* was his god. Finally this old man learned about God and the priest told him that he had to leave off praying to that rock. The old man was worried by this. He wanted to do what the priest said but he was frightened of what might happen to him if he stopped praying to that rock. Finally he gathered together his best pipe and a fine knife, and several twists of the old Bay tobacco and left his camp to paddle along the river to where the rock was.

There was one younger fellow there who was watching him. He wanted to know what the old man was going to do so he followed him along on the shore and then he positioned himself in the bush where he could watch what the old man was up to. When the old man came to the rock, he beached his canoe and then stood up in front of the rock and prayed to it for the last time. He said that because he was now baptised he could no longer pray to the rock as he had always done, but that he had brought his last offering to the rock so that it would not be angry with him. He put down a clean piece of caribou hide and he carefully laid the pipe, the knife, and the tobacco out on the ground before the rock. Then he departed. That younger man came out, laughed at the old man, and took all of the offerings that he had left there.

Soon again the old man paddled along the river past the rock. He looked and saw that his offerings were gone. "This is good, *nimosōm*" ("my grandfather"), he said. "I am happy that you are not offended. I feared your anger before but I see that you have accepted my offerings. You have taken the tobacco and smoked it already."

CHAPTER 7
ācimōwina: *wītikōw* Encounters and Medicine Stories

Barren Lands *wītikōw*
Narrator: Albert Umferville

You probably hear lots of stories of the *wītikōw*. Well, this one comes from Moose Lake [east of The Pas]. One time I was there trapping and I heard this one told to me by an old fella. Anyway, the story starts out with this trapper and his family way up north, out there in the barrens. Of course, in the barrens, there's hardly any trees. So anyway, they were there this one night and they heard someone prowling around outside their tent. And the dogs were very scared. This wanted to come in. And every once in a while they'd hear something squeal. That was the dogs. Pretty soon there was scratching at the door.

That man said, "We'd better not let him in. I know who it is. It's the *wītikōw*. It's eating up our dogs out there." So they were pretty scared. So come morning, they packed all their stuff and they started off. They started going south. And in the evening they made an igloo out of snow.

The same thing happened that night. They heard something prowling around. But they didn't have no dogs that night because they were all eaten up. They were travelling by foot on snowshoes. So the old man, he loaded up his rifle and sat by the door all night long. He could hear him [*wītikōw*] walking round and round outside. The next morning, he went away.

So he says, "Wife, children, we'd better get going." They didn't have any sleep that night again. Pretty soon they came to where there were trees. There was lots of [snow] drifts. So the old man said, "We'll dig into the drift. But we'll have to dig a long ways so he won't be able to find us." So they dug and made a long tunnel into the drift. Zigzagged back and forth. They were trying to fool the *wītikōw*. So this *wītikōw*, it came there that night, and they could hear it walking up there on top of the drift. And he had a long stick that he was poking into the drift, trying to find where those people were. Couldn't find them.

So they started off again in the morning and they were very tired because they didn't have any sleep again that night. So they came to a log cabin. So they went into this log cabin and the man got a few nails and nailed the windows shut and put a bar across the door so he (*wītikōw*) won't be able to come in. And he was prowling around there all night. Come morning, he wouldn't go away. So that man told his wife to boil a large kettle of water. So the wife went to work and she boiled that hot water. And then he opened the door and there was the *wītikōw* standing out there. All he could see was his teeth. Lips were all chewed away. And he told him to come on in. So the *wītikōw* come in and sat down. He gave him something to eat. He couldn't have enough. He wanted more. Pretty soon he ate up everything. And the man told his wife, "Well, is the water already boiled?" She said yes. So he told the *wītikōw* to come here. Told him that if he wanted more to eat there was something in the pot there. So the *wītikōw* came walking over to where the pot was. He bent down to look and the man shoved his head into the hot boiling water and killed him.

So after he killed the *wītikōw*, he cut lots of dry wood and he made a big fire and threw the body on top of the woodpile. Every time he threw it on there, water would come out of the body of the *wītikōw* and drown the fire out, and he'd have to make it all over again. And he worked all day, all night, all day. And toward evening there was only one little bit of a bone left. So he had to cut more wood and he burnt all that bone until there was nothing but just ashes. And that's how they got away.

Discussion

Although the monster in this narrative is somewhat atypical in accepting conventional food from humans, its voraciousness and consumption of abnormal food such as dog flesh conform to general images of *wītikōw* behavior. Also conventional are the exposed teeth and the cremation of the body to prevent reanimation; as in "*mīsīl* Dumas Kills a *wītikōw*" in the previous chapter, the drowning of the fire by the melting ice in the monster's body adds an additional element of suspense. The "igloo" referred to here is an emergency travel shelter made by tossing snow into a mound and then excavating a small chamber inside.

Laurie River *wītikōw*
Narrator: Sidney Castel
One thing I'll tell you about, this *wītikōw*. It's a very interesting story. There was this old man here who ran away from that guy *wītikōw*. I'm telling you the story now. Well, this guy he seen the *wītikōw*. He was spring trapping. He was lifting his traps in the morning īno, it was in the afternoon. That *wītikōw*, you know, it doesn't come around until at night when people go to sleep, when it wants to make a sudden attack. Mostly in the evenings. So this guy is still alive. You

know that guy we passed down there? That's my cousin. He was lifting his traps in the evening, see? And he sees this—while he was lifting his traps he thought somebody was looking at him. With them things you could notice. You could feel when something was trying to hurt you or do something. He felt that. So he looked around down there and there was a *wītikōw*. Ready to jump on him. So he shot him twice with a twenty-two and he started running. So those things, they're something like Dracula. He flies and he's got a cape on him, covering himself.

So he [cousin] starts running. He was coming to a portage. He came to the rapids. There's falls there, running water about a hundred yards. And this guy, he runs down there and he sees the *wītikōw* coming in front of him, cutting him off. So he just come across and jumped over that river, that rapids, right across. And he landed there [opposite side] and he saw that *wītikōw* jump too and fall right in the middle of that river and drown.

And so this guy, he was scared and so nervous that he couldn't go any further. He just sat there. Because he had jumped from so far away, he just fell down and couldn't get up again. He was scared. That's about forty-five miles from here. There's a river we call Laurie River (Cree *maskwōwakan sīpīy* "bear-backbone river"). It's about a hundred feet across. It's a wide river. It was getting dark and he was supposed to be back by this time. His partner he was trapping with, he went and looked for him on this side of the river. So they heard him hollering and he was there across the river. It's a pretty big river. When you're scared, you can do anything. He turned his head around and he saw that guy coming. That *wītikōw* jumped right over and fell right in the middle of the river. So he's swept down river. That thing drowned because the water's so strong. They never found him either.

Discussion
The narrator amplified his remarks about flying and cape-like garments by referring to another story in which *wītikōw* tracks were followed through the snow and found to stop suddenly in the middle of an expanse of undisturbed snow. The potential victim's awareness of the monster's proximity is paralleled in other stories, and his life-saving leap across the Laurie River illustrates the conviction that otherwise impossible achievements can be accomplished in the extremities of need.

P.B. and *wītikōw*
Narrator: Johnny Bighetty
P.B. and Bruce Anderson, the Swede trapper from South Indian, were out trapping. One day, while he's checking his traps, P.B. starts to feel lonesome. He felt tired. He didn't feel like working or eating. They say that people begin to feel sad like that when there's a *wītikōw* somewhere going around. So he lifts his traps and

he's walking home along the shore of the lake and he sees something's footprints there. And those prints are all webbed across like a fishnet. He was just stiff with fright. It looked like something had been walking there which had mukluks made out of heavy fishnet.

P.B. got back to camp and told Bruce what he saw. Bruce laughed at P. and told him he was superstitious. P. still felt scared. The next day, they went back there to look at the tracks. They were still there and from his canoe P.B. could just catch sight of something moving around back in the bush away from the shore. That night, all the dogs in their camp were nervous. They howled all night and the fur on their backs stood up on end. The next night, they heard something bothering around their camp while they were in the tent. Bruce stuck his head out and saw the *wītikōw* standing in the brush right by the edge of the camp. He yelled at it and it ran away.

The next day, P.B. went to set up a little camp further out along their trapline. The old people always said that the *wītikōw* would hang around and bother people for three days and then kill and eat them on the fourth day. Well, now it's the fourth day and P.B. is still feeling sad and scared. No appetite, just dragging himself around. He tried to set up a camp in the bush. And just then he heard gunshots in the distance. Right away, he felt this great relief and his appetite came back. He travelled rapidly back to their old camp. There he found Bruce standing there with his thirty-thirty. He'd killed that *wītikōw* as it was coming into their camp. The feet were webbed just like the prints it left. They burned the body.

Discussion

This story is especially detailed with respect to the emotional condition of an intended victim; in addition to being aware of the monster's presence, P.B. experiences anxiety, depression, and anorexia and it is said that the *wītikōw* purposely produces these conditions in its victims to render them more vulnerable. It is interesting that all three of these symptoms are often associated with transformation into a *wītikōw*, and it may be that the story implicitly intimates the possibility of such an event. The webbed feet are not attested in other physical descriptions of *wītikōw*, and are among a number of variable features particular to single narratives. An unexplored element of irony juxtaposes the White trapper's initial disparagement of P.B.'s fears with his subsequent personal encounter with the monster.

Moose Lake *wītikōw*
Narrator: Albert Umferville

When I was around sixteen, I was trapping near Moose Lake which at that time was a non-treaty town east of the reserve at The Pas. An older guy I knew there took me to a spot in the middle of the village. There were willows growing in a circle surrounding this spot and nothing was growing from the earth. In the ground you could see the imprint of knees where someone had been sitting.

A long time ago, he said, a *wītikōw* had camped there. She would just sit there during the day. At night she killed and ate the people's dogs. The people got to be more and more frightened. They didn't have a strong medicine man there at the time so they sent south and asked a Saulteaux medicine man to come there. He went to where the woman was sitting and told her to leave the place. She said that she was going to stay right there and that as soon as she had eaten all the dogs she was going to begin eating the people. She was going to stay there until all the people were eaten and then move on. That Saulteaux doctor began to sing. He called up a big storm like a whirlwind. The wind picked up the *wītikōw* woman and carried her off. After that, nothing would grow where she had been sitting and you could always see the marks of her knees on the ground.

Discussion
In addition to evidencing the *wītikōw*'s proclivity for dog meat as a substitute for human flesh, this narrative introduces another association consistent with *wītikōw* symbolism, a capacity to impart barrenness or infertility to the earth.

Nelson House *wītikōw*
Narrator: Sidney Castel
There was a man who came back after killing a *wītikōw*. He was at Nelson House and he's still alive. He killed it with a little hatchet. He killed that guy. And he said that thing was a woman! That guy, he went deaf because he was so scared. Because that thing grabbed him right from the back. He was running up and grabbed him. And when he turned around, he could see it, eh? He went deaf and dumb.

Discussion
Mr. Castel's brief account emphasizes again the fear that the *wītikōw* inspires in its potential victims and also the lingering disorders, mentioned in other accounts, that afflict the survivors of *wītikōw* encounters (Merasty 1977: 23).

Introduction to the Medicine Narratives
The eight accounts that follow concern practices conventionally labeled "sorcery" or "witchcraft" in English. Crees recognize different modalities of such practices that are lexically represented by at least ten distinct nouns and/or verbs with distinguishable meanings. The Cree noun *maskīkīy* is usually glossed into English as "medicine" and typically refers to the botanical preparations used in traditional medical practice. The noun *maskīkīwīðiniw* "medicine person" signals

an individual knowledgable about such practices. The noun *macimaskīkīy* "bad medicine" refers either to preparations that subvert the welfare of others or to the use of such devices; their users are *macimaskīkīwīðiniwak* "bad-medicine-people." Additional inquiry is needed to ascertain whether Crees, like the Ojibwa discussed by Black (1977) include hunting and love medicines within an encompassing "bad medicine" category, and also whether the noun *macimaskīkīy* refers appropriately to the full range of contexts exemplified in the narratives below. The liquid potion in "Sled Medicine" is *macimaskīkīy*, but the effective means of sorcery include also object intrusion ("Insect Medicine," "Hair Medicine"), the exteriorized soul of the sorceror ("Dr. Young and the Saskatoon Medicine Man"), and the shaking lodge. Crees suggested that these different means were sometimes combined, although each could occur singly. It follows that the inclusive use of the English gloss "medicine" here is tentative.

Athletic prowess and improper sexual behavior are represented as provoking retaliatory sorcery in these stories, and the sorcerer is conventionally identified as an older individual. A strong competitive orientation is evident in the manner in which Crees discuss sorcery and is evidenced here in the first "Dr. Young" story as well as in the *manicōw* narrative above. Sorcery is also recurrently associated with outsiders and with residence in unfamiliar communities.

Sled Medicine
Narrator: Albert Umferville
Various people were reluctant to race their dogs in the Trapper's Festival at The Pas because they were convinced that a certain Saulteaux was using medicine to win. Someone said that they had seen him remove a small bottle from his pocket, pour liquid from it onto his hands, wipe his hands over his whip, and then whip the trail in an "X" pattern behind him. All the other teams would be slowed up when they had to cross over that spot.

Hair Medicine
Narrator: Albert Umferville
A man from Brochet was visiting in The Pas and he was fooling around with one of the local girls even though he was engaged to be married up here. Her father took a liking to him and decided that he would be a good son-in-law so he told that man to marry his daughter. Then later on, someone told him that the man was already engaged and he was angry when he found out. When he left to go back to Brochet, that old man sent bad medicine ahead of him. He began getting a bad pain in his arm about half-way to Brochet and he was crippled up by the time he got here. He went to see an old medicine man here who asked him if he had done anything to make anyone angry while he was in The Pas. So he told the doctor the

story. The doctor told him that the only way he could cure him was if he married *his* daughter. Well, the young man had to agree to that and so the old doctor put a poultice on his arm that he had to wear for several days. His arm recovered quickly. When they removed the poultice, they found that a long hair had come up out of the arm.

Soccer Medicine
Narrator: Albert Umferville
I was playing soccer one time when I was visiting Prince Albert and I was scoring a lot of goals. Probable I got some old man related to someone on the other team mad at me. My leg cramped up really bad. My aunt who lived there gave me a garter to wear and my leg got better immediately.

Insect Medicine
Narrator: Albert Umferville
There was one man who got an old man mad at him by playing around with his daughter. So he was leaving. And before he left, the old man told him, "Before you reach the portage, you'll know me." At the first portage, that man began to feel something in his ear. He was nearly going crazy. When he got home to Moose Lake, they sent for a Saulteaux doctor who put a poultice on the man's head. When they took it off later they found a dead insect in the man's ear. No one had ever seen that kind of insect and no one could say what it was.

Enlargement Medicine
Narrator: Jeremy Caribou
There was this old man. When he was a young man he used to be a trapper. He used to trap up north here and he used to catch a lot of fur. He used to go to The Pas or somewhere else—Prince Albert, Saskatchewan, I think. There was a dance and he was dancing with a nice-looking woman there. And right away he gets ideas. So sure, he takes her outside. But that woman was married. And it just so happened that this girl's father-in-law, he was one of the kind that jinxed people. So *i-pawākanawāt* ("he uses sorcery against him"). So after this guy gets back to his trapline, he found this enormous thing growing here. Way too big. So that old man fixed him.

Dr. Young and the Saskatoon Medicine Man
Narrator: Albert Umferville
Dr. Young was a well-known Cree doctor around The Pas. He was apprenticed to an old medicine man when he was younger. The old man was teaching him everything. They used to travel together and one time they traveled to Edmonton

and Saskatoon. They were having different kinds of games in Saskatoon and Dr. Young was competing against some of the local young men at wrestling and horseback riding. He was better than any of them and he always beat them. A local medicine man who was related to some of these men was angry at Dr. Young.

"That's not so good that that old man is mad at you," Dr. Young's teacher told him. "You'd better do something to appease him." Dr. Young followed this advice. He got together a bunch of goods—traps, knives, and blankets—and he brought them to that old man's *mīkiwāp* as a peace-offering. That old man was still mad. He didn't want any of the presents.

"Take 'em out!" he said. "Get out of this village!" That meant that the old man was going to fight Dr. Young. Dr. Young and his teacher packed all their possessions into their canoe and began paddling back towards The Pas.

On the first evening that they were traveling, Dr. Young began to feel awful. They stopped and camped for dinner, and then began traveling again. Dr. Young was feeling worse and he told his teacher that they'd better stop again. They stopped. The old man told Dr. Young that the medicine man from the village was trying to get him. He brought canvas out from the canoe and told Dr. Young to get underneath it. Then the teacher began to sing. The wind began to blow very hard and it started to snow heavily. The teacher kept singing and finally all of the bad weather passed. Dr. Young felt a little better. They camped the night there.

The next night, just as had happened earlier, Dr. Young began to feel really sick. They were traveling around nightfall. A strong rain storm blew up. The teacher sang again and the rain storm passed away. Again Dr. Young felt better and again they camped that night.

The third day of traveling, Dr. Young again began to feel ill around evening. His teacher told him that he had helped him two times and that now he was going to have to take care of himself. The old man said that on this, the third night, that medicine man would come himself to where they were camped. He told Dr. Young to cut three pieces of canvas in eight, ten, and twelve square-foot dimensions. He made Dr. Young lie down on the ground and then covered him with the pieces of canvas. He then told Dr. Young that if he had the power to jump up to his feet and pass through the canvas without tearing it or making a hole in it, he'd be able to beat the other medicine man himself. In the bush they could hear the sound of someone traveling toward them. He was singing a song about how he was going to kill Dr. Young. That witch had sent his ghost (or *ahcahk* "soul") to kill Dr. Young. This is like Dr. Strange in the comic book. He can stay in one place and send his ghost somewhere else. He would send out his ghost to do the dirty work. Dr. Young jumped up and passed right through the canvas without tearing it. That scared the ghost and it went back into the old man's body and didn't bother them after that.

Dr. Young's Love Medicine
Narrator: Albert Umferville

There was a girl at The Pas who wanted to get a boy to fall in love with her so she went to see Dr. Young and asked him for some medicine. He was reluctant to make it but he finally agreed to do so, and the girl said she would pay him ten dollars and a bottle of wine. They made arrangements that he would come to her house and bring the medicine and receive his payment there.

The night before Dr. Young was going to come, the girl had a party. They ran out of wine and didn't know where they could get any more. Then she thought of the bottle she was saving to pay Dr. Young. In those days, the bottles had wax stoppers and dark glass so you couldn't see how much was inside. She took a lot of the wine out of the bottle and then sealed it up again. The next day, she told her brother to give the wine to Dr. Young when he came and to tell him that she'd pay him the money later.

When Dr. Young came with the medicine, he knew that she was trying to cheat him. He left the medicine for her but told her brother that it wasn't going to work. That night she put some of the medicine in her boyfriend's tea. He drank it. Suddenly, instead of falling in love, he jumped up, slapped her in the face, and left.

Can't Refuse Medicine
Narrator: Albert Umferville

At The Pas, there was an old woman who used to live alone in a tent. All of the kids were scared of her because their parents told them not to go there or to bother her. The parents would tell the kids that the old woman knew how to make bad medicine. One time my mother and my mother's sister had a lot of moose meat so they decided to give some to that old lady. The old woman liked the moose meat and she said that she would give them something. She gave them a package of leaves wrapped up in a little leather bag. She told them that if they put some of the leaves under their tongue and asked for anything, no one would be able to refuse them. They took that medicine home and hung it up right by the door. They didn't know if it would work or not.

A few days later, both women went into town to go to the store. They decided to take the medicine along and try it out. They got to the store and were joking with the clerk who worked there. My aunt put some of the leaves under her tongue and asked the clerk for five dollars. He gave it to her right away. He just went over to the money box and got it out and gave it to her. They both laughed a lot over that.

Later on, at home, they decided that that medicine was too strong and that they might get into some kind of trouble if they kept it. So my mother threw the leaves into the stove. That medicine was so strong that when it burned, it exploded.

There was an explosion and all the stovehole covers were blown into the air.

Goldsand Lake *wīhtikōw*

There was one guy here that turned to *wīhtikōw* out at Goldsand Lake. There was one guy from Brochet and another guy from Southend on Reindeer Lake. And *acīkwas* from Granville Lake met the guy [from Southend] over there [near Goldsand Lake]. That was his brother-in-law and they had a camp in there.

So earlier the guy from Brochet—he had a daughter and he wanted the son of the guy from Southend to marry his daughter. But he was half-Chipewyan [Athapaskan tribe to the north]. So the man from Southend said he didn't want to. Said he didn't want his boy to marry a dog. He said that with a translator: "I don't want my boy to marry a dog." So the man from Brochet got mad. He said, "Wait. His son is going to eat him this coming winter."

So they move in at Goldsand Lake and they were there during the fall. The young guy [son] used to go out with his sister, shooting rabbits in the fall. They were out one evening shooting rabbits. They came back to the tent they had out there and they found a bear in it. Already, it was late fall when the guy killed it. Killed the bear right away. Drag him out of the tent, cut the head off right away, threw it in the fire. He's going crazy. Made fire right away and threw the head in there. Half-cooked and he started eating it. His sister asked him not to do that, but no, he wouldn't listen.

After they went back to the main camp, the guy got sick and he wouldn't eat. No, he wouldn't eat and he doesn't sleep at night. Well, they know he was turning crazy and they gotta' keep him at night so he wouldn't kill people. So finally it was getting about the end of November. Those two old people [*acīkwas* and the man from Southend], they couldn't trap. They were keeping this guy. He was in bed all the time, he doesn't talk, doesn't eat. And the guy from Southend was watching. He was keeping the boy at night. The sick guy had his face covered with his blanket. And he heard something like chewing and he went to see what he was eating. He was eating his moccasins. This guy took his moccasin off and was eating it. Half-gone already. His father took the moccasin and said, "Good thing you don't eat the whole moccasin, it would've killed you." The sick guy said, "I'll start on you after I'm through eating that thing."

So the guy went and woke the old man [*acīkwas*] and said, "We've got to take care of him. Got to kill him." So he got a rope and choked the guy there. That was either them or him. To kill him, they choke him with a rope. This old man [*acīkwas*] went back to Granville Lake after that and they took the body in to Southend and buried it over there, I guess. Ever since, everytime someone camps in that camp where they had the house, they find a bear where that guy [*wīhtikōw*] was sleeping. Bear every winter. So finally nobody bothered going there because there'd be a bear there. They kill it every time, but there's another one every winter. The bear doesn't even put anything—he just sleeps right where the guy was sleeping. That's how bad that Chipewyan was, eh? He sent that. The guy would eat that bear so he'd turn crazy. He ate the head-part raw. He turned sick, wouldn't eat. Turn to *wīhtikōw* then.

Discussion

Mr. Colomb's narrative obviously refers to an instance of what in the literature is conventionally referred to as "windigo psychosis," although the circumstances are too far removed in time to permit its inclusion as an unquestionable case of cannibalistic obsession. Crees typically specify prior cannibalism, spirit possession, dream predestination, and death by freezing as etiological factors producing the windigo condition. Any of these can be linked with sorcery, as in this narrative where the vengeful Chipewyan induces, through unspecified means, a spiritual disorder that compels the victim to eat half-cooked meat from the head of a bear. Consumption of half-cooked or raw meat is elsewhere, as in the *mistacayawāsis* myth, represented as a proclivity of windigos. The subsequent symptoms—anorexia, sleeplessness, threats to kill others—also figure in other myths and in factual accounts of windigo behavior.

Antoine Dumas's Prophecies
Narrator: Jeremy Caribou

My grandfather, he was some kind of prophet, eh? He got his insights from dreaming. But he used to be able to tell from the environment. He sees in the dream what the environment's going to be like. Like that day he sat like this and he squats on the ground beside the fireplace. He's facing the west, eh? This way he says, "You're going to see a lot of things in your later life. But now you're just a little boy. You know nothing. You don't know—you're just a little boy. You have no knowledge of what's to become later," he says.

"From the west I see this water. Water problems. This is exactly the problem we have now today. You're going to have trouble with that water. That water is not going to supply you all your life. There's White men over there that plugged up water. They're fooling around with that water. They're ruining the land to the north."

"I look to the north, they're over there again. They're there ahead of you. They're digging holes in the ground. And they're taking money from the ground [mining]. And they got these big highways over there." He didn't call them highways. It was *miskanaw* ["trail," "road"], that's what he called highways. "And they're hiding that money all over the north from you. And then they have a snake passing—crawling through your land. Right by your reserve there. There's some kind of a snake." It's not a snake. It's metal. White man's machinery. This is what we call a train today. He told me I would see this.

And to the east, same as to the west. All kinds of land that's going to be ruined. They have mines over there too. They have dams. I guess that's what he meant about the river. They have water passages that are not made by *kicimanitōw* ["God"]. Now it's Manitoba Hydroelectric. And he looks that way and he says, "Oh, it doesn't look too good."

Then he faces the south, he looks this way. "Oh, from the south," he says, "there's lots of White people coming. And they'll bring a lot of things that are good. Both good and bad for the people of the north. And the people are going to try to live with them, alongside them."

He was right. Oh, I tell you, eh? All these things that that old man told me about that were going to involve my life, they're accurate so far. He even told me about the bomb. And that I'm going to see these jets flying overhead going faster than lightning and sounding like thunder. He told me about these things. But then I was a boy. I never knew those things existed. I never knew they would exist. They didn't exist period then. But nowadays I see all these things. But this fellow, he know about these things before, eh? *Fifty years* before. And some of the people said that he was a bullshitter. I think they were wrong. He was right. The old man was right. He foretold these events fifty years in advance. Fifty or sixty years in advance. *nimosōm* ["my grandfather"] Antoine Dumas. That's my mother's dad. He was an incredible philosopher. He used to tell things about religion. About the things that are going to happen. But those people didn't see the evidence of what he was talking about. Didn't see any evidence of it, eh? So they said, "Ah, he's full of garbage. What he's saying is impossible. Never possible that a snake will crawl across Pukatawagan. Not snake-animal." But today they see the train go crawling across the country like a snake. They see it. They see these big jets. Airplanes. That didn't exist then. What he foresees comes true, eh? *ī-kiskīwīhikit* ["he prophesies"]. *okiskīwīhikiw* ["prophet"], that's the man who can do that. That's when you can tell the future exactly the way it is today.

They dreamt it. Some of them, they said it just like him, they used to see it. Like him, he used to sit in the sun. They used to sleep in the sun and sometimes that sunset, they used to do it with the sunset. *kicimanitōw* would tell them. Or whatever god they believe in. They call it the Great Spirit, eh? That must be the same God people talk about nowadays. That's the only being that could give knowledge and wisdom, eh? It relates to the fact that's where he got his wisdom. I cannot deny that he was telling the truth. Nothing but the truth.

CHAPTER 8
ācimōwina: Humour

Introduction

As Basso (1979) and others have pointed out, a rich legacy of North American Indian humour—farce, satire, slapstick, and comedy noir—has been submerged beneath stereotypes of savagery, nobility, and congenital stoicism. Humour, of course, predominates in the *wīsahkīcāhk* cycle and figures also in many stories relating to the introduction of Catholicism. I have grouped together here a residuum of comic stories—some fabricated and some regarded as records of real eventsīthat illustrate other dimensions of Cree humour.

As in Euro-Canadian society and elsewhere, sex and the elimination of bodily waste are often considered humorous in and of themselves. Sexual joking often makes use of metaphors whose constituents are animals or activities relating to hunting. *maskwa* "bear" is a humorous euphemism for "penis" and one person, when asked about the location of a bear, remarked with a poker face that he thought he had a *maskwa* in his pants. The verb *nāciskwī* "hunt bears" is similarly a humorous metaphor for chasing women. Metaphor also enters into humorous nicknames, the most striking example of which was "Mosquito Airport", applied to a bald individual. A derisive form of humorous insult metaphorically likens the butt to a lifeless object; speakers may use syntactically inanimate pronouns and verbs with an effect broadly comparable to the English phrase "You thing." Exotic animal metaphors occur in some contexts; an otter pelt mounted on a stretcher was pointed out to me, for instance, as "Churchill River alligator." Sarcasm was seldom encountered, although irony and/or incongruity appear frequently in both jokes and narratives. Johnny Bighetty's joking reference to a lynx herd on his trapline brought appreciative laughter both because the lynx do not herd and because such herds would have been immensely desirable during a year of high prices for lynx pelts.

No distinguishable genre of Whiteman jokes appears to exist; jokes are told of Whites but they do not differ materially from those told of Indians or animals.

That some humorousness appears to accrue to Whites is suggested by the frequency of *wīmistikōsiw* "Whiteman" as a dog name and a nickname for infants and small children. Incongruous or incompetent behavior by Whites in the bush is considered funny. The term *mōnīyās*, now a disparaging epithet for Whites in contrast to the neutral *mōnīyāw*, is said earlier to have referred more narrowly to Whites who were incompetent in the bush. One particularly popular story involved a White tourist who arrayed himself at night in a dressing gown and bedroom slippers while on a guided hunting trip in the bush.

Any adequate analysis of Rock Cree humour would require, of course, material transcribed in Cree and analyzed with a bilingual speaker. The stories below are provided as interim data on a little-known aspect of Subarctic Algonquian culture. The accessibility of the humour to non-Crees is highly variable. The listener left unmoved by *wīsahkīcāhk*'s use of *nistīs* "my elder brother" to address a baby may nonetheless appreciate the spectacle of the great hero stumbling blindly through the bush with a caribou skull stuck on his head.

Trapper Tricks *wītikōw*
Narrator: Jeremy Caribou
This fellow's name was Sam and he was out trapping with his mother and dad. They were camped out on the river. On the first point of the river, that's where they had their camp. So this *wītikōw* sneaked up to their camp. And, of course, they got into their canoe and ran away to the next point. There, they got off and camped again. But no sooner had they camped than *wītikōw* arrives there again. So they got into their canoe again. And he [Sam] says to his dad, "You leave me at this point here and I'll fix that *wītikōw*." So he went up to a big spruce tree and he cut it about three feet high. And he took his clothes off and he made a dummy sitting, just like it was someone sitting next to the fireplace. After he made that dummy, then he builds the fire. And after that, he goes and hides himself beside the lake there, behind the willows. And not very long after, sure enough, comes the *wītikōw*. He's going to sneak up to that guy, there, squatting over the fire. So this guy, he looks at the *wītikōw*; he's not very far from him, just a little ways. He see this guy just bunch himself up like this for a spring. He went after this guy squatting by the fire. And he got ahold of him right in the middle. Right here in the shoulder he grabbed that stump.

And he started to cry. That was a stump there that was standing, it wasn't human. "So that's the first time I ever hear *wītikōw* cry," he says. So that's the biggest story I could ever tell anyone," he says. So that's the end of the story. He took off.

Drowning the Moose
Narrator: Albert Umferville

This is the story of an old man and his wife and a moose. This old man and this old lady, they were traveling, going someplace. And while they were traveling, they saw a moose swimming on the lake. So they took after it in the canoe. Well, when they got to it, they ran that canoe right up on its back.

And the old fellow says, "Give me something. I want to drown him."

"We haven't got nothing."

"Well," he says, "gimme your skirt." So the old lady took off her skirt and handed it over to the old man. And he throws it over and tries to get it over the moose. But the moose went working to rip the cloth with his front hooves and he knocked it into the water, so he [old man] didn't have nothing.

So he says, "gimme something else." He says, "Gimme your blouse." So the old lady pulled off her blouse and give him that. So he tried to put it over the moose's mouth again, and the moose done the same thing and knocked the blouse away.

So, "What else you got?"

"I got nothing," the old lady says.

"Well," he says, "gimme your underwear." So the old lady pulls off her underwear. And of course I guess she was a big woman. And he tried to pull it over the head of the moose. The moose done the same thing yet. Well, so it was up to him now, so he rips off his shirt and he puts it over the moose's head and ties it around. The moose knocked that away so he figured, "Well, I guess there's no use."

"I'll jump on him," he says. "I'll use my knife," he says, "and when we're just close to shore, I'll try and cut his neck." Course they were way out in the lake and the old lady was all by herself in the canoe so she had to paddle. So she got left behind. Pretty soon they come to a long narrow island. Well, the old fellow didn't know what to do. He stayed right on the moose's back. Well, the moose got too sore. He tore right clean through that island and out on the other side and out into the water again. Away he'd gone. So the old lady, she had to paddle all the way around the island to chase after the moose and the old man. And he was sitting on top of the back of the moose. Oh, it was quite a way to go. So he's going along. So he decided, "Well, maybe I should have a smoke. I've got a long ways to go anyhow." So he lights his pipe.

And while he was going along, there was a priest and a guide coming along in another canoe. So they saw this smoke. So this fellow says...he turned around to his guide and he says, "I've never seen that island before. Someone must be making a fire over there because I see some smoke there. Let's go and investigate." So they started to go toward the island. They thought it was an island. But when they got closer, they saw it was a moose and a man on top of it.

He says, "What are you doing there?"

He says, "I'm riding a moose."

He says, "You got anything to kill it with?" He says, "I've got my knife. That's all."

"Well, I'll tell you, we'll pull up alongside, you jump into the canoe and we'll go along until he gets close enough to the island, another island, where we'll shoot it for you."

"Okay."

"Well," he says, "where's your wife?" "Oh, she's coming along back there." "All by herself?"

"Yeah, she's paddling." Well, they got to an island and they shot that moose before he got too close to the island and they dragged him ashore. So they started skinning and in the meantime the old lady comes up with his canoe and she's all bare. No clothes on.

"What happened to your old lady?" the priest asked.

"Oh, we were trying to drown that moose," he said, "so we had to use all her clothes."

The Voluble Wolverine
Narrator: Henry Linklater

My son was out trapping and having a lot of trouble with the wolverine. The wolverine was stealing furs from every trap along his line. One time, he's crossing the lake with his dogs and he saw the wolverine way off ahead of him on the ice. He drove his dogs up toward the wolverine and stopped. He grabbed his gun, pointed it right at the wolverine and got ready to shoot.

"Wait a minute!" yelled the Wolverine. "It wasn't me! [who plundered your traps]."

"Sure it's you!"

"No, it wasn't me! Leave me alone and I'll buy you a skiddoo (snowmobile) for Christmas!"

Edmund Sinclair in the Chimney
Narrator: Johnny Bighetty

This story comes from High Rock and it happened when Edmund Sinclair was a young man about nineteen or twenty. At that time all the log cabins around here had clay stoves and clay chimneys. Edmund's girlfriend was inside one of these cabins and he wanted to go in and see her. This was in the night. He kept knocking at the door, but she must have been asleep because there was no answer. Edmond really wanted to see his girl because he'd been in the bush a long time. Finally, he figured that the clay chimney would be big enough to let him through and he climbed up on the roof. Then he starts going down the chimney feet first. At first he's okay but after he's about halfway down he begins thrashing around and yelling for help. All his yelling woke up his girl-friend. She got scared. She thought a *wītikōw* was climbing down her chimney after her. So she builds big fire to burn this *wītikōw*. Then she runs outside and starts yelling for help. People come there from the other houses and she tells them she's got *wītikōw* in her chimney. Edmund is still in there. He's all covered with smoke and he's getting hotter and hotter so he begins roaring like a *wītikōw*. Finally, someone recognized his voice and they ran in and put out the fire. They hauled Edmund out of the chimney. He was black all over from head to foot.

The First Bush Pilot
Narrator: Johnny Bighetty
opimisihōwitāk was hunting in the bush and heard loons on a lake nearby. He stealthily approached the lake. When he got there, he found that the loons had flown away but that a bunch of swans were swimming around some distance from shore. They were too far away to shoot so *opimisihōwitāk* took off all his clothes, found a large rock, and lowered himself into the water, his plan being to approach the swans from underwater and grab them by their feet. He crept closer and closer underwater and finally, finding himself directly beneath the swans, grabbed several of them by the feet at once.

Those swans were scared and they began yelling for help. They began to spread their wings and try to take off flying. *opimisihōwitāk* was hungry and he held on to those swans. Suddenly they took off and flew up into the air with *opimisihōwitāk* still holding on tight. Pretty soon they were up above the treetops. The old man started to try to think what to do. The swans were flying faster and faster and they're taking him further and further away from his clothes and gun. Those swans flew out over a lake and he thought, "I intend to say goodbye to these swans now." He let go and fell down through the air into the lake.

Jimmy Bighetty Rides a Moose
Narrator: Johnny Bighetty
This story happened about fifty years ago to Jimmy Bighetty from Pukatawagan. He used to fish during the summer at Sisipuk Lake and one afternoon he was hunting moose. Finally he saw a moose in the lake some distance from shore and he began to think about how he could kill it. He only had a twenty-two so he had to get up real close. His wife was with him in the canoe. He left the gun with her in the canoe and walked along the shore. He planned to grab the moose from underwater and hold it while his wife paddled up and shot it. He jumped into the water and went along holding himself down with a stone. Unknown to him,

a strong wind had blown up and his wife was having trouble paddling the canoe fast enough to keep up with him.

Finally he saw the moose legs standing there in the water. Just then, the moose turned and stepped on him. First, it stepped on his shirt and then it was standing on his butt [laughs]. That startled the moose and it jumped away and started swimming toward the middle of the lake. Jimmy grabbed a rear leg and hung on and finally he managed to get up on that moose's back like he was riding horseback. In the distance, he could see his wife struggling to catch up and yelling, "Don't let go of that moose!" Jimmy took a good grip on the horns. The moose swam fast and soon outdistanced the old lady. The moose reached the shore, ran for half a mile across a portage, then went into another lake. It swam across that lake, came out again at a second portage, and then went into another lake. Jimmy was still hanging on. He reached into his pocket and found something like a nail or a little knife. He reached around and popped the moose's eyes with it. That moose couldn't see where it was going then. He finally grabbed that moose's head and slipped his shirt over it and pulled it down into water and drowned it. He finally got that moose. Back at the second portage he found his wife who was still paddling against the wind. They went and butchered the moose and dried the meat.

The Dumb Partner: The Lost Ducks
Narrator: Caroline Caribou
An old man was out on his trapline with his grandson. After hunting a long time, the old man killed two ducks. He instructed his grandson to throw them in the water, by which he meant to clean them and put them in the kettle. The grandson took the ducks and threw them in the water.

The Dumb Partner: The Cat Impersonator
Narrator: Caroline Caribou
It used to be real hard for men to meet their sweethearts in the old days. The parents were real strict. The parents decided who was going to get married to whom and they would forbid communication with ineligible suitors. One boy wanted to see his girl but he knew that her father didn't approve of him. So he got his friend to help him. He planned to sneak into the girl's lodge really quietly without disturbing her relatives. He told his friend, "In case the old man wakes up, make a noise like a cat. He'll think that's all it is and he'll go back to sleep." They snuck over to the lodge that night and the one boy tried to get in under the sides. He made too much noise and the old man woke up.

"Who's there?" he said.

"*posīs*" ("cat"), said the friend. The old man chased them out of there with a stick, and that boy gave his friend hell.

The Dumb Partner: Feasting in Heaven
Narrator: Caroline Caribou

Two hunters were very hungry. They'd been out in the bush for a long time hunting but they couldn't kill anything. Finally, they killed two partridges which they decided to leave for the morning. The more foresighted of the two warned the other not to eat them during the night because they would need them in the morning. They went to bed. In the morning, the cautious man got up.

"I had a wonderful dream," he said. "I went up to Heaven and had a big feast." He went over to cook those partridges and they were gone.

His partner said, "I knew you were going to Heaven to have a feast, so I had a feast right here in camp while you were gone."

The Dumb Partner: Scabby Suitor
Narrator: Phillip Bighetty

A man, desiring to speak with his sweetheart's father and arrange marriage in the appropriate way, planned with his partner to create a good impression. Knowing that the old man valued both industry and modesty, he expected that he would be asked about his hunting and trapping gear. He planned, therefore, to deprecate modestly his possessions. His partner would then "correct" him by saying, "He's too modest. His outfit is in fine shape." The partner, though, was kind of stupid.

They went to see the girl's father and, as expected, the latter began to query his prospective son-in-law about his hunting, trapping, and fishing equipment.

"How many nets do you have?"

"I've only got one worn-out old net," replied.

"He's too modest," interrupted the partner. "He has several nets and they're all in good repair."

"Well, how about outboard motors?"

"I've only got one broken old motor," said the suitor.

"My partner is too modest," interrupted the friend. "He has three new motors."

"Yes," said the old man. "What about your trapline? Are there many beaver houses there?"

"Only a few and they're nearly trapped out," said the suitor.

"He's being modest again," said the partner. "He has a big line with many beaver colonies."

The questioning continued and the old man was impressed favorably with both the assets and the modesty of the suitor. There had been cold weather lately and the suitor had a small frostbite scab on his cheek. The old man remarked conversationally that it had been cold and asked whether the suitor had been frostbit badly.

"No, I only got this one little scab," said the suitor.

"He's being too modest again," piped up the partner. "He has scabs like that all over his body. He just now picked them off. He's usually covered with scabs."

CHAPTER 9
Texts: Animal Marriages

Introduction

The two texts presented here were narrated in February of 1979 by Mrs. Angelique Linklater of Brochet, Manitoba and translated with the assistance of her husband Mr. Henry Linklater, Pierre Merasty, and Muggs Merasty. The dialect is Woods Cree, exhibiting the characteristic falling together of /ē/ and /ī/ together with considerable free variation between the two. The occurrence in most positions of Plains Cree /y/ in place of Woods Cree /ð/ in "The Bear Husband" resulted from the fact that Mrs. Linklater wrote out the narrative in Cree syllabics and, with the exception of intermittent "breakthroughs," read aloud from the written text. In northern Manitoba, and perhaps elsewhere, the syllabics are strongly associated with Plains Cree and persons reading them often substitute /y/ for /ð/.

    Mrs. Linklater's speech exemplifies a characteristic that is remarked upon by Cree speakers at Pukatawagan and Granville Lake and which John Nichols (personal communication) has noted also in the speech of a Swampy Cree speaker from The Pas. Mrs. Linklater frequently lacks preconsonantal /h/ in positions where Pukatawagan and Granville Lake speakers retain it. Additionally, as Nichols notes, the loss of aspiration is often accompanied by vowel lengthening; the sequence of short vowel plus /h/ plus consonant becomes long vowel plus consonant: *pīwinahki* "he scatters it" > *piwināki*. Neither the lengthening nor the loss of aspiration occur consistently with word-final /hk/ which is often realized as a velar fricative. This feature is remarked upon as "funny" by Pukatawagan speakers who associate it with such communities along the provincial border as Sandy Bay, Southend, and Sturgeon Landing. Mrs. Linklater was born at Southend and moved north to Brochet early in her life. The loss of aspiration indicated in the texts is characteristic of certain other Brochet speakers. The generational stratification of this variation, if any, would be an interesting subject for further inquiry.

    The accuracy of the transcriptions has benefited greatly from the generous assistance of John Nichols; nonetheless, the quality of the tapes renders the discrimination of vowel length less exact than would be desirable in some instances. Passages marked with empty brackets were not audible or intelligible to myself or my collaborators. In some instances, these passages prevent the satisfactory translation of adjacent sections of text. For example, near the conclusion of "The Beaver Wife," a teenager cautions a young boy not to reveal the sex of the surviving beaver, but the lacuna renders it difficult to tell who is speaking and to whom.

The organization of the texts into lines is based on pause groupings in Mrs. Linklater's speech. Following Tedlock's (1983) conventions, adjacent lines correspond to pauses of two seconds or less while periods between lines indicate longer pauses. No pauses greater than two seconds occur in "The Beaver Wife," although they are present in other texts from Brochet, Granville Lake, and Pukatawagan. Since "The Beaver Husband" was for the most part read from a prepared text while "The Beaver Wife" was related extemporaneously, it is not surprising that the latter contains significantly longer stretches of speech between pauses.

The translations themselves attempt to steer a middle course between Bloomfieldian "literalism" and the objective to communicating literary and poetic qualities of the text. Recent criticism of literalist approaches to translation from American Indian languages (Tedlock 1983: 37–38), although unquestionably cogent as concerns problems of style, seemingly are skeptical as regards the possibility of aesthetically satisfying renderings that retain syntactic and lexical characteristics of the originals. The translations worked out here experiment with such an approach, although the success of the results is at best partial. Canons of stylistic adequacy are usually set aside in favor of relatively literal glossing, as with the recurrent and inelegant but semantically consistent use of "his/her younger sibling" for *osīma* in "The Bear Husband." The problem of translating such particles as *ēkwānī*, *īkwa*, and *īyako* is handled rather opportunistically. The ubiquitous *ēkwānī/īkwānī* is glossed consistently as "so" and the others are sometimes glossed differently in varying contexts although never with senses rejected by Cree consultants. In cases where the same particle occurs twice in a line, the gloss typically occurs only once in the translation. Use of these particles in combination with pause groupings to delimit lines (cf. Bright 1979) would be an alternative and potentially useful approach to the graphic presentation of these texts.

The Bear Husband (Cree)
Narrator: Angelique Linklater

pīyakwāw īsa mīna kayās,
pīyak iskwīw ī-kīy-ōtinikot maskwa.
īyako ītōkwī, kayās iskamikōcihk,
kā-kī-wīcayāmāt
anihi maskwa.
ēkwānī ītōkwī
ōma
māna kā-ti-takwākik
ka-ti-kāksināk.
ēkwānī ēkōsē kāy-itwīt ana maskwa,
"īkwa.
nītē wī-natonītān
ī-ta-kita-piponisiyāhk,"
kāy-itāt
otiskwīma.

ēkwānī ī-sipwītīcik
ī-natonāk—ī-natonāk, ana
maskwa
ita-kita-mīywāsinīyik kita-wātīhkīt.
ēkwānī kwayis ītōkwī wayāw kāy-
tōtīcik.
ēkwānī kitātawē kā-wāpatahk
ita kwayis i-mīywāsiniyik kita-wātīhkīt.
ēkwānī ēkwa
kā-wātīhkīt,
kā-ti-wātīhkīt ōma.
īkwānī
īsa
kā-misi-pawīkitot [laughs],
 kā-misi-pawīkitot.
"hāw namwāc," itīw
maskwa.
"ki-ka-miskākowīnānaw.
kiyām sipwītītān ōtē isi,"
kāy-itwīt īsa.
īkwānī

kā-sipwītīcik
kitātawē ē-wāpatahk
ita kītwām

ta-wātīhkīt
awa ēkwa.
[ ]
mitōni wayāw isi
namwāc ēkwa—
namwāc ēkwa—
namwāc ēkwa pawīkitow.
īkwānī, "namwāc awiyak ka-
miskākonaw,"
itīw.
ēkwānī ēkwa kā-pītokwatācik
maskōsīya
kita-swapacik.
īkwānī—
īkwānī pītokīwak ispī
ī-mīkiskayik. īkwānīka-pī-pipon,
ka-pī-pipon.
nipāwak pātīma ī-nipayamiyāniwak.
"ka-kwīskīsīkwaw," kāy-itwīt īsa ana
iskwīw.
īkwānī ītōkwī kā-ti-sikwāhk māna ōma
kā-pākānōtīhk

īkwānī īsa kisīyiniw.
"ni-wī-nātāwak īkwa
ni-ka-miskowāwak
ita kāy-ayācik," itīw.
īkwānī kā-sipwītīt nōhcimihk īsa ēkōta
ēkōta kā-wāpamāt mōswa.
īkwānī īsa kā-nipahāt, kīwīhtataw
wīyās.
kītwām sāsamīna sipwītīw pīyakwan
ispaðīyik.
sāsamīna nipahīw mōswa.
ī-sākōtiðimikot maskwa.
īkwānī kītwām
ī-wāpāhk.
īkosī kāy-itwīt:
"namwāc mistawāc
ni-ka-sākōtiyimik maskwa."
īkwānī kā-sipwītīt. kā-wāpatāk

ita nistam kā-nōmakī-wātīhkīt.
sīmāk īkosē kāy-itwīt,
"īkōta ēsa kī-pawīkitōw."

īkwānī kā-sipwītīt wayāw itōtīw.
īkwa—
īkwānī īsa ana maskwa kāy-itāt
iskwīwa,
otiskwīma,
"ki-wī-miskākonaw kipāpa.
māka kīspin nipahici—
kīspin nipahici
kīspin mistahe pīwināki nimīkom
kītwām ni-ka-pasikōn īkōta ohci.
īkwa ka-wītamātin," itīw otiskwīma.
"kīspin kitātawē wī-nōtinikīyani
kanawīmik mōswa ospakīkana mitātāt.
īyako aniki ta-paciyiclk."
īkwānī kisīyiniw
miskam owāti.
īkwānī ka-cīkahahk iskwāhkitīmihk.
"pīyakwayēwik," kāy-itāt,
īkwānī nīkan nāpīmaskwa
nisīkāc kā-wayāwītacimot
ēkōta kā-nipahāt.
īkwānī iskwīw wīsta
wayawitācimow
māka iyiniw ispayīw īkōta.
īkwa wīstawaw
nīso maskōsisak kā-wayawīcik
wīstawaw
māka iyiniw ispayīwak.
īkwānī ana kisīyiniw
tipīyāk ī-kī-pakōcīnāt anihi maskwa
ēkosīsi nakatīw
īkwa.
īkwānī kā-kīwīhtahāt.
kā-kīwīhtahāt otānisa asici osisima
ka-takosīkwaw wīkiwāhk.
kwayis miyīyitam ana nōcōkwīsiw
ī-wāpamāt otānisa asici osisima.
īkwānī īkōta ī-ayāwak
pāpakīkinōkīw ana iskwīw

asici pīyak osīmisa,
oskinīkīskwīsisa.
wīstawāw awāsisak miyīyitamwak
ī-wī-ci-mītawīmācik nīso awāsisa.
īkwānī ēkosē kāy-itwīcik,
"māti anima mītawītan
maskokācōsīwin mītawīwin," itwīwak
awāsisak.
"aniki nīso nāpīsisak
īyako aniki ta-maskwōwiwak."
īkwānī ēsa kā-sipwīðimītawīcik.
"māka tātākonamok mistikwa
tāpiskōc mōkomāna,"
itwīwak.

īkwānī sipwīpātāwak ī-itwīcik,
"nācaskwītan! nācaskwītan!"
īkwānī aniki nīso nāpīsisak
nācipahēwak māna tapasīwak kotakak
awāsisak īkwa
ī-ka-kita-kācitinikocik anihi. osītāwak
wīkiwām mistikwa ōci.
ī-cimatācik [ ] wīkiwāhk
*   ka-pītokīyāmocik.*
īkōta namwāc ka-pī-ispātāwak
nīso napīsisak. kitātawē mīkwāc ōma
ī-mītawīcik aniki nīso nāpīsisak.

ī-kisīwimītawīcik īkōta maskosisak
*   kā-ispaðīcik.*
kākiyaw nipahēwak awāsisa.
īkwānī tēpwīwak iyiniwak,
"nipatākīwak maskosisak," itwīwak.
īkwānī nipahēwak maskosisa.
kwayis kisīwāsiw ana iskwīw
pītokīpātaw wīkiwāhk ī-y-otītināt
mōswa ospakīkana
kākiyaw nipahēwak iyiniwa.
nayīsta pīyak osīmisa namwāc
nipahēw,
anihi oskinīkīskwīsisa
wīcihik ī-pakīkinīkit. kīsihk askaw
*   āsawāpīw.*

nīso osīma ī-kī-sipwītīyit nāpēwa.
ī-kī-natonawācik iðiniwa aniki
nāpēwak
kinwīs kī-ayāwak īkwānī
ītōkwī kitātawē pīyak ana nāpēw
    kā-pī-tōtīt
nōhcimihk.
sīmāk wāpamīw awa iskwīw
maskwa ispayīw
kā-nacipahāt osīma.
īkwānī sīmāk ana nāpēw
nitawī-pwākastawīyāmōw
īkosē īsa
kāy-itwīt tāwic ī-ayāt,
"ōtī ati-nīkan wī-itātwāwi iyiniwak
tāy-itwīwak: 'īyako awa osīmimāw
nāpēw.'
īyako nīya," kāy-itwīt īsa.
sīmāk mitoni ī-yōtīk
ī-misāk nipīy
ī-mamākakamāskāk. īyako ana nāpēw
    kā-kī-itwīt īsa
kayās.

īkwānī wīsta kitātawē ana nāpēw
kā-pī-tōtīt nōhcimihk.
īyako wīya sīmāk kiskīðitam
ī-nipatākīyit omisa.
māka namwāc wāpamik
omisa.
īkwānī ēsa
ēkosē kāy-itāt osīmisa ana iskwīw,
"māti pitama piminawasōw.
ta-mīcisowāhk."
īkwa wīya ispīci matahikīw.
kwayis māka
ī-kitimahāt osīmisa, ī-pāpakamawāt.
mīkwāc ī-mātahīkit ana iskwīw.
kitātawē kā-pimōtikot osīma.
īkwānī kā-nīcipayit pakīkinohk
ōci. īkwōnī kā-pī-takosīhk ana nāpēw
kakiwīcimīw osīmisa,
"tānsī kāy-itākiminaniyik?"

kā-kī-wītamawīw ostīsa.
"ēkosē," kāy-itikot,
nitawī manīy kicayānisa, kanakī
nayāta.
īkwa nīya
akōpa asici mīciwin.
ōtē [ ] ni-kī-miskāwānānak iyiniwak
kā-kī-natonawākīcik.
ēkōta ka-nitawī-wīcayāmānawak.
īkwānī kapoh,
īkwānī tāpwē sipwītīwak
osīmisa tasic.
itakōsīkwaw ita kāy-ayāt iyiniwa.
asici mōstawēwak kākīyakīkway.
"tānsē," kāy-itāt [ ] wīkiwāhk.
anima tēskwa.

The Bear Husband (English)
Narrator: Angelique Linklater

Once then and long ago,
one woman was taken away by a bear.
Just this way it must have been, long ago in the past,
that she lived with him,
that bear.
So it must be
this way
that autumn comes on and
it becomes cooler.
So then that bear says,
"Let's go.
Let's search for the place where we'll pass the winter,"
he says to
his woman.

So they go off traveling.
He searches—he searches, that
bear,
for where it will be good for him to make a den.
So it must be very far that they travel.
So presently he sees
where it will be very good for him to
make a den.
So then
he makes a den.
He proceeds to make a den in this way.
So
just then
he farts powerfully. He farts powerfully.
"Oh no," he says to her,
that bear.
"We will be found.
Well, let's go off elsewhere,"
he says then.
So
they go off traveling and
presently he sees
where again

he will make a den
now.

[ ]
It is very far away.
Not this time—
Not this time—
He doesn't fart this time
Now, "No one will find us,"
he says to her.
So then they bring in the grass
for their bedding.
So—
So they go inside when
it is late autumn. So winter comes,
winter comes.
They sleep until midwinter. "Turn over,"
    that woman says then.
So it must be that spring approaches and
the ground is cleared of snow.

So then the old man.
"I intend to search for them now and
I will find them
wherever they are," he says to them
    [relatives].
So he goes off travelling in the bush there
and there he sees a moose.
So then he kills it and brings meat back to
    his camp.
Once again he departs travelling and once
    again it happens.
Once again he kills a moose.
He is being overcome by the bear
So again
the next day
he says in this fashion:
"Surely
that bear will not overcome me."
So he goes off traveling. He sees
where first he [bear] begins to make a den.

Right away he says in this fashion:
"Right there he farted.
"So he departs traveling and very far
    he goes."
Now—
So then that bear says to
the woman,
his woman,
"Your father will find us.
But if he kills me—
If he kills me—
and if he scatters much of my blood
    around, from that place I'll rise up
    from there.
Now I will tell you," he says to his
    woman,
"if presently you are going to do battle
you keep ten moose ribs.
Just in that way you will use them."
So the old man
finds his den.
So he cuts a hole at the entrance. "All of
    you come out," he says to them.
Now first that male bear
slowly crawls forth
and just there the old man kills him.
So that woman herself
crawls forth
but just there she transforms into a human
    being.
Then themselves
two bearcubs crawl forth
and themselves
transform into human beings.
So that old man
merely gutted that bear and that way he
    discards him then.
So he brings them home.
He brings home his daughter and his
    grandchildren
and they arrive at his lodge.
That old woman is very happy
to see her daughter and grandchildren.

Now just there they stay and
that woman prepares moosehide
with one of her younger siblings,
a teenage girl.
The other children are happy about it
    themselves and want to play with the
    two children.
Now they say in this fashion,
"Please, let's play that bear hunt game,"
    the childen say.
"Those two boys
in that way will be the bears.
"So then they go out to play."
"But you carry sticks
as pretend knives,"
they say.

So they run off and they say,
"Let's hunt bears! Let's hunt bears!"
So those two boys
chase them and then the other chidren run
    for fear that they will catch them. They
    build a lodge from sticks.
They build [ ] a lodge and run inside.
They aren't able to get in there,
the two boys. Presently amidst all this
    [horseplay],
those two boys are playing.
They play roughly just there and they
    transform into bear cubs.
They kill all of the children.
So the people cry,
"The bear cubs are killers," they say.
So they kill the bear cubs.
Very enraged is that woman [mother].
She runs inside the lodge and seizes
the moose ribs and
she kills all of the people.
Only her younger sibling does she not kill,
that teenage girl
who helps her tan moosehide. Often from
    then on she looks out watchfully.

Her two younger siblings, adult men, had
    gone off.
Those men had gone looking for other
    people.
A long time they stayed there now and
it must be that presently that one man
    [younger brother] came there
through the bush.
Right away that woman sees him
and transforms into a bear
and charges at her younger sibling.
So right away that man
runs hastily into the water
and then in this fashion
and far from shore he says,
"There when the future comes, the people
    will say about him:
'Just this, that male younger sibling of
    hers.'
Just this, myself," he says then.
Right away the wind blows strongly up
and the water becomes turbulent
with great waves. Just this that man said
    then
long ago.

So presently that man himself
    [second brother]
comes there through the bush.
In this way he immediately knows himself
    that his older sister is a killer.
But she doesn't see him,
his older sister.
So then
in this fashion that woman says to her
    younger sibling,
"Stop working and cook. We'll eat."
Meanwhile she scrapes hair from the hide.
But she is very
cruel to her younger sibling and strikes her
while she [woman] is scraping the hide.
Presently her younger sibling [brother]
    shoots her with an arrow.

Now she pulls down upon herself
    [in dying] that moosehide
there. Now that man comes up and
he asks his younger sibling,
"What is it that happens here?"
She told her older brother.
"Well then," he says to her,
"quickly prepare your clothing, at least
    one pack.
And myself [I will gather]
blankets and food.
There [ ] we found them, those people
    who searched for me
and just there we will rapidly go and stay
    with them."
So then
really they set off travelling,
his younger sibling with him.
He leads them to where those people are
    staying
and after a long time they arrive. "Hello,"
    they say to them [   ] at the lodge.
That is finished.

Discussion

Although Petitot (1884: 46–63) obtained another version of this myth from the Cree of Lake Athabasca, it does not occur in other published sources on Cree literature. McClellan (1970) provides an authoritative distributional study of a related myth from Athapakan and Northwest Coast sources.

A terse horror story, the myth begins with the encounter between a human woman and a bear; the woman becomes a bear and they live as husband and wife. They pass the winter in hibernation and the bear-woman gives birth to two cubs. The woman's father divines their location, kills the bear in a disrespectful manner, and is reunited with his daughter who, together with the cubs, resumes human form when she emerges from the bear's den. The woman and her children return to human society where she tans moosehide and the two boys play with the other children. With grim and ironic inevitability, the boys are appointed as the "bears" in the bear-hunt game; this catalyzes their transformation into cubs and they kill their human playmates. The others in the camp kill the cubs and the enraged mother in turn destroys them, sparing only her younger sister. Thereafter the bear woman watches warily for the return of two of her adult brothers who had gone in search of another camp. They return separately. The first is chased into the water by his sister and he drowns. The second approaches the camp undetected and kills his sister with an arrow after divining that she is murderous. Together with the surviving sister, he travels to another camp where they are welcomed.

The narrative is "temporally" situated in the remote past where in many myths animals are represented as possessing physical and cognitive characteristics of human beings. However, in this myth, contemporary distinctions pertain and humans and animals are represented as differentiated in appearance and practices. The woman, for example, undergoes a physical transformation into a bear during her absence and the ursine couple are described as preparing and occupying a den for hibernation during the winter. Such attributes of the bear as speech, hominid intelligence, and spiritual power are consistent with some Crees' assessments of bears in the present. A number of other contemporary beliefs about bears are exemplified in the narrative. For example, the initially enigmatic passage in which the bear "farts powerfully" after digging the first den was explained by Mr. Linklater as a form of ursine divination. It is said that when bears fart at this time it prognosticates the discovery of the winter den by hunters and that bears consequently go elsewhere and dig another den. The passage in which the woman tells the bear to turn over at midwinter reflects another Cree conception of bear behavior during hibernation, although it may also, in this context, suggest the initiation of sexual relations. Additionally, the passage in which the woman's father is diverted from his search by encounters with moose reflects the belief that bears can exert control over other animals and send them across the trails of approaching hunters in order to prevent the discovery of their dens. The old man is twice distracted in this way but becomes cognizant of the bear's strategy and continues the search. Finally, the bear's threats to "rise up again" if his remains are treated disrespectfully are consistent with ritual obligations pertaining to the carcasses of bears and other large game animals. The bear specifically refers to the act of scattering his blood around at the kill site as a ritual offense. Crees who observe these regulations today cover blood spilled on the ground with snow or moss; animals are butchered on clean pine boughs which are then burned. As predicted, the father contemptuously guts the bear and discards the carcass, compounding the insult of incorrect butchering with the offense of wasting meat.

With its movement between animal and human habitations and conditions, "The Bear Husband" readily lends itself to structural interpretation; the marriage and the cubs functioning as unsuccessful mediators between human and animal domains. Those partisan to social anthropological perspectives could elaborate a subtext in which the *mésalliance* represents tensions and conflicting obligations between consanguineal and affinal relatives. The incidental remarks of Mr. and Mrs. Linklater indicate that they interpreted the story as a comedy of errors or horrors arising from ambiguities in human-animal relationships. That the story is not a moralistic fable exemplifying the inherent danger of animal-human or human-bear miscegenation is clear from other myths in which the progeny of such unions are heroes or in which the marriages end "happily" as in "The Beaver Wife" text which follows. To Mr. Linklater, the cycle of killings that followed the woman's return to her human family were consequences of the bear's prophecy and the old man's disrespectful treatment of the bear's carcass. He regarded the bear's threat to "rise up again" not as a reference to literal regeneration but rather as predestining the materialization of his personality and vengeance in the transformations and murders committed by the two children and by the woman. The murders are, from this point of view, a posteriori irruptions of the bear's anger over the old man's contemptuous treatment. This interpretation is consistent with modifications in human-animal relationships that are brought about through such marriages in other myths. For example, characters who have been married to animals or who possess an animal parent typically avoid eating the flesh of animals of the same species, as in the myth of *maskōkōsan*. From this point of view, the old man's aggressive treatment of the carcass assumes special gravity, resulting not in the conventional sanction of bad hunting luck but in the death of himself and his family.

The occurrence of the moose and of moose body parts is clearly an important thematic element in the myth. The bear initially diverts the old man from his search by sending moose across his path and instructs his wife to use ten moose ribs as knives if she intends to fight. Rather ominously, the bear woman is set to work tanning and scraping moosehide when she returns home and the story emphasizes that she is continually at work with it. Finally, when her brother shoots her with an arrow and kills her, she pulls the moose hide down over herself in dying. The particular significance of the moose in these contexts requires elucidation but it is clear that the animal and its products function throughout to effect a disjunction between the woman and human society.

The Beaver Wife (Cree)
Narrator: Angelique Linklater

*pīyakwāw īsa mīna kayās, nāpew
pīyak nāpēw,
kapin nitē kapīsitēy ī-nitē-nipāt
    pawiscikosihk.
īkwānī īsa
kitātawē owīcīwākana īkosē kāy-itikot,
    "ī-namatītīt." pātimā ī-tipiskāk
    ī-kīwīt.
īkwa ēsa
īkōta anima tātokīsikāw īkwānī [ ]
    pawiscikosihk, ē-ayāðik īkōta
    ī-nitē-nipāt ī-kisikāšik.
īkwānī pēšis īkōta ī-pawātāt,
pēšis pawātīw ōta iskwīwa. ī-sākihāt
    anihi iskwīwa īkōta kā-pawātāt
    anta pawiscikos.
pātimā māna ī-tipiskāšik wā-kīwīt.
īkwānī pēyakwāw ēkosīsī,
īkwānī nānōsamāc ī-kī-namatīt.
    kā-natonikot īkwa owīcīwākana
    kā-wicāmāt anta ī-natonahk.
namwāc, tātīpwīw nōhcimihk
    namwāc miskawīw.
namwāc nantētī tīpwīšiwa. īkwānī—
    īkwānī tāpwī pīšis namwāc īkwa
    natonowīw.
īkōta māka īsa ana nāpēw, ana
    oskinīkiw,
        ī-pwākastēpašihot pawiscikosihk.
īkwa ītōkwī īkwa ana nāpēw pīšis īkwa
    amisk īkwa ispašīw īkōta anima.
ī-isi-pē-pwākastēpašihot amisk īkwa
    ispašēw īkōta anima.
ītōkwī kinwīs ēkōta anima ēkwa,
īkwa nāpēwak kāy-itwīcik—[a false
start; no dialogue ensues]
kāy-iskīcik īkwa, kāy-iskīcik īkwa,
īkōta anima.
īkwānī īkōta anima kāy-iskīcik
    kā-kapatisīpinīwak amiskwa.*

*kitātawē ana nāpīmisk [ ] mina
    kapatisīpinīwak
anihi amiskwa.
īkōta kā-nipowit ana nāpēw
kā-kī-namatīt.
īkwānī ēsa kā-kospit ē-kospicawīwak
    ana nāpēw tantē ē-ayāt nītī
    pakwanikamikohk.
nāpēs īsa, nāpīsis, kā-pī-nasīpēpahtāt
    ēkōta [singsong voice].
"kāða wītamaw ana nāpēw,
kāða wītamaw ana oskinīkiw
tāntōwī amisk kāy-iskohayāhk,"
itīw [ ] ana oskinīkis.
"ayhāw," itwīw ana oskinīkis [ ].
īkwānī ana nāpēw kā-kī-amiskōwit
    ēkōta wītapimīw anihi nāpīsa.
īkwānī īsa ikosē kāy-itāt,
"īkwānī tāntatō nipahēwak?"
    āta-wītamawīw.
"pēyak māka namwāc," itīw,
"awīða māka kāy-iskohācik,
nōsī!" kāy-itwīt ana nāpīs.
tāpwī pokoh īsa ana nāpēw, tāpwī
    pokoh
kā-nasīpētpātāt tāpwī pokoh
    pwākastēpaðihōw.
īkwānī kītwām [ ] kītwām [ ]
    kī-amiskōwiw, kī-wīcāmīw anihi
    nōsīmiskwa.
anima tēskwa.*

The Beaver Wife (English)
Narrator: Angelique Linklater

Once then and long ago, a man,
one man,
remains there and always sleeps there by
    the small rapids.
So then
presently his friend says in this fashion
    about him, "He is a long time absent."
Eventually he comes home at nightfall.
Now then,
every day now just there at the small
    rapids he stays and dreams there
    during the day.
So until right there he dreams of her,
until he dreams of a woman. He loves her,
    that woman whom he dreams of
    there at the small rapids.
Eventually at nightfall he comes home.
So one time it happens
so that he was long absent and not to be
    found. His friend looks for him,
the one he stays with there looks for him.
No, he calls for him in the bush but he
    fails to find him.
Not from anyplace does he call back to
    him. Soīso really he finally ceases to
    search for him.
But now that man, that young man, leaps
    into the small rapids there.
Then until it must be that that man
    changes into a beaver there.
He leaps into the water there and changes
    into a beaver then.
It must be a long time later at that place
    that
the men then say—[a false start; no
    dialogue ensues]
They chisel open beaver lodges then, they
    chisel open beaver lodges there.
So just there they chisel open beaver
    lodges and they will pull out beavers.
Presently [ ] they pull out that male
    beaver,
that beaver.
Right there stands that man
who had been missing.
So then he goes up and they take the man
    up the bank where he stays in a tent.
Then a boy, a little boy, runs down to the
    bank just there [singsong voice]
"Don't tell that man [the beaver-man],
don't tell that young man
the kind of beaver we left living in the
    lodge,"
that teenaged boy said to him [little boy].
"Alright," he says to that teenaged
    boy [ ].
So that man who had been a beaver sits
    together with that boy just there.
So then he says to him in this fashion,
"So how many beavers do they kill?"
Alas, he tells him.
"All but one," he says to him,
"which they left alive in the lodge.
A FEMALE!" says that boy.
Really right away, really right away then
    that man
runs down to the bank and really right
    away leaps into the water.
So once again [ ], once again [ ] he is
    able to be a beaver and to with dwell
    with that female beaver.
That is finished.

Discussion

Other versions of this myth have been recorded from Cree (Skinner 1911: 104–07) and Eastern Cree/Montagnais-Naskapi sources (Turner 1890: 339–40, Savard 1979: 24–26, Bauer 1971: 36–49, Steager 1976: 175–96, Bell 1897: 1–8). Some of these account for the lodge-building behavior of beavers as an innovation introduced by the transformed human.

Mrs. Linklater's version is relatively attenuated in comparison with many of those noted above. The myth relates the experiences of a young man who passes his days sleeping and dreaming by a rapids, a behavior which his companion remarks upon as odd; in the evenings, he returns to their camp. During the day, he dreams of a beautiful woman with whom he falls in love. The woman of whom he dreams is in actuality a beaver and the young man joins her by leaping into the water and becoming a beaver. His friend searches in vain for him and then gives up. A long time later, men of the young man's band are cutting open beaver lodges near the rapids and pulling out beavers. They pull out the young man who has been living with his beaver wife and he reassumes human form. They take him up to an empty tent on the bank while the beaver hunt continues. His old companion, divining what has happened, warns a small boy not to tell the young man that they have left one beaver living in the lodge, the female with whom he had been living. The boy thoughtlessly tells the man this and he runs down the bank, leaps back into the water, and, once again in the form of a beaver, rejoins his wife.

Unfortunately missing in the text is a section of the myth that Mrs. Linklater added as an afterthought. She remarked that once the man had entered the water, he perceived the female beaver as a beautiful woman and her lodge as a well-appointed human dwelling. The wood which they ate, he perceived as conventional human food. This philosophical emphasis on multiple perception is represented elsewhere in this collection by *maskōkōsan*'s mother's perception of the bear as human, by the identification of humans as moose by the anthropophagous *wīhcikōsisak*, and by the contrasting definitions of the same objects in "Wolverine, Wolf, and Dog."

References Cited

Ahenakew, Edward. 1929. "Cree Trickster Tales," *Journal of American Folklore* 42: 309–53.
Ahenakew, Beth and Sam Hardlotte (eds.). 1977. *Nehiyaw A-tayoka-we-na (Cree Legends): Stories of Wesakechak*. Saskatoon: Saskatchewan Indian Cultural College.
Allouez, Claude. 1899. "Relation of 1669–1670." In Reuben G. Thwaites (ed.), *The Jesuit Relations and Allied Documents*, vol. 54. Cleveland: n.p.
Aubin, George F. 1982. *Ethnographic Notes from Golden Lake. Papers of the Thirteenth Algonquian Conference*, William Cowan (ed.). Ottawa: Carleton University.
Barnouw, Victor. 1977. *Wisconsin Chippewa Myths and Tales and Their Relation to Chippewa Life*. Madison: University of Wisconsin Press.
Basile, Marie Jean and Gerard E. McNulty. 1971. *Atanukana/Legendes Montagnaises*. Universitt' Laval, Centre d'Etudes Nordiques, Collection Nordicana 31. Quebec.
Basso, Keith. 1979. *Portraits of the Whiteman*. Cambridge: Cambridge University Press.
Bauer, George W. 1971. "Cree Tales and Beliefs," *Northeast Folklore* 12. Orono, ME: The University Press.
Bishop, Charles A. 1981. "Territorial Groups Before 1821: Cree and Ojibwa." Pp. 158–68 in June Helm (ed.), *Handbook of North American Indians*, Vol. 6, *Subarctic*. Washington, DC: Smithsonian Institution.
Black, Mary B. 1977. "Ojibwa Taxonomy and Percept Ambiguity," *Ethos* 5: 90–118.
Blair, Emma H. 1911–1912. *The Indian Tribes of the Upper Mississippi Valley and the Region of the Great Lakes*. 2 Vols. Cleveland: Arthur H. Clark.
Bloomfield, Leonard. 1930. *Sacred Stories of the Sweet Grass Cree*. National Museum of Canada Bulletin 60, Anthropological Series No. 11.
———. 1934. "Plains Cree Texts." In *Publications of the American Ethnological Society* 16. New York.
———. 1957. *Eastern Ojibwa*. C. Hockett (ed.). Ann Arbor: University of Michigan Press.
Boas, Franz. 1914. "Mythology and Folk-Tales of the North American Indians," *Journal of American Folkore* 27: 374–410.
Brassard, Denis. 1980. "Three Montagnais Myths: A Structuralist Approach," *Anthropologica* 22, no. 2: 187–202.
Bright, William. 1979. "A Karok Myth in 'Measured Verse'," *Journal of California and Great Basin Anthropology* 1: 117–23.
Brightman, Robert A. 1977–79. Fieldnotes on Rock Cree.
Brown, Jennifer S.H. 1977. "James Settee and His Cree Tradition: An Indian Camp at the Mouth of Nelson River Hudson's Bay." In William Cowan (ed.), *Actes du Huitième Congrès des Algonquinistes*. Ottawa: Carleton University.

———. 1982. "The Track to Heaven: The Hudson Bay Cree Religious Movement of 1842–1843." Pp. 53–64 in William Cowan (ed.), *Papers of the Thirteenth Algonquian Conference*. Ottawa: Carleton University.

Brown, Jennifer and Robert Brightman (eds.). 1988. *The Orders of the Dreamed: George Nelson on Cree and Northern Ojibwa Religion and Legend, 1823*. Winnipeg: University of Manitoba Press.

Canada, Department of Indian Affairs. 1889. *Annual Report of the Department of Indian Affairs*. Ottawa: S.E. Dawson.

———. 1899. *Annual Report of the Department of Indian Affairs*. Ottawa: S.E. Dawson.

———. 1900. *Annual Report of the Department of Indian Affairs*. Ottawa: S.E. Dawson.

———. 1901. *Annual Report of the Department of Indian Affairs*. Ottawa: S.E. Dawson.

Chamberlain, Alexander F. 1890. "The Thunder-Bird Amongst the Algonkians," *American Anthropologist* 3: 51–54.

———. 1891. "Nanibozhu Among the Otchipwe, Mississagas, and Other Algonkian Tribes," *Journal of American Folklore* 4: 193–214.

Clay, Charles. 1938. *Swampy Cree Legends*. Toronto: Macmillan.

Cockburn, Matthew. 1985. "Like Words of Fire: Lore of the Woodland Cree from the Journals of P.G. Downes," *The Beaver* 315, no. 3: 37–44.

Coleman, M. Bernard, Ellen Frogner and Estelle Eich. 1962. *Ojibwa Myths and Legends*. Minneapolis: Ross and Haines.

Cooper, John M. 1934. "The Northern Algonquian Supreme Being," *Catholic University of America Anthropological Series* 2: 1–78.

———. 1936. "Notes on the Ethnology of the Otchipwe of Lake of the Woods and Rainy Lake," *Catholic University of America Anthropological Series* 3.

Coues, Elliott (ed.). 1897. *New Light on the Early History of the Greater Northwest: The Manuscript Journals of Alexander Henry and of David Thompson*. 3 Vols. New York.

Cresswell, J.R. 1923. "Folktales of the Swampy Cree," *Journal of American Folklore* 36: 404–06.

Curtis, Edward. 1928. *The North American Indian* 18. New York: Johnson Reprint Co. Darnell, Regna.

1974. "Correlates of Cree Narrative Performance." Pp. 315–35 in R. Bauman and J. Sherzer (eds.), *Explorations in the Ethnography of Speaking*. Cambridge: Cambridge University Press.

Davidson, D.S. 1928a. "Some Tête de Boule Tales," *Journal of American Folklore* 31: 262–74.

———. 1928b. "Folktales from Grand Lake Victoria," *Journal of American Folklore* 41: 275–82.

Denig, Edwin T. 1952. "Of the Crees or Knisteneau," *Bulletin of the Missouri Historical Society* 9, no. 1: 37–69.

Dixon, Roland B. 1909. "The Mythology of the Central and Eastern Algonkins," *Journal of American Folklore* 22: 1–9.

Dusenberry, Verne. 1963. *The Montana Cree: A Study in Religious Persistence*. Uppsala: Almqvist and Wiksells Boktryckeri Ab.

Ellis, Henry. 1748. *A Voyage to Hudson's Bay by the Dobbs Galley and California, in the Years 1746 and 1747*. London.

Faries, R. (ed.). 1938. *A Dictionary of the Cree Language*. Toronto: Church of England.

Fisher, Margaret W. 1946. "The Mythology of the Northern and Northeastern Algonkians in Reference to Algonkian Mythology as a Whole." Pp. 226–62 in F. Johnson (ed.), *Man in Northeastern North America. Papers of the Robert S. Peabody Foundation for Archaeology* 3.

Fleming, R. Harvey (ed.). 1940. *Minutes of Council: Northern Department of Rupert's Land, 1821–1831*. London: Hudson Bay Record Society.

Fogelson, Raymond. 1965. "Psychological Theories of Windigo Psychosis and a Preliminary Application of a Models Approach." In Melford Spiro (ed.), *Context and Meaning in Cultural Anthropology*. New York: Free Press.

Franklin, John. 1823. *Narrative of a Journey to the Shores of the Polar Sea in the Years 1819, 1820, 1821, and 1822*. London.

Godsell, Philip H. 1938. *Red Hunters of the Snows*. Toronto: Ryerson.

Graham, Andrew. 1969 [1767/1791]. *Andrew Graham's Observations on Hudson's Bay, 1767–91*. Glyndwr Williams (ed.). London: Hudson's Bay Record Society.

Greenberg, Adolph and James Morrison. 1982. "Group Identities in the Boreal Forest: The Origin of the Northern Ojibwa," *Ethnohistory* 29, no. 2: 75–102.

Hallowell, A. Irving. 1926. "Bear Ceremonialism in the Northern Hemisphere," *American Anthropologist* 28: 1–175.

———. 1942. "Conjuring in Saulteaux Society," *Publications of the Philadelphia Anthropological Society* 2.

———. 1955. *Culture and Experience*. New York: Schocken Books.

———. 1976. *Contributions to Anthropology: Selected Writings of A.I. Hallowell*. Raymond Fogelson (ed.). Chicago: University of Chicago Press.

Hamilton, J.C. 1894. "Two Algonquin Legends," *Journal of American Folklore* 7: 201–04.

Henry (the Elder), Alexander. 1901 [1809]. *Travels and Adventures in Canada and the Indian Territories Between the Years 1760 and 1776*. J. Bain (ed.). Boston: Little, Brown.

Hewitt, J.N.B. 1926. "Ethnological Researches Among the Iroquois and Chippewa. Explorations and Field-Work of the Smithsonian Institution in 1925," *Smithsonian Miscellaneous Collections* 78, no. 1: 114–17.

Honigmann, John J. 1956. "The Attawapiskat Swampy Cree: An Ethnographic Reconstruction," *Anthropological Papers of the University of Alaska* 5, no. 1: 23–82.

Howard, James H. 1977. *The Plains Ojibwa or Bungi*. Lincoln, NE: J. and L. Reprint Co.

Hudson's Bay Company Archives, Winnipeg, Manitoba. 1794. Remarks Going Up the Churchill River. Also During the Winter of 1795 by Goerge Charles. B/83/a.

———. 1822–23. Indian Lake Journal, 1822–23 by George Charles. B.91/a/8.

———. 1838. Indian Population of Nelson River District. B239/z/10.

———. 1889. Nelson River District Report (Fort Seaborne). D.25/6.

Isham, James. 1949. [1743–49]. *James Isham's Observations on Hudson's Bay, 1743 and Notes and Observations on a Book Entitled "A Voyage to Hudson's Bay in the Dobbs Galley, 1749."* E.E. Rich (ed.). London: Hudson's Bay Record Society.

Jenness, Diamond. 1935. "The Ojibwa Indians of Parry Island: Their Social and Religious Life," *National Museums of Canada Bulletin No. 78*, Anthropological Series 17.

Kinietz, Vernon W. 1965. *The Indians of the Western Great Lakes, 1615–1760*. Ann Arbor: University of Michigan Press.

Knight, James. 1932. *The Founding of Churchill*. J.F. Kenney (ed.). Toronto: J.M. Dent & Sons.

LeJeune, Paul. 1897a. "Relation of What Occurred in New France in the Year 1633." In Reuben G. Thwaites (ed.), *The Jesuit Relations and Allied Documents*, vol. 5. Cleveland: n.p.

———. 1897b. "Relation of What Occurred in New France in the Year 1634." In Reuben G. Thwaites (ed.), *The Jesuit Relations and Allied Documents*, vol. 6. Cleveland: n.p.

Maclean, John. 1897. *Canadian Savage Folk: The Native Tribes of Canada*. Toronto.

Marano, Louis. 1982. "Windigo Psychosis: The Anatomy of an Emic-Etic Confusion," *Current Anthropology* 23, no. 4: 385–97.
Mason, Leonard. 1967. *The Swampy Cree: A Study of Acculturation*. National Museum of Canada, Anthropology Papers 13.
Masson, Louis F.R. (ed.) 1889–1890. *Les Bourgeois de la Compagnie du Nord-ouest*. 2 vols. Quebec.
Merasty, Marie. 1974. *The World of Wetiko: Tales from the Woodland Cree*. C. Savage (ed.). Saskatoon: Saskatchewan Indian Cultural College.
Morriseau, Norval. 1965. *Legends of My People the Great Ojibway*. Toronto: McGraw-Hill Ryerson.
Morton, Arthur S. 1973. *A History of the Canadian West to 1870*. Toronto: University of Toronto Press.
Nabakov, Peter. 1978. *Native American Testimony*. New York: Harper Colophon.
Norman, Howard. 1982. *Where the Chill Came From*. San Francisco: North Point Press.
Paget, Amelia. 1909. *People of the Plains*. Toronto: Ryerson.
Pentland, David. 1978. "A Historical Overview of Cree Dialects." In W. Cowan (ed.), *Papers of the Ninth Algonquian Conference*. Ottawa: Carleton University.
Petitot, Emile. 1886. *Traditions Indiennes du Canada Nord-ouest*. Paris.
Radin, Paul. 1914. "Religion of the North American Indians," *Journal of American Folklore* 27: 335–73.
Radin, Paul and A.B. Reagan. 1928. "Ojibwa Myths and Tales," *Journal of American Folklore* 41: 61–146.
Rasles, Sebastien. 1900. "Letter…to his Brother." In Reuben G. Thwaites (ed.), *The Jesuit Relations and Allied Documents*, vol. 67. Cleveland: n.p.
Ray, Arthur J. 1974. *Indians in the Fur Trade*. Toronto: University of Toronto Press.
Robson, Joseph. 1965 [1752]. *An Account of Six Years Residence in Hudson's Bay from 1733 to 1736 and 1744 to 1747*. Toronto: Johnson Reprint Co.
Rossignol, Marius. 1938. "Cross-cousin Marriage Among the Saskatchewan Cree," *Primitive Man* 11: 26–28.
——. 1939a. "Property Concepts of the Cree of the Rocks," *Primitive Man* 12, no. 3: 61–70.
——. 1939b. "The Religion of the Saskatchewan and Western Manitoba Cree," *Primitive Man* 11: 67–71.
Russell, Frank. 1898. *Explorations in the Far North*. Iowa City: University of Iowa Press.
Savard, Rémi. 1979. "Contes Indiens de la Hasse Cote Nord du Saint Laurent," *National Museum of Man Mercury Series*, Canadian Ethnology Service Paper 51.
Simms, S.C. 1906. "Myths of the Bungees or Swampy Indians of Lake Winnipeg," *Folklore* 19: 334–40.
Skinner, Alanson. 1911. "Notes on the Eastern Cree and Northern Saulteaux," *Anthropological Papers of the American Museum of Natural History* 9, no. 1: 1–177.
——. 1914. "Political Organization, Cults, and Ceremonies of the Plains Cree," *Anthropological Papers of the American Museum of Natural History* 11: 513–42.
——. 1916. "Plains Cree Tales," *Journal of American Folklore* 29: 341–67.
Smith, Huron H. 1932. "Ethnobotany of the Ojibwe Indians," *Bulletin of the Milwaukee Public Museum* 4, no. 3: 327–525.
Smith, James G.E. 1975. "Preliminary Notes on the Rocky Cree of Reindeer Lake. Contributions to Canadian Ethnology." Pp. 171–89 in D.B. Carlisle (ed.), National Museum of Man, Mercury Series, *Ethnology Service Paper* 31.

———. 1976a. "On the Territorial Distribution of the Western Woods Cree." In William Cowan (ed.), *Papers of the Seventh Algonquian Conference*. Ottawa: Carleton University.

———. 1976b. "Notes on the Wittiko." In William Cowan (ed.), *Papers of the Seventh Algonquian Conference*. Ottawa: Carleton University.

———. 1981. "Western Woods Cree." *Handbook of North American Indians*, Vol. 6, *Subarctic*. J. Helm (ed.). Washington, DC: Smithsonian Institution.

Speck, Frank G. 1915. *Myths and Folklore of the Timiskaming Algonquian and Timagami Ojibwa*. Canada Department of Mines Geological Survey, Memoir 71, Anthropological Series 9.

———. 1925. "Montagnais and Naskapi Tales," *Journal of American Folklore* 38: 1–32.

Stevens, James. 1971. *Sacred Legends of the Sandy Lake Cree*. Toronto: McClelland and Stewart.

Swindlehurst, Fred. 1905. "Folk-Lore of the Cree Indians," *Journal of American Folklore* 18: 139–43.

Tedlock, Dennis. 1983. *The Spoken Word and the Work of Interpretation*. Philadelphia: University of Pennsylvania Press.

Teicher, Morton I. 1960. *Windigo Psychosis: A Study of a Relationship Between Belief and Behavior Among the Indians of Northeastern Canada*. Seattle: University of Washington Press.

Thompson, David. 1962. *David Thompson's Narrative, 1784–1812*. R. Glover (ed.). Toronto: Champlain Society.

Thwaites, Reuben G. (ed.). 1896–1901. *The Jesuit Relations and Allied Documents*. Cleveland: n.p.

Vandersteene, Roger. 1969. "Some Woodland Cree Traditions and Legends," *Western Canadian Journal of Anthropology* 1, no. 1: 40–64.

Wolfart, H. Christoph. 1973. "Plains Cree: A Grammatical Study," *Transactions of the American Philosophical Society* 63, no. 5: 1–90.